BAZAAR BIZARRE

BAZAAR BIZARRE

Not Your Granny's Crafts

Greg Der Ananian

VIKING STUDIO

VIKING STUDIO
Published by the Penguin Group
Penguin Group (USA) Inc., 375 Hudson Street,
New York, New York 10014, U.S.A.
Penguin Group (Canada), 90 Eglinton Avenue East, Suite 700, Toronto, Ontario, Canada M4P 2Y3
(a division of Pearson Penguin Canada Inc.)
Penguin Books Ltd, 80 Strand, London WC2R 0RL, England
Penguin Ireland, 25 St. Stephen's Green, Dublin 2, Ireland
(a division of Penguin Books Ltd)
Penguin Books Australia Ltd, 250 Camberwell Road, Camberwell, Victoria 3124, Australia
(a division of Pearson Australia Group Pty Ltd)
Penguin Books India Pvt Ltd, 11 Community Centre, Panchsheel Park, New Delhi – 110 017, India
Penguin Group (NZ), Cnr Airborne and Rosedale Roads, Albany, Auckland 1310, New Zealand
(a division of Pearson New Zealand Ltd)
Penguin Books (South Africa) (Pty) Ltd, 24 Sturdee Avenue, Rosebank, Johannesburg 2196, South Africa

Penguin Books Ltd, Registered Offices: 80 Strand, London WC2R 0RL, England

First published in 2005 by Viking Studio,
a member of Penguin Group (USA) Inc.

1 3 5 7 9 10 8 6 4 2

Copyright © Greg Der Ananian, 2005
All rights reserved

LIBRARY OF CONGRESS CATALOGING IN PUBLICATION DATA
Der Ananian, Greg.
Bazaar bizarre : not your granny's crafts / Greg Der Ananian.
p. cm.
ISBN 0-14-200506-1
1. Handicraft. I. Title.
TT157.A54 2005
745.5—dc22   2005046113

Printed in the United States of America
Set in Rotis Sans Serif
Designed by Liney Li

This book is for my mother,

Priscilla Der Ananian,

who once told me that I was the

closest thing to a daughter she'd ever have.

I love you, Mom.

ACKNOWLEDGMENTS

It's difficult for me to know where to draw the line when thanking people. I could go on for pages if I were to acknowledge every person who has brought me to this point in my life. As far as this book is concerned, however, I would be remiss in not thanking certain persons individually:

My agents Marc Gerald and Caroline Greeven of The Agency Group have changed my life. I felt like Lana Turner when they "discovered" me at Bazaar Bizarre 2003. Without their guidance, support, and belief in my abilities, writing a book would still be one of those things that *other* people do. On the other end of the life-change hotline was Megan Newman at Viking, who took a chance on me when she gave this project the green light. My editor Kristen Jennings has been my literary Sherpa throughout the project. Talk about rocky terrain—without her feedback I'd have lost my way. Kate Stark in Viking's marketing department rounds out my team of handlers. Whenever self-doubt has crept into the picture, I've recalled Kate's enthusiasm and fabulous shoes for motivation.

I need to thank Eva Cherniavsky not only for her invaluable remarks—or should I say *reMarx*—about the arts and crafts movement, industrialization, women's labor, and the domestic economy; but for being my longtime mentor, champion, and good friend. Nedra Friedman has been a guide for many years, but her advice and support through this often overwhelming process has been critical. Literally telling ambivalence to shove it, she taught a picker and a grinner that fear, faith, and forgiveness can work together. Tiffanie Reid will always be one of the great loves of my life. Fielding my 2 A.M. panic-ridden phone calls, she always listens to my kvetching with endless patience and love, whipping anxiety into purpose with the usual ease. Thanks to Emily Arkin for furnishing me with a copy of *The Clockwork*

Muse, a book that taught me some important lessons about budgeting time and that some very famous authors were much lazier than I am. Her second career as my own personal tech-support line also deserves major credit. Since volunteering to help organize Bazaar Bizarre in October 2003, Mary Jo Kaczka has been my close friend and crutch—not to mention my book proposal's sample chapter.

Of course, I am indebted to the wonderful artists who contributed to this book. Their love for their crafts makes this book what it is. Thanks to Joe Tanis and Colleen Walker for shooting the beautiful photos you'll see, and to Craig Bostick for bailing my ass out of a sling with his illustrations. Thanks also to those who modeled for photos.

I am the luckiest person alive to have the family that I have. My parents Paul and Priscilla Der Ananian, after my thirty years on this earth, continue to astound me with their unwavering support and boundless love. My brother Paul, sister-in-law Jen, and their daughter—my brilliant and beautiful niece Ashley—remind me of family's importance as I take a step back to watch them begin the next generation of Der Ananians. I would feel incomplete if I didn't at least mention the animal members of my family: my kitties Tron and Jett, as well as my parents' bichon Becky. Each used her magic pet powers to make me feel special and loved.

During the late stages of this project I unexpectedly found myself in the hospital, only to discover that my skull was home to a golf-ball-size brain tumor. Coming through that ordeal was nothing less than a miracle for me. I continue to be amazed by the achievements of modern medicine and the dedication and skill with which the women and men in the field heal the sick. More important, perhaps, is the transformative power of love that I have felt from not only family and friends but also from complete strangers. No matter what your religious or spiritual beliefs, I defy anyone not to be moved by the knowledge that scores of people you don't even know are thinking of and praying for you. I just wanted to take a moment to express my gratitude for the astonishing love and positive energy I was fortunate enough to have surrounding and protecting me during a difficult time. I am truly a better person for it.

CONTENTS

CONTENTS

x

INTRODUCTION

I was but a wee flaming homosexual when my mother wisely took me under her wing and taught me the ladylike skills of knitting and cross-stitch . . . and so began my love affair with crafts. Working with my hands made me feel good in a Marxist sort of way, and I learned at an early age that being able to make something from nothing was extremely rewarding. As I got older, my interest in crafts waned because the spectrum of traditional craft imagery didn't represent me.

Dissatisfied with stencils of country ducks and painted wooden slices of watermelon, I decided to use what I'd learned as a child to express my own interests. To my surprise and delight, a lot of my friends were experiencing the same kind of personal renaissance. How exactly to share these objets de craft was a project upon which we embarked. The result? Bazaar Bizarre.

Bazaar Bizarre began in 2001 in the Boston area as a hodgepodge of friends and acquaintances cobbling together their handcrafted DIY wares to sell and staging an offbeat entertainment extravaganza. Crafts have long been denigrated as a feminized form of expression, but Bazaar Bizarre represents an impulse to revalue the abilities our mothers and grandmothers taught us, while making them our own. It's as much about tradition as it is about change. In the ensuing years, BazBiz has added additional cities to its roster and is now one of the most eagerly anticipated craft events of the holiday season on both coasts.

This book is but a sampling of the artists featured at past Bazaars. Each has designed a project specifically for this book, all of which I think are great as is but are very easily customizable. In fact, when I was asking each crafter to participate, I stipulated that his or her project should be basic in nature so that you the reader could make it your own without delay.

DISCLAIMER

My use of the terms "punk" and "punk rock" in this book refer principally to a set of values and aesthetics that run counter to most established trends of cultural production and consumption. While it's true that I was in a "punk" band for many years (Prettypony—heard of us? Thought not), I make no claim to having any sort of musicological expertise or rarified historical knowledge when it comes to the punk pantheon. Sure, I love punk rock, but I will most certainly lose any pissing contest when it comes to punk trivia. In my opinion, punk encompasses a much broader sphere of culture than just music. I only mention all of this because after living in Bloomington, Indiana, for seven years (a small town where there's nothing to do except be a nerd and start a punk band), I know how fussy you punk nerds can be about these things. I hereby reserve my right to be punk identified despite my unironic horrible taste in music. ("Horrible" according to the vicious and threatening Post-its left on my dorm room door by one unfortunately coiffed Iggy Pop fan and cooccupant.)

How to Use This Book

Yes, Bazaar Bizarre is a how-to book full of fun projects for you to do. However, things aren't that simple. Each chapter will introduce you not only to a project and skill but also to an artist as well. My hope is that the combination of the artist's words and designs will sketch a picture of what it might mean to be a "punk-rock" crafter. You'll notice that every chapter's project has a different rating of difficulty. Some could indeed be considered beginner, while others may require a bit more courage to attempt. But hey, if it comes out looking a little messed up, so much the better—we're not in this to fulfill everyone else's wishes about what crafts are *supposed* to be, right?

Read every chapter even if you aren't ready to try the project. The designs are intentionally basic. That is, whether you're a veteran punker newly trying your hand at crafts or a dyed-in-the-wool granny trying to get in touch with your inner Johnny Rotten, this book can be a fun jumping-off point: a place from which to start customizing, personalizing, and generally rampaging . . . with a glue gun. Maybe you'll see a familiar technique presented with materials you'd never thought to use, or perhaps you'll encounter an entirely weird opportunity to incorporate something mundane sitting in your junk drawer. The point is to unlock all the great ideas you already have inside you.

Chapters

Each chapter is divided into several sections, so you can expect a fairly similar format from each chapter.

CRAFTER BIO

Each chapter contains a bit of info about the artist who originally created the project. These anecdotal passages vary a lot from artist to artist. Even though I wrote the words, I asked each crafter to supply me with some biographical info that they'd want presented in the book. Some were verbose, and others extremely brief. Some bios were strictly factual and chronological, while others were downright strange. The biographical blurbs were some of the most fun parts of the book to write.

CRAFTER Q & A

Everyone filled out a little questionnaire that I came up with. It's not meant to be too serious, but I think if you give some thought to the crafters' responses you can learn a lot. These Q&As are all presented in the artist's own words.

GLOBAL TECHNIQUES

In this portion of the chapter, you'll find some generalized guidelines about a particular crafting genre as a whole. In some cases, there will be books, Web sites and resources you can go to for further information. Some projects are more unique skillwise than others, so there might not be a genre to which it belongs, per se, but you'll still find some useful hints to keep in mind before you get started.

DiFFiCULTY

I've given each project a general difficulty rating on a scale of 1 to 5. Don't let this scare you off. In most cases it just indicates how *involved* or complex a project is, as opposed to any indication of your chances of being able to actually make it.

TiME LiNE

Here you'll find a general idea of how long the project might take from start to finish. I've also included some crafting stimuli suggested by each crafter. The 45-spinner symbol indicates something to listen to while you work: could be a radio show, a book on tape, or in most cases an album. The filmstrip icon indicates something visual to look at, but I learned that, like myself, a lot of the crafters in the book "watch" the same things over and over again while they work. That way they don't necessarily need to have their eyes directed at the TV. With a movie you've seen a zillion times, you can watch it more or less in your head, glancing up occasionally from your work. The video suggestions are also useful for passive time during which you may have to wait for glue or ink to dry, water to boil, or inspiration to strike. Mostly the suggestions are for fun and to give you, the reader, another little peek into the feverish brain of the artist.

SHOPPiNG LiST

Pretty self-explanatory. It's a list of materials you'll need to complete the project. Lots of them you can probably find in your house—especially if you're already an artist or crafter. Some lists will have notes if the supplies are highly specialized, while others will be more obvious.

STEP BY STEP

Just what it sounds like. This is the meat and potatoes of the project, where I take you through each, well . . . step. You'll be able to follow a numbered list of instructions, with further information contained in subtext for each. If you are making a project for the second or third time, you may not need to scrutinize the detailed info as much.

At the end of this section in each chapter you will find any necessary patterns, images, or templates you'll need to complete the project. These designs are optional in many cases. You may feel comfortable creating your own imagery from the get-go, but they're there if you need something to get you started.

SERVING SUGGESTIONS

Here you'll find some variations on each project along with ideas for presentation if you're thinking of giving the project as a gift. These few suggestions are designed to get you thinking of your own ways to customize the craft.

CONTACT INFO

Wanna get in touch with the crafty guy or gal responsible for the fun time you had making the project? Here's where you'll find e-mail addresses and Web sites to reach out and touch another crafter.

CRAFTOIDS

In between chapters you'll find these tasty morsels. Maybe it's a word search, or a story of a historic crafter, or just my perspective on some aspect of crafting as a way of life. Each is a must-read gem, I promise.

Nice Basket!

Any cookbook or DIY manual gives you a list of essentials to keep on hand. A well-stocked larder or toolbox makes for an easier endeavor. Plus, if you always have necessities readily accessible, you'll spend a lot less cash buying supplies when it's time to get started.

Many of the projects in this book have an overlapping shopping list. When you head out to your local arts and crafts purveyor, buy certain items in the economy size if you can. Having replacement blades, glue sticks, needles, brushes, staples, and other "staples" within reach can help you avoid a lot of Maalox moments when you hit a bump in the road—or should I say a run in the nylon. And wouldn't you rather have a Certs encounter with a cute 'n crafty cashier while you're *not* soiling your undies due to the epoxy that's hardening beyond your control back at the apartment?

A crafter, however, cannot exist on store-bought goods alone. In fact, your goal should be to buy the absolute *minimum*. We're crafty, damnit, and that means using what we have to make what we need. You gotta have your bin, junk box, barrel, whatever. See stuff on the street? Pick it up. Save your junk mail, or at least cut out the goofy pictures from the ads you get before recycling. Save jar lids, popsicle sticks, mint tins, empty shampoo bottles, soda pop caps. Think of yourself as the magpie of the art world, and line your nest.

Unfortunately, we can't always simply "harvest" our tools from our surroundings. In such cases, I recommend the following list to get you going:

- **Aleene's Tacky Glue:** A BazBiz essential. Proclaims itself "the crafter's favorite" and I'd have to agree. Dries clear and flexible. Even the dusty gold bottle with its scalloped border is kinda tacky.
- **Bone folder:** While I've never seen one actually made of bone, and it certainly wouldn't *fold* one, this is an extremely versatile tool. It's useful for making sharp, clean creases as you might expect, but it can do so much more. Try using it to poke out a sewn corner when you turn your project right side out. As a burnisher (a round-tipped rubbing tool), it can't be beat. I could go on all day, but you'll discover your own uses for this must-have.
- **E-6000:** I know many crafters that swear by this self-touted industrial-strength glue. Of course, keep it away from huffers. It's abrasion resistant, flexible, water-proof, and paintable. What else could you ask from glue?
- **Embroidery floss:** I recommend DMC brand. It's the most widely available in your run-of-the-mill craft store. And at about a quarter a skein, you can't beat the price. Yes, you can embroider with it, but it's also the cornerstone of cross-stitch, and comes in a zillion pretty colors. I suggest tracking down some sturdy plastic Bestway bobbins around which to wrap it. Makes it a lot easier to dispense and keep neat and tidy.
- **Fusible interfacing:** This behind-the-scenes iron-on material adds stability to almost any fabric-based project, allowing you to use materials that might not normally be up to the task you have in mind for them.
- **Glue gun:** These come in high temp and low temp. Choose one based on how liquid you want the glue to come out and how quickly you want it to dry. Unless you buy some superchic one, there ain't no way it's gonna run you more than ten bucks.

You can get miniglue guns for as cheap as two bucks, and certain novelty glue sticks (like the awesome colored or glitter ones) only come in the minigun size.

- **Needles and Pins:** That's how it begins. Find yourself a nice assortment pack of sharp sewing needles in different sizes. Try crafting your own fun pincushion for that big box of straight pins you're gonna pick up. They even come in pretty colors.

- **No-sew fusible tape:** Sticks fabrics together . . . without sewing (hence the moniker no-sew)! It's a minor miracle for hems or temporarily laying down rickrack, grosgrain ribbon, a million and one trims, or a fabric label.

- **Paintbrushes:** Go ahead and spend a little money on one nice paintbrush in each size you think you might need. Remember to keep in mind what you might use it for—you may need to get one for chemicals and one for water-based media. And keep 'em clean!

- **Sewing machine:** If you have one, great. Learn how to use it, and take it in for a tune-up and lube job once a year! Just trying out the different settings and stitches on scraps of fabric can be very educational. Take my advice and don't screw with the thread tension unless you really know what you're doing, or I promise you'll regret it. If you don't have a sewing machine, consider getting one. Borrow one first, and when you're ready to buy, find a high-quality unit. That way you'll only ever have to buy one in your lifetime.

- **Tackle box:** Screw the craft store—go to the hardware store for this one. Look online for hunting and fishing Web sites. The Plano brand makes one for every conceivable need. My mother bequeathed me her Plano Magnum II. How butch is that?

- **Thimble:** When you're trying to push a needle through several layers of fabric or run a dangling thread through a number of tight stitches, your tender finger will be glad you spent the 99 cents.

- **X-acto knife:** I do love this particular brand, but there are also small utility knives (Olfa makes a nice one) with snap-off blades that are great when you cut a lot of heavier materials.

CROSS-STITCH
PROJECT: DiRTY PiLLOW

ARTIST: *Greg Der Ananian*

On a recent car trip to the big and tall outlet, my mom and I figured out that I must have been about ten years old when she taught me how to cross-stitch. Through the intervening years, the one bit of needlework lore that stuck with me more than any other was this: The sign of a truly great stitcher is that the backside of her project will look as nicely finished as the front. It was one of those inner-cross-stitch-circle ideals that I am still trying to attain. I'd ask myself: Why should it matter? No one ever sees the back of your project. If you were to ask this question of a seasoned stitcher like my mom, you might get a reply like "Well it doesn't really matter, but . . ." which of course means it really does matter—even though it doesn't.

I am nowhere close to approaching the Hannibal Lechter precision that typifies my mother's needlework, but I'm improving—the front sides of my projects are nice and even, with all the stitches going the same way; even the old ladies that brave the horrors of Bazaar Bizarre comment on their uniformity. But why would I, Evil Mistress of Underground Crafts, care what Grandma thinks?

Contrary to the potential conclusion of an uncritical observer, BazBiz isn't out to destroy grannies with all our punk-rock nonsense. That very granny-seal-of-approval is a crucial part of the BazBiz creed—or at least my own value system. For instance, when I would cook for my Armenian language class, and some ladies from the old country would comment on the deliciousness of my *Kataif* or *Yalanchi*, my chest would swell with pride. Of course I *always* try and enter a room boobs first anyway because I heard Sly Stallone say in an interview once that it gives you good posture

1

and makes you look buffer than you really are. Anyway I'm getting off topic here.

My point is that every BazBiz crafter I know *loved* the time she spent learning how to make stuff. Mastering a skill in which you've become interested is always fun. No one had to drag me kicking and screaming to aspire to be a great stitcher like my mom . . . even if our tastes were divergent. It wasn't like I was chained down in the basement with my bag of cotton loops and plastic loom in some *Mommie Dearest* pot-holder sweatshop. I was sitting on the couch next to mom watching CBS soaps (*As the World Turns, Guiding Light, Search for Tomorrow* —remember that one?). My conclusion? When we find a way to truly *own* our crafty skills by imprinting them with a meaningful personal voice, we get to sit back down on the couch with mom. And believe me when I say that when I visit the folks, I'm still sitting next to Mom during *Guiding Light.*

Growing up, when I got in trouble at school, it was usually the result of some problem that arose in my art class. By elementary school standards, I was a bit of a renegade artist, although I don't know if I was a Serrano-or Mapplethorpe-caliber troublemaker or just a smart-ass. My art wasn't even visually objectionable—there was no nudity, profanity, or vulgarity of any kind (that didn't come until college). The controversies always arose due to a conflicting artistic vision between me and my art teachers—Mrs. Piles in elementary school and Ms. Wagers in high school.

I should mention that as a youngster, my idea of artistic vision consisted of drawing Garfield and Odie for my classmates or reimagining the PacMan family in various domestic vignettes. As the resident "art kid" at school, pretty girls in Izods with upturned collars used to ask me to draw unicorns or if certain colors in their wardrobe clashed. Being a fourth-grade boy, no matter how sissified, I had no idea what the hell they were talking about. The point is that I had some modicum of artistic ability and I learned to use it to make trouble.

Briefly in the fifth grade, I was the pride and joy of my art teacher, Mrs. Piles, due to the leg up I had in the needle arts thanks to Mom. My needlework projects were usually quite stellar. But just as I earned my teacher's praise, I decided to reject her authority by destroying my precious needlepoint project with a pair of scissors. I don't know if I was motivated by a need to reject the approval from an authority figure to maintain a bad boy status or if it was just one of those psychoimpulsive things I used to do as a kid. But without those antics, I never would have been able to savor the irony of a low grade in effort alongside a high grade in achievement. It was such a slap in the face to the hegemony of Paul P. Gates Elementary.

Despite engineering a gallery installation whose gay-porn factor induced threats of police action in college, my crowning art controversy had to be getting kicked out permanently from Ms. Wagers's "senior portfolio" art class in high school. This lady *hated* me for some reason—probably because of my cheeky sense of style and devil-may-care attitude. Week after week she would attempt to humiliate me in front of the other students by doing things on the order of removing my self-portrait from the wall and throwing it into the garbage while she lectured the class on how they should be offended that my "trash" was hanging alongside their hard work. I finally endeavored to portray our conflict in my final project—a comic entitled "Art Man vs. Art Bitch." She didn't seem to appreciate my efforts to exorcise our demons by putting our differences on paper. It was a big hit with my classmates but got me thrown out of the class, right into a parent-teacher-vice-principal-guidance-counselor-and-me meeting. I was never more proud to be a Der Ananian than when my parents rallied around me to tell Ms. Betts off.

I have no idea what Ms. Wagers or Mrs. Piles would have to say about me, but I

4

think all of the trouble I've found myself in when it comes to art has served me in very good stead. I'll have to ask their opinion when I bring them autographed copies of this book.

What is the difference between an "art" and a "craft"?

That's a toughie. This is one of the key questions that drives both Bazaar Bizarre the event and *Bazaar Bizarre* the book. My goal, however, isn't to necessarily *answer* this question. I think I just want to highlight it. I am not certain it even warrants an answer. So why ask? When I think about the relevance of the question, I believe parties interested in maintaining the distinctions between the two terms offer most of the definitive conclusions. This wouldn't really bother me except for a tradition of sexism and exclusion when it comes to art.

What is your earliest crafting memory?

I think it was making pot holders for my mom with those loops with the plastic loom. I am aware of craft objects that I made prior to my pot-holder production because I see them at my folks' house, but I don't *remember* making them.

What was your best crafting moment (idea, inspiration, etc.)?

Best? I think the inspiration for Dirty Pillows. It brought me back to a place I liked being but had left because it got boring, or, at least, it no longer satisfied my needs.

What was your worst crafting moment
(a huge mess, project gone horribly wrong, etc.)?

Worst? I think it was in preparation for Bazaar Bizarre 2002 when I incorrectly mixed a batch of Enviro-tex epoxy resin that never quite dried. So the Fagnets I was making never got *really* hard (never a good sign in epoxy or . . . other things).

What is your favorite craft you've ever seen?

There are a few, and of course it's tough to choose. Josh Yeager's shrines are extremely beautiful (see page 149). I like crafts that have the ability to combine irony with sentiment; crafts that can take a critical step back once in a while but still be earnest.

Who made you the crafter you are (who introduced you to crafts, taught you crafts—whether or not it is the one you do now)?
Mom—without question.

What are your crafting goals?
To maintain a lifestyle that allows me the time to craft.

Kraft or Kraftwerk?
Kraft cheese and macaroni—I mean *macaroni and cheese*—tastes better while listening to "Das Modell."

Who is your fave crafty celeb?
Pamela Anderson. I hear she knits like crazy, and she seems like such a nice person. I love the idea of an absolute bombshell who knits. Martha is incredible, too, and she got a raw deal. You know, my mom actually called a local Boston TV station to protest when they pulled her show from the air.

What is your fave craft resource (Web site, store, dumpster, etc)?
Well for actual craft objects I'd have to say Bazaar Bizarre. I mean where else can you find this kinda stuff? For craft supplies, I dunno . . . I pick a lot of stuff up off the street or save packaging from items I've bought. Of course I love Michael's, but something about spending so much time and money there bothers me—damn that college education!

Global Techniques

So where to start? I think the most important thing to know is that counted cross-stitch is *not* needlepoint, embroidery, or anything else. It's *only* counted cross-stitch. I say this because people are always commenting on my "needlepoint" or "embroidery," and it drives me up the freaking wall. While I concede that historically cross-stitch evolved as some sort of splinter craft from embroidery, it has matured quite nicely into its own formal technique.

The oldest complete cross-stitch design (and I warn you that I'm running on Internet info here) was found in a Coptic tomb in Upper Egypt, dating back to circa

A.D. 500. I was hoping to discover that, like knitting, cross-stitch had some unlikely über-masculine origins (Scottish fishermen invented knitting by adapting the knot-tying of their nets), but the date of origin was all that was mentioned in the article. Not that the feminine nature of something should disturb me. Anyone who's ever met me knows I have sissy pride. It's just that I wanted it to be invented by pirates. And honestly, could you not see Johnny Depp in *Pirates of the Caribbean* doing cross-stitch as he marauded the seven seas in all that eyeliner? So in my head, maybe I'll just preserve that fantasy. And who's to say that those wacky Coptic priests didn't incorporate cross-stitch into some gruesome human sacrifice ritual. I know absolutely nothing about ancient Coptic rites, but hey, anything's possible.

There is an excellent counted cross-stitch tutorial by Kathleen M. Dyer that I found online that goes into lots of detail in a very clear way. The URL is http://users.rcn.com/kdyer.dnai/faqs/xstitch_tut.html. For our purposes here, though, I am just gonna go into a few cross-stitch basics that you'll need to know to complete this project.

CLOTH

There are more than a couple of choices when it comes to the cloth you can use as a surface for your satiny stitches. Stitch count is the first thing to think about because no matter what kind of cloth you choose, it will come in a range of counts. The count is the number of stitches that you must make to cover 1 inch of cloth. This does not mean the stitch count is the number of stitches in a square inch—it is the number of stitches in a row that add up to 1 inch. The higher the count, the smaller your stitches will have to be. A smaller thread count might work best for beginners because it requires less dexterity or familiarity with the technique. Also, remember that the higher the thread count, the smaller your finished design will be. The smaller the count, the more likely you are to have bits of cloth showing from behind your stitches, which I have used before in a calculated way for a more rustic country look. This makes for a number of other necessary considerations, such as how many strands of floss you'll use, but more about that in a bit.

In addition to the count, there's the type of cloth. Type is generally designated by the way it's woven.

Aida cloth is the most widely available and, in my opinion, the easiest cloth on which to work. It's commonly pronounced "ay-dah." I'm always stopping myself from saying "eye-ee-dah," like the opera. Aida cloth is so easy to use because its weave creates a visible grid. One knows exactly where to stick his needle—an unfortunate rarity among men. If only there was an Aida analogue for every aspect of life. Aida cloth is what we'll be using for this project.

Linen seems, in my limited deviance from the Aida path, to be the most popular second choice. Linen comes in both "natural" and "even" weaves. Natural weave will have some variation from strand to strand, while even weave is uniform throughout. My mom swears that linen is easier to work on than Aida, but I don't buy it. Linen does not have an obvious grid, and cross-stitching on linen involves stitching "over 2" or skipping strands of the cloth. Truth be told, I am very intimidated by linen, but I am getting more used to the fact that it's much more versatile than Aida for sophisticated patterns. There are some designs that require linen because of their division of stitches, and so forth. Linen does look much more pro, and you can usually find a wider range of colors. Small-scale designers that target advanced stitchers will hand dye and sell their own linen cloth. Hand-dyed cloth can look somewhat mottled though, which—depending on your design—either works or doesn't. The graphic nature of my designs works best with saturated, solid colors. And by "graphic" I mean stylized and iconic as opposed to explicit, although all definitions certainly apply.

FLOSS

I'll just go ahead here and recommend DMC brand 6-strand embroidery floss because that's what I always use. There are other brands, but you'll never find them unless you go to a specialty needlework shop. Plus, I have never ever encountered a pattern that did not include DMC colors and numbers in its palette. Occasionally a pattern will call for a specialty thread such as metallic Balger or some such, but again these will usually only be found at needlework shops. Additionally, these threads are often used in conjunction with regular embroidery floss. For instance, a pattern may have a design using 1 strand of specialty thread combined with 1 strand of DMC. That, of course, brings me to the topic of strands.

Six-strand embroidery floss comes in skeins about 8 ½ yards in length. Depending on the count of your cloth, you will use a different number of strands. The most common seems to be 2 strands. I think this is because most mainstream cross-stitch is done on a range of counts (14 to 18) where 2 strands provide a nice thorough coverage (i.e., you can't see the cloth underneath) without overcrowding the holes in the cloth. I would recommend 3 strands for counts 11 and lower. When I bring home a new color, I always wind the skein onto a bobbin (Bestway is my fave bobbin). This makes organization much easier, plus you can get these big key-chain things that allow you to have a ring holding only the colors you are using on your current project. When you need to prepare a length of floss to work with, unwind all 6 strands of the desired length, cut, and "peel off" 2 strands. You can wind the remainder back onto the bobbin or just leave it sitting out if you know you're gonna use it right away. I would never recommend a partial cut of the floss. Always cut all 6 strands and then separate.

NEEDLES

I use size 24 tapestry needles. There's not much more to say on the subject I guess. Although, I recently learned a trick for easier threading. I believe most people know about sucking on the end of the floss or thread to make it pointy enough to fit through the eye of the needle, but it turns out you can also suck on the eye of the needle. I dunno much about the physics of saliva (well, as they pertain to needle threading), but the combo of these two sucking moments seems to help for some reason. I find that a little spit can help out in most life situations. At this point I am gonna go against every instinct that is telling me to pass on about a zillion double entendres and innuendos concerning sucking, saliva, and threading needles. They're all really obvious, and I certainly think I've laid plenty of pervy groundwork elsewhere in this book. Think of this as an instance for *you* to be the naughty one. Otherwise we'd be here all day. It reminds me of a *Golden Girls* episode where Rose, in trying to advise Dorothy without the aid of a Saint Olaf story, ends up telling three simultaneously because she simply can't stop herself. I guess I'm that way when it comes to immature dirty jokes.

PREPARING YOUR FABRIC

There are a lot of things people do to prep their fabric, from rinsing and pressing to basting a grid right onto the cloth. I pick my battles when it comes to being anal (oh God, it's starting again). Except for deciding on its color and count, all I do to my fabric is cut it out. Measure your pattern and calculate the size of the finished piece based on your stitch count.

Sometimes the pattern will give you measurements based on a range of counts, but it's easy to calculate if it doesn't list this info. For instance, if a design is 100 x 100 stitches and you were using 14 count Aida, you could determine that your finished piece would be about 7 1/8 inches square by dividing the number of stitches by the fabric count (for each dimension). I always round up each dimension at least to the half inch. That leaves you with a 7 1/2-inch square working area. Now just add 3 to 4 inches along each edge as a safety/buffer zone and you know how big to cut your fabric—for this hypothetical, I think an 11- to 12-inch square would be a safe size.

It's funny, my mom always advised me that in cooking you can always add more, but you can never take away. In cutting your fabric, you can always trim, but you can never add. Imagine the frustration after days and days of work, when you run out of space because you miscalculated your design's center or something. Trust me when I say that it *really* sucks.

STARTING AND ENDING STITCHES

Making the very first stitch on a blank piece of cloth can be kind of intimidating if you're not used to it. When beginning a project, cross-stitchers, unlike a lot of other needle-and-thread crafters, do not tie a knot at the end of their floss to secure the beginning stitch. A knot would have to be fairly large to prevent the floss from pulling through the hole (which will stretch easily because of the weave). In addition, knots all over the back of your project would give you a really bumpy and lumpy finish on the front.

So instead, when you begin a cross-stitch piece, you leave a length of thread on the underside that you can secure under your subsequent stitches. I don't have any big scientific way of doing it. I find where I wanna start (I almost always start at the center), pull the needle through, and just leave an inch or

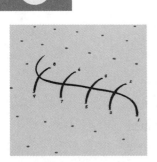

so dangling on the under side of the fabric and start stitching, holding the loose end in place against the fabric with my finger. For the first few stitches, I just turn over the cloth each time and make sure to catch the beginning of the floss under the loop created on the backside with each stitch. It's not rocket science, and you'll get the hang of it quickly.

When you already have a chunk of your stitching done, starting a new strand of thread when one runs out or switching colors is much easier. Just run your needle through a few stitches on the backside of the piece close to where you want the new stitches to begin. Just be careful on the first stitch not to pull so hard that the thread comes all the way through. Until you are sensitive enough to feel subtle changes in tension, you'll probably have to turn your project over as you pull the first stitch.

To finish stitches when you get to the end of your thread or when you need to switch colors, you will also run it through some stitches on the backside and then snip. When finishing stitches, you don't have to worry about it accidentally pulling the end of the thread through the fabric. Try to do it neatly though.

THE CROSS-STITCH

The cross-stitch is the only stitch we'll be using in this project. There are many others, most commonly backstitching, which is used for outlining. But we're just gonna discuss the actual cross-stitch. It's an X. There are actually different schools and techniques when it comes to making an X from traditional to Danish. I say screw all this. I operate by two basic rules:

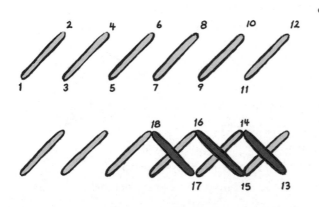

- **Cross-stitches (an X) should always always always have the / on the bottom and the \ on top.** I generally make a row of / in one direction and then come back on top of them with \. Technically I think this is Danish, but I end up using a zillion permutations to navigate my way around the cloth. Just give it some time, and you'll figure out what works for you, and I bet you'll end up using a mélange of techniques just like every stitcher I know.

- **Stitch with the least amount of traveling possible.** I try never to skip more than one square at a time when stitching, although sometimes you have to. It doesn't always matter because either you'll be covering that area with more stitches later anyway, or there are already adjacent stitches through which you can tunnel on the backside. Okay . . . tunneling through one's backside?

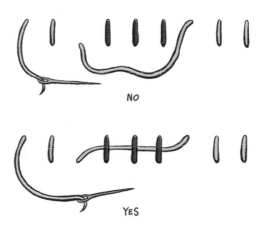

NO

YES

DIRTY PILLOW: CHERRY PIE DIFFICULTY ✪✪✪✪✪

TIME LINE Prepare yourself for something of a time commitment with this project, especially if it's your first go-round with counted cross-stitch. I cannot do this project in one day. My hands just will not work long enough to keep stitching until completion. I'd have to say the stitching part takes a good solid 8 hours at least, and the assembly/sewing of the pillow—while basic—is gonna run you another 2. I recommend boxed sets and/or series for your audio-visual pleasure.

Bea Arthur on Broadway: Just Between Friends; Berlin Philharmoniker, Herbert Von Karajan, Conductor: Tchaikovsky 6 Symphonien (Deutsche Grammophon); any David Sedaris audio book (these are perfect for a road trip if you can stitch in the passenger seat without getting carsick—I cannot).

Alien; Aliens; Alien 3; Alien: Resurrection; Scream; Scream 2; Scream 3; any HSN (Home Shopping Network) show lasting more than 2 hours, although I can't recommend host Colleen Lopez enough. Her hair and knowledge of semiprecious stones are impressive—I think HSN hosts must actually become educated in gemology. When megashill Suzanne Somers stops by for one of their "pajama parties" you truly learn a lot about capitalism, and why foreign people hate America.

SHOPPiNG LiST

THE FABRIC-CRAFT STORE

- **DMC 6-strand embroidery floss** You'll need 1 skein each of DMC colors 304, 311, 3716, 3852, 3855, 603, 666, 745, 814, 995, 996. Sometimes projects require newer DMC colors that are tricky to find. For instance, at Michael's they'll stock the necessary floss only as part of a "newest colors" set or some bullshit. So you end up paying like fifteen bucks for the one color you need. The solution, as always, is the Internet (unless you happen to know of a specialty needlework or even a cross-stitch store). Herrschners.com is my fave. You can find any color you want and buy single skeins for like thirty-nine cents apiece.
- **Aida cloth** It's hard to find many good colors at your run-of-the mill fabric store. It usually comes precut in tubes and is overpriced. If you can, find a cross-stitch specialty shop where they can cut it for you. They'll have a much better selection of colors. I would advise against a stitch count higher than 16 (stitches per inch) for this project. First timers may wanna stick to 14 count Aida.
- **Fusible interfacing** To add stability to the reverse of the stitched Aida cloth.
- **Backing fabric** Pick something pretty, and thematically related if you can. There are about a zillion cherry prints out there. You only need a 9-inch square, so I'd just look for remnants. Or you could always pick up a yard if you like the fabric. Keep your basket stuffed . . . no, wait that's gay porn. Stocked is what I meant.
- **Fusible tape** We'll use this for pressing some hems, which will give the back of the pillow a very finished look.
- **DMC size 24 tapestry needles** They come in packs of six and they're cheap.
- **Embroidery hoop** I recommend the tension-oriented "spring-loaded" ones as opposed to the wooden ones or even plastic ones with the screw tension mechanism. Just much easier, plus you can throw 'em in the dishwasher!

- **Scissors** Nothing special, but you might wanna pick up a little pocket-size pair. You could alternatively get this little medallion thing that looks like a flower that cuts thread. These are good because you can't bring scissors on a plane, and my mom had an expensive pair confiscated forever by TSA.
- **Bobbins** Not like sewing machine bobbins. These are flat plastic-card things around which to wrap your floss after you unroll the skein. It's a pain and takes time, but it's really worth the extra minutes. Bestway bobbins are the hands-down best, but you have to find 'em online unless you can find them in a specialty shop. The DMC bobbins suck because the notches where you are supposed to hook the end of your floss are too loose, and they don't even hold the floss in place.
- **Bobbin ring** It's like a giant key ring. Find 'em next to the bobbins in the store.
- **All-purpose sewing thread** Coates & Clark Dual Duty or whatever all-purpose thread you like. Re: color choice—it's a matter of taste. I think an invisible color looks just as nice as a contrasting one—like western stitching or something.

RIGHT IN YOUR VERY OWN HOME

- **Iron and ironing board** It's an iron. It's an ironing board.
- **Sewing machine** I wouldn't try hand sewing this one.
- **Hand-sanitizing gel** You need to actually wash your hands before you start, but I keep some gel handy since the alcohol in it dissolves the oil on your skin that can stain your project.

Step by Step

I'm really proud of this design. The challenge was to come up with something that fit the Dirty Pillows brand aesthetic, but wasn't *completely* vulgar like the rest of my stuff. My agent told me that there's a difference between "naughty" and "outright dirty," and that I should probably keep that in mind. So, if you wanna see the really X-rated stuff, you'll have to contact me, my Web site, or come to the bazaar. In the meantime, you'll have to settle for some clever innuendo and pretty colors.

GETTING STARTED

1. If you don't already have the necessary colors in your box, get 1 skein of DMC 6-strand floss for each required pattern color (refer to the DMC palette numbers on the chart—*bring your list to the store*) and wind each skein onto a bobbin.
This will be way more than enough floss for the project. Buy the bobbins if you don't already have 'em.

2. Choose your fabric.
There are a lot of options here. Colorwise I would recommend laying out your bobbins of floss (or skeins if you're still at the store) and trying to choose a fabric color that will contrast nicely. I used pale blue for this book's example, but I think a drab green would work as well. Use your own taste, but remember that a color that lacks sufficient contrast to your design will make things more difficult. White is almost always safe, but not the most thrilling. Dark colors work well, but the fabric can show through the stitches, which looks more rustic to me. This can vary with the number of strands you use and the stitch count of the cloth—again, it's a matter of taste. As far as the actual cloth goes, if this is your first cross-stitch project, I would stick with 14 count Aida cloth. I have done this for a long time, and I still generally don't go higher than 16.

3. Cut your fabric (or have the store cut it) into a 10- x 10-inch piece.
If you have the store cut it, go 12 x 12 inches. I am very fussy about cutting and I cut along the lines created from the holes in the fabric—I'm anal, what can I say. The store does not care about this kind of accuracy, so the extra inches of fabric are worth the pennies, and you can trim it at home.

4. Find the center of your fabric.
Since this is a square, it's pretty easy. If it's off by a stitch or two, I don't think it's the end of the world. I usually fold the piece in half, making a crease, vertically and horizontally. I stick an extra needle through the center stitch to mark it so I can remember where it is (make sure you go down through one hole and up through the next so the needle won't fall out; which it will, if you don't).

5. Start stitching at the center of the fabric.

Find the center of the pattern (which will be marked with bold grid lines and arrows at the edge) and look to see what color floss you'll use for your first stitches (in this case, the center stitch would be DMC 666 Christmas Red Bright). Remember, for this project (and most cross-stitch) you'll use 2 strands at a time, so you'll have to separate the strands out as you cut from the 6-strand skein or bobbin.

Start by anchoring your floss using the technique described in the previous section. My advice is to just keep working from the center out. Always start a new piece of floss or color building from *adjacent* pattern grids as opposed to working in "islands." I know it gets tough; craving variety you'll wanna change colors. When you do start a new color, just don't stray too far from the previous block of stitches.

6. Once you have finished the cross-stitching, take a breather.

That's right. Step 5 is a biggie, but it just kind of is what it is . . . just follow the pattern. This project doesn't have any specialty stitches, so it's pretty straightforward.

7. If you need to, hand wash your project in the sink or a dish tub.

Sometimes oils from your hands or the embroidery hoop can stain your fabric—sorta like ring around the collar. To clean it up, I recommend dissolving a laundry booster such as Oxy-Clean in a small amount of hot water, and then adding cold water to fill the tub. Place your project in the water, and let it soak for a few hours. Rinse it *very* well.

8. Lay out your clean project on a towel laid on a hard surface to dry.

You can place a second towel over the project, and a heavy book to sorta prepress it.

9. Once the project is completely dry, iron out the wrinkles on the cotton setting, using a little steam if you need to.

Make sure you use an ironing board, but if you don't have one, you can use a towel on a hard surface—just nothing too bumpy.

10. Iron an 8-inch square piece of fusible interfacing to the back of your finished stitching.

The original piece of Aida cloth is 10 x 10 inches, remember? Leave a 1-inch border around each edge. Use the grid of the weave to place it accurately. This selvage will be usable for fraying and fringing, but it is not the greatest for holding a secure seam. The interfacing is useful because when sewing a loosely woven fabric like Aida to a "regular" cotton fabric, it helps things kinda hold together.

11. Choose a piece of cotton fabric for the back of your pillow, and cut it into a 9-inch square. When I made this project I chose a cherry print.
If it seems a bit lightweight, use some interfacing on it as well.

12. Press a half-inch hem along each edge of the backing fabric square using your fusible tape.
I recommend pressing a half-inch hem, then laying down the fusible tape, and repressing with the tape in place to secure. This will leave you with an 8-inch square to match the interfacing on the back of the Aida. When you sew it to the Aida cloth, you'll have a 1-inch margin all the way around. If you like, you can snip a half-inch square from each corner of the backing, preventing the corners from being too bulky when you hem the fabric.

13. Sew Aida to the backing fabric.
Align the hemmed backing fabric to the 8-inch square of interfacing on the back of the Aida and pin together with straight pins, wrong sides (the sides without the print) together, all the way around the square, leaving about 2 inches open for stuffing. Sew together with your sewing machine using a straight stitch setting and backtacking for a secure seam. You can sew as close to the edge as you like, but I recommend just placing the presser foot's right edge flush with the pressed edge of the backing square.

14. Stuff the pillow with polyester fiber. Good and full.
I use a chopstick to really jam it in there.

15. Finish sewing the remainder of the open seam.
The fringed edge of this design makes it really easy when it comes to the sewing because there's no turning inside out of anything.

16. Now it's time to fringe the raw Aida cloth edges.

It's silly how easy this is to do, and how super-pro it ends up looking. Just take one of your tapestry needles and stick it into one of the holes closest to the corner of the pillow and slide it outward from the edge. This'll get you started. I recommend only removing as many strands of the Aida as are between each hole at one pass. Otherwise, things can get knotty—and we wanna keep 'em strictly *naughty*. Repeat this for each side of the pillow, obviously.

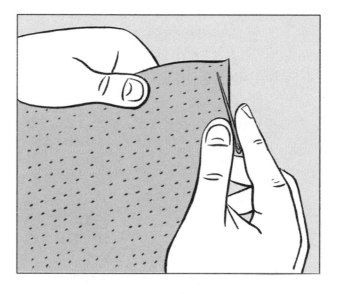

17. Now just sit back and admire your suggestive stitchery!

Now I bet that was long and hard, but that's the way we like it, right?

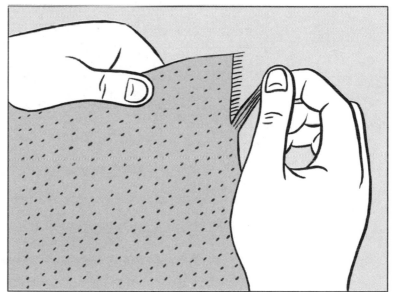

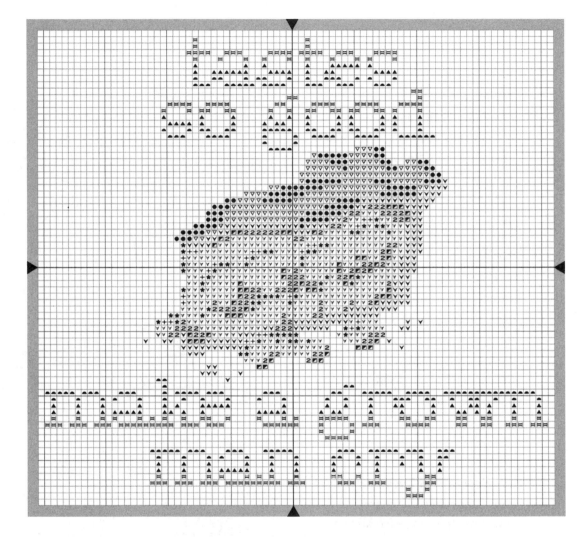

Pie Pattern—whole. The thicker lines mark every 10th stitch. Don't confuse this with the stitch count of the fabric. They are not related. The 10-stitch divisions in the pattern are just to help you count easily. The stitch count of the fabric, remember, just tells you how many stitches fit in 1 inch of the cloth. The lines with triangles at the ends represent the center of the pattern on each axis.

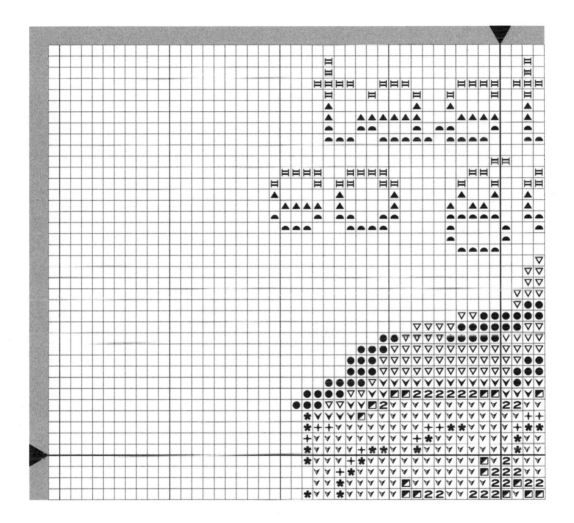

Pie Pattern—quadrants. These four enlarged quadrants will show you the pattern in greater detail. You'll notice that I've included a 4-stitch overlap (of which you can keep track by the triangles).

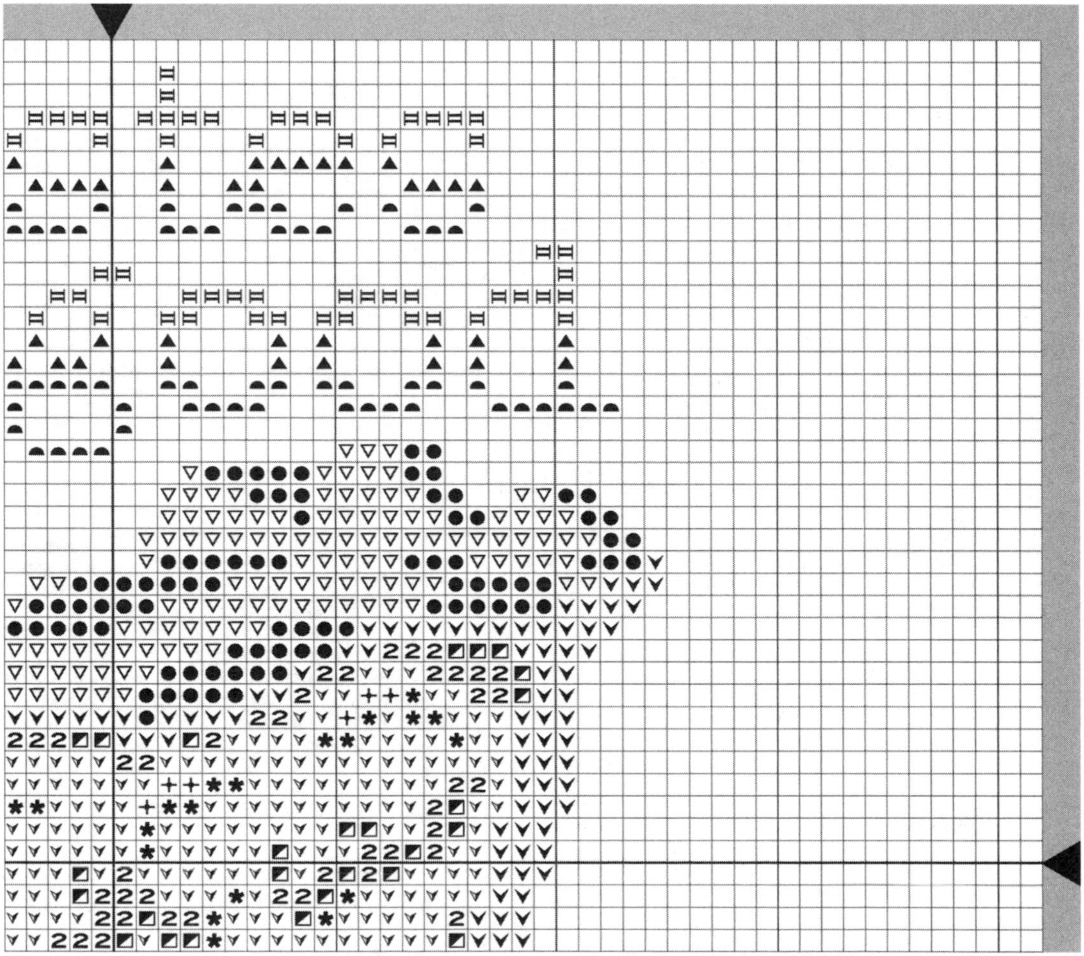

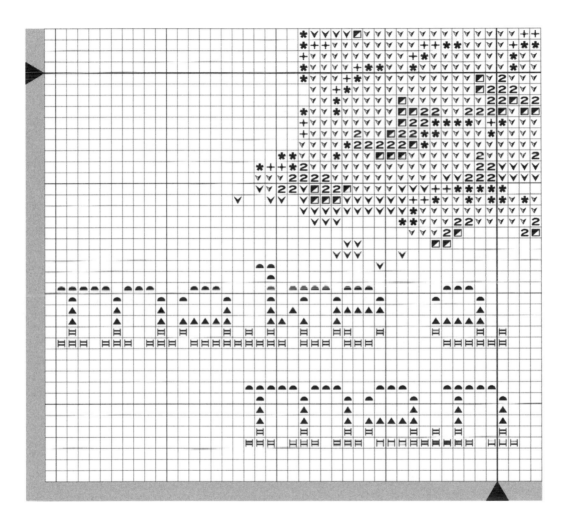

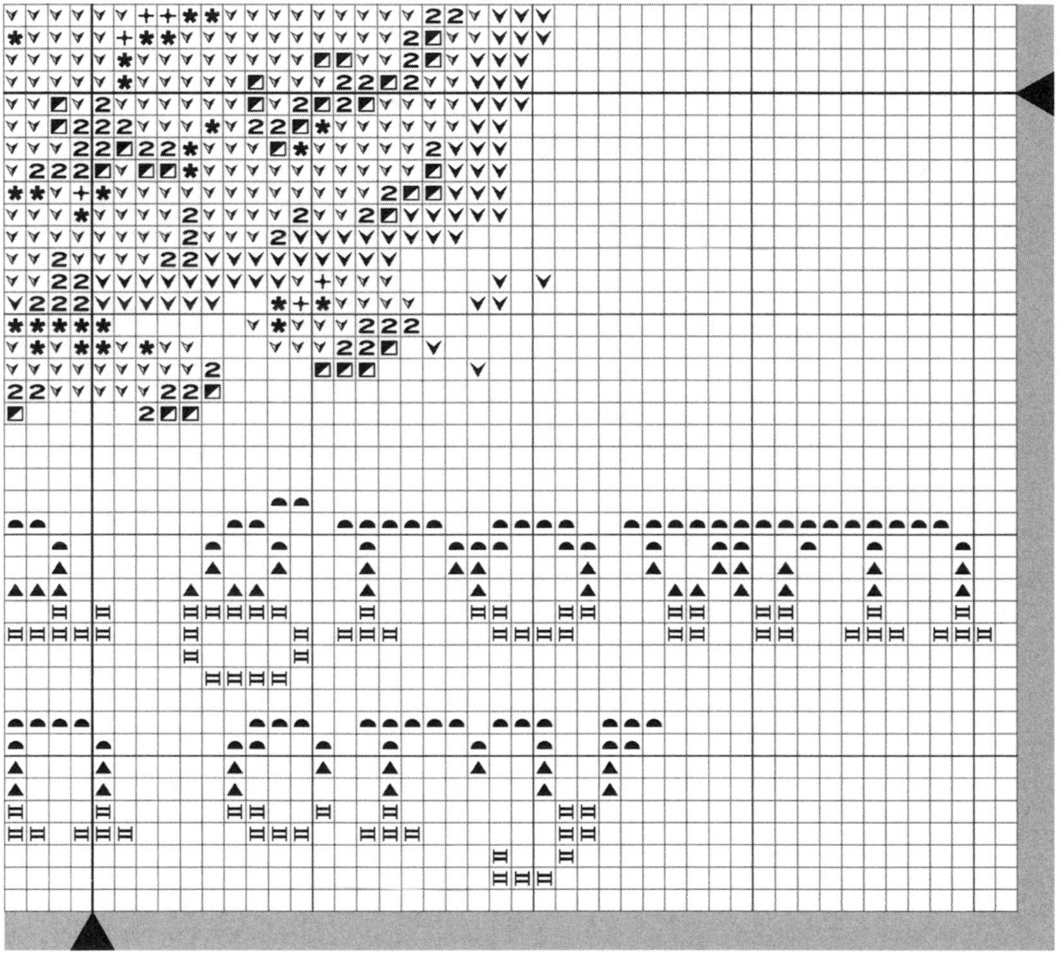

SERVING SUGGESTIONS: FRAMED CROSS-STITCH

This project makes a great pillow, but if you don't want or need a pillow, there are other modes of presentation. Cross-stitch makes great framed art if you do it right. Complete the project up through step 9. That's where we'll take a little turn in the road. For this design, I'd recommend getting a DIY frame set and a sturdy piece of foam core.

You can buy custom frame kits that each come with two (opposite) sides of a frame. That way you can create a frame with the exact dimensions that you want. Just buy 2 pair of 9-inch frame sides, get it?

Cut the foam core into a 9-inch square, and glue 2 to 3 layers of Poly-fil batting onto it. Once the glue has dried and the batting is securely on the foam core, do your best to center the cross-stitched piece onto the foam core. Tack the middle of each side to the back of the foam core using a straight pin or thumbtack, sorta wrapping the cross-stitch around it.

Place this assemblage into the frame so that the cross-stitch puffs out on the other side. Secure everything in place with glazier's points (available in the framing department of the craft store).

As for finishing, do what my mom does, which is cover the back of the project with a cut-up brown bag, an old printed gift bag from the closet, origami paper, etc. Trace the frame onto the paper, or at least measure out a square that's the same size of the frame's exterior edge. Sparingly apply a bead of tacky glue or use a glue stick around the edge. Make sure to smooth out any bumps with your finger, and make sure you have a good seal all the way to the paper's edge. Then mist with a sprayer or dampen with a paper towel—you don't have to wait for the glue to be dry before you dampen the paper. As it dries, the paper will become taut. This looks *really* pro. Of course, do all this before attaching any hardware like one of those jagged frame-hangy things (actually, self-leveling picture hangers).

Contact Info

Wanna get in close personal touch with me and stay a-*breast* of my goings-on?
Then check out http://www.dirtypillows.net/ or send me an e-mail at
mama@dirtypillows.net. Just don't call me looking for baked goods (except maybe
my hot-crossed buns). There is a Filipino bakery called Betsy's Cake Factory that used
to have the phone number that I have now. You would not believe how many calls I
get a day with people screaming cake orders at me in a foreign language. Evidently
this Filipino phone book refuses to remove the listing. I really should just take up
baking. I'd have a built-in clientele. Evidently Betsy's does—or at least did—a lot of
business.

CHERRY PiE PALETTE

Here's the legend/key/palette or whatever you wanna call it for the cherry-pie pillow
pattern. Remember that for this project you'll use 2 strands when stitching.

SYMBOL	DMC ID	DESCRIPTION
2	DMC 304	RED VY DK
⊟	DMC 311	NAVY MED
+	DMC 3716	DUSTY ROSE LT
∨	DMC 3852	STRAW VY DK
●	DMC 3855	AUTUMN GOLD LT
✳	DMC 603	PINK MAUVE MED
▽	DMC 666	CHRISTMAS RED BRIGHT
▽	DMC 745	YELLOW VY LT
◨	DMC 814	GARNET DK
▲	DMC 995	ELECTRIC BLUE DK
⬤	DMC 996	ELECTRIC BLUE MED

Arachnephobia

She was talented, hot, and had a bad attitude—at least that's what the gods thought. The gods: aka "the man" of ancient Greece. Anyway, not only was Arachne's weaving amazing but her very presence at the loom was something to behold. According to myth, nymphs were said to abandon their frolicking—and you know how they love to frolic—to watch her weave. She was so good, evidently, that her fan base thought she must have studied with Athena, who was literally the *goddess* of weaving. Being an independent, self-educated gal, Arachne was kinda pissed that people assumed she needed some authority figure's help and/or approval for her craft.

So Athena got wind of this and in a kind of patriot-act covert op, approached Arachne disguised as a crone, warning her to watch her step vis-à-vis the whole weaving thing. Arachne promised the old gal that she'd be fine and sent her on her way with some baklava and an assurance that, if push came to shove, she could hold her own against Athena and would even concede victory to the Olympian debutante if she really did best her in competitive weaving.

In a subsequent intimidation tactic, Athena ripped off her disguise (or however immortals disrobe), *totally* freaking out the nymphs. Arachne kept her cool and threw down the loom. Now Athena was no slouch, of course, but she wove this predictable, patriotic scene replete with Poseidon's saltwater-spring misstep and her own fabulous olive tree gift to the city that then named itself Athens. And honestly, it *was* gorgeous.

CRAFTGOLD

Arachne, in true Bazaar Bizarre fashion, refused to toe the party line and do the whole traditional bit. Instead, she wove a beautifully and brutally honest depiction of Zeus (perhaps a Hellenic proto-Clinton) engaged in his well . . . "mythical" peccadilloes (all rapes, by the way): Leda with the Swan, Europa with the bull, Danaë and the golden rain shower (c'mon—*golden shower?*).

Maybe it was her incredible skill or perhaps her choice of materials and threads, but despite Arachne's unflinching and somewhat vexing honesty, Athena had to admit that the tapestry was flawless. In what could only be considered blatant censorship (and in my opinion poor sportsmanship), Athena tore the tapestry to pieces and destroyed the loom. Further, she smacked Arachne with her shuttle and transformed her into a spider. Was that really warranted?

The moral: I guess you can't beat city hall, but at least there are crafters out there refusing to take it lying down. That's Bazaar Bizarre in a nutshell: Unsettling though it may be to our forebears, we stick to our glue guns and find our own representation at those times when we have none.

SOAP MAKING

PROJECT: **ANARCHY SOAP**

ARTIST: *Mary Jo Kaczka*

Soap is fun, it smells good, and everybody loves it. It makes a great gift, and it's perfect if you know someone who really stinks. It's a lot more subtle than taping a bow to a Speedstick. With soap you get a lot of bang for your buck—an integral facet of the crafting experience. Why would you put all the time and effort into something if it was gonna break the bank on top of everything? After the initial cash layout, soap is actually really cheap to make. Like any recipe, you may have to buy pricey ingredients, but you certainly won't come close to using them all up on one project. Fragrance and pigment can be used over and over and over again.

This project brings back memories of living in Bloomington, Indiana, and how I wish I'd had Mary Jo's anarchy soap then. Walking down Kirkwood Avenue past People's Park, I'd see the young, crusty punks and ask myself why did anarchy have to smell so bad? How does a lack of bathing dismantle state machinery? If I'd had a few of these soaps to hand out to those misguided Sids-Vicious-in-training, many innocent personal relationships could have been spared and employment maintained.

Yummy smells and a bold graphic look give this project an impressive design, but it's still a very beginner-friendly endeavor. For fragrance, Mary Jo tried out grapefruit, and it was a big hit. You can use the grapefruit scent detailed in the directions below, or lime, lemon, and orange would all be great. I always like my projects to reflect my favorite fruit: me. Now if only I could find an artist to develop a Dead Kennedy's dentifrice . . .

I met Mary Jo in October of 2003 when she volunteered to help organize the first Los Angeles edition of Bazaar Bizarre. She jumped in headfirst and was an absolutely essential part of the success of our West Coast team. Mary Jo has been working in tour and event production for over ten years, and she brought

her impressive expertise to Bazaar Bizarre. Mary Jo is a fellow Gemini, born June 12, the oldest of five. Four years at an all-girl Catholic high school engendered an obsession with bad boys and rock (yet she took accordion lessons for a decade). Hailing from Denver, Colorado, Mary Jo moved to the Whitley Heights neighborhood of Hollywood, California, and freelances as a tour manager and event producer. She has worked on tours with bands such as Bauhaus, the Eagles, Skinny Puppy, and King Crimson, in addition to spending five summers on the Vans Warped Tour. She's also helped organize events such as the Coachella Festival. Even though she never broke 1000 on her SATs, she makes a pumpkin bread truly worthy of the description "honor roll."

CRAFTER Q+A

What is the difference between an "art" and a "craft"?
I think the biggest difference is that a craft is art that you can physically use for a purpose—jewelry, pottery, stuffed animals, soap, etc. There is art that is designed to be interacted with, but to me, what differentiates a craft from interactive artwork is that it also has

a use that is more than merely interacting for an aesthetic reason. For example, a vase can be used to put flowers in. Jewelry can be worn. Stuffed animals can be slept with at night.

Also, to me, crafts must be handmade. A mass-produced bar of soap is not a craft, but a handmade one is. The lines between arts and crafts are pretty blurred nowadays, though, because many crafts are designed to push the limits of what might be considered a craft, into the realm of art. Inversely, crafts can potentially become art: For example, at art museums you'll see lots of examples of Native American pottery as art. But essentially, those items are crafts, as I see it.

What is your earliest crafting memory?

My mom would save everything she could think of in a box: yarn, glue, glitter, empty dishwashing soap bottles, empty jars, construction paper, etc. Then if we were bored or just had some time during the day, she'd pull it out and say, "Make something from this stuff."

What was your best crafting moment (idea, inspiration, etc.)?

My best crafting moments were when I was at summer camp as a kid. There was a whole craft building with a candle-making studio, leather-craft room, stained glass-making studio, etc. Since the camp was in the middle of the forest in Colorado, you could just run outside and grab a stick or a rock or anything and use it in your crafts. Also these rooms were so incredibly stocked with everything you'd need to make stuff that you could really just go for it and do any idea you came up with.

What was your worst crafting moment (a huge mess, project gone horribly wrong, etc.)?

I was pouring some melted soap into a mold when the bottom broke, and soap went everywhere. Cleaning soap off your kitchen floor is not as easy as you'd think it would be—especially when it's an inch thick!

What is your favorite craft you've ever seen?

Not really sure, there are so many great ones. Favorite ones I've seen lately are biggerCritters. I love the nontraditional stuffed things. (NOTE: biggerCritters are unusual stuffed "animals" made by Krissy Harris: www.biggerkrissy.com.)

Who made you the crafter you are (who introduced you to crafts, taught you crafts—whether or not it is the one you do now)?
I'd have to say my mom (see above).

What are your crafting goals?
No real goals other than to keep making stuff! I'd like to sell some kind of product that I make, but I enjoy giving it away so much that I doubt it will ever happen. Also to help show people that crafting is a form of art for the masses.

Kraft or Kraftwerk?
Kraftwerk, definitely! (And I have a backstory to go with that—I was the tour manager for Kraftwerk's 1998 U.S. tour, so I have a special fondness for them.)

Who is your fave crafty celebrity?
Rosey Greer (NFL legend most famous for his needlepoint—Google him!).

What is your fave craft resource (Web site, store, dumpster, etc.)?
The hardware store and salvage yards for inspiring me with ideas (and many interesting items!) and www.soapcrafters.com and www.soapwizards.com for soap-making stuff.

Global Techniques: Soap-Making Basics

The world of melt-and-pour soap is a universe of creative opportunities. Hard-core traditional soapsters may prefer the more chemistry-intensive soap-from-scratch methods, but in those cases you're spending so much more time actually producing the soap medium before you even begin to get creative visually. In addition, soap from scratch can only be set once, preventing you from remelting scraps or salvaging a mistake. Pigment and fragrance must be added to the entire batch, and once you're done, you're done. No second chances here. Melt-and-pour is a much more forgiving medium when it comes to both design and finances.

Soap molds that you can buy in the soap-making aisle of your local craft supply store might be a good place to start, but I say ditch the prefab molds ASAP. In addition to a complete paucity of interesting designs, the scale of your project is very predetermined and usually way too ladylike for the renegade crafter that you aspire to be. Instead, look around you and keep a crafty eye out for vessels that might make interesting molds. A good intermediate step might be investigating molds that were made for nonsoap projects: candy and candle molds to name two. What about cupcake tins and tiny loaf pans? Almost anything that could contain a liquid can be a mold. You are only limited by your punk-rock imagination. Mary Jo has made some great soap out of children's sand toys and novelty ice cube trays. Check out your 99-cent store— always a treasure trove of junk from whence your next masterpiece might spring.

Dropping stuff in soap is a really fun thing to do. I am sure you've encountered the soap with other little soap cubes trapped inside. This is pretty basic stuff. Mary Jo recently showed me a bar of soap with a cute little plastic pig in it. For the more chichi, froufrou end of the soap spectrum, try herbs for fragrance or oatmeal as an exfoliant. Remember, however, that soap will not "preserve" the items dropped within. This means that if you decided to submerge a bunch of raspberries, before long you will have rotten raspberry soap. I like things like glitter, bugs, or even a severed finger. Now that's punk!

There is melt-and-pour soap formulated specifically to better allow ingredients to hover suspended rather than sink to the bottom or float to the top. Before you lay out the extra cash, however, experiment and see if you can't get things to stay put by stirring, keeping your little scuba divers in motion until the soap begins to firm up. You can usually get things to remain suspended this way.

ANARCHY SOAP DIFFICULTY ✪✪✩✩✩

TIME LINE The active time in Mary Jo's project is broken up into fairly reasonable 20- to 30-minute chunks, with longer periods in between when you will be waiting around for the soap to set up and dry. That's time enough to review some essentials (and I don't mean oils). Try passing the time with these albums and movies:

The Ramones: *The Ramones;* Styx: *The Grand Illusion;* Gary Numan: *Replicas*

This Is Spinal Tap; Ice Castles; Hedwig and the Angry Inch

SHOPPING LIST

THE CRAFT STORE

- **Opaque white melt-and-pour soap**
- **Clear melt-and-pour soap**
- **Fragrance (soap fragrance, essential oils)**
- **Pigment** Choose one color—Mary Jo chose green for her project. You can use soap colorant or food coloring.

THE HARDWARE STORE

- **One 3-inch long section of 2-inch diameter PVC pipe** Orchard Supply Hardware had 12-inch sections of PVC that they were happy to cut down to size. Most hardware stores will cut it for you if you ask nicely. You may want to get the PVC cut slightly longer than 3 inches to make it easier to get the hardened soap out of it later.

- **One 3-inch-long section of 3-inch-diameter PVC pipe** Again, you may want to get the pipe cut slightly longer.
- **4- x 2-inch sheet of tin or aluminum (but not foil)**
- **Tin snips** Or I'm sure you can have the hardware store cut it for you if you bring your measurements.

RIGHT IN YOUR VERY OWN HOME

- **Microwave-safe (not metal or Styrofoam) mixing bowl in which to melt soap (if microwaving)**
- **Pot with metal/glass bowl that can fit inside to make double boiler**

(if using stovetop)
- **Rubbing alcohol in a spray bottle**
- **Vaseline**
- **Saran wrap**
- **2 thick rubber bands** You may wanna have extras on hand.
- **Cleaver or heavy-duty knife**

Step by Step

NEGATIVE SPACE:

1. Coat the inside of the 2-inch diameter PVC pipe piece with petroleum jelly.
Try to achieve a very thin coating, but do ensure that the PVC is coated completely.
Remember: lube, lube, lube!

2. Cover one end in plastic wrap and secure with a thick rubber band—like a little drum.

3. Place PVC wrap-side down on your pouring surface.
Put the PVC somewhere that it won't be moved. You can't pick it up until the melted soap hardens, or it will leak all over the place, and you'll have a huge mess. Unbelievably, soap is hard to clean up.

4. Take your 4- x 2-inch tin piece and snip a 1-inch cut perpendicular to the bottom, 1 inch from each of the short sides. This is going to be the first part of a slot assembly.

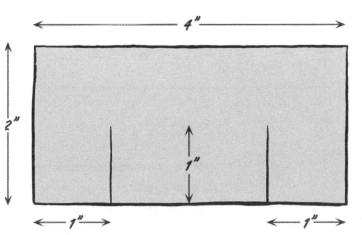

5. Fold the 4- x 2-inch tin piece in half so that the folded piece is 2 x 2 inches. Don't fold it flat. Make it look more like a tent.

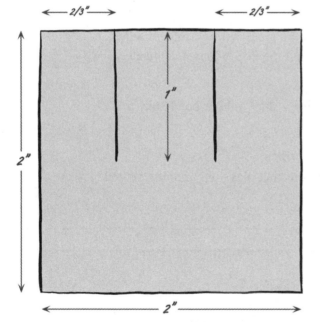

6. Take your 2- x 2-inch tin piece and snip a 1-inch cut perpendicular to the top (well "top" cuz it's a square) 2/3 inch from each of the sides. This is the second half of your slot assembly, which will create the separate pieces of the negative space.

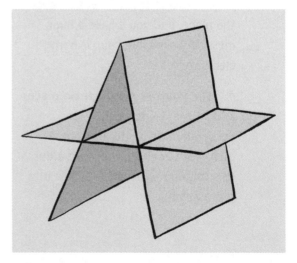

7. Join the two pieces by matching up the slots on the bent and straight segments and shimmying them together. You should have a 3-D anarchy symbol at this point

8. Stand up your tin assembly in your 2-inch diameter PVC pipe, which should be ready and waiting on your pouring surface.

9. Melt clear soap in microwave or on stovetop.
If melting in microwave: Check every 30 seconds until melted to be sure the soap melts without boiling. If melting on the stovetop: Melt the soap in a double boiler. It's very important not to let the soap boil. Boiling will trigger a chemical change in the soap that will prevent it from setting properly.

10. Add pigment to melted clear soap.
With color and fragrance there is no set method or amounts. Just "season" to taste. The color will remain true as the soap sets, so there's no need to second-guess.

11. Add fragrance to melted clear soap.
Don't get too crazy right off the bat. A little goes a long way. Like Mom always says: "You can always add more, but you can never take away."

12. Pour melted clear soap into 2-inch diameter PVC pipe piece.
If using a PVC pipe that is slightly longer than 3 inches, be sure to only pour the soap up to the 3-inch mark, which you should premeasure with a Sharpie. Make sure this mold is where you can leave it to harden. *Do not* attempt to move the mold. I suggest placing the empty mold onto a saucer or on a cookie sheet for added portability once it has hardened.

13. Spritz with rubbing alcohol to remove any bubbles from the soap's surface.
Don't ask me why this works—it just does.

14. Allow to cool and harden for 30 to 45 minutes.
Don't succumb to the temptation of cooling the soap in the freezer or refrigerator! Water droplets will form on the surface of the soap, making it sticky and slimy, as well as less adhesive in the following steps.

15. Once soap has completely hardened, remove plastic wrap and push soap out of the PVC piece.
If you use a pipe that is slightly longer than 3 inches, you can invert the PVC onto the counter, hollow end down, and push the soap through.

16. Separate the negative space pieces of soap from the tin divider.
You may have to jiggle this a bit. If you are having trouble separating it, and if the soap is *completely* dry, you can stick it in the freezer cuz freezing things makes 'em shrink a little.

POSITIVE IMAGE

17. Coat the inside of a 3-inch diameter PVC section with petroleum jelly.
Slippery!

18. Cover one end in plastic wrap and secure with a thick rubber band.
Stretchy!

19. Stand negative space soap sections in center of can, using a butter knife to separate them slightly while maintaining their overall circular formation.
This doesn't have to be absolutely perfect. Rules are for chumps and slaves of the state!

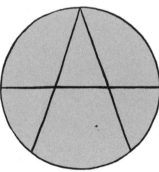

Step 15

Step 16

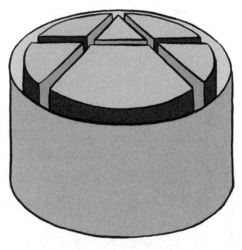

Step 19

20. Melt white soap in microwave or on stove top.
Remember to check every 30 seconds—no boiling!

21. Add pigment to the melted white soap.
Even though you'll be using the same color pigment (which of course you don't have to), it will be contrasting cuz the negative image is clear while the positive is opaque.

22. Add fragrance to melted white soap.
Take a big whiff and remember that even though it smells friendly, this soap is badass.

23. Spritz negative space sections with rubbing alcohol.
This'll make it cling better.

24. Carefully pour melted white soap around edges of negative space sections until melted white soap barely covers them.
You might wanna give each section piece a jiggle just to make sure there are no air pockets.

25. Spritz with rubbing alcohol to remove any bubbles from the soap's surface.
Bubbles, be gone!

26. Set aside to cool and harden for about 30 to 45 minutes.
Not in the freezer or fridge.

27. Once soap has completely hardened, remove plastic wrap and push soap out of PVC piece.
Push it out! Shove it out! Waaaay out!

28. Remove a thin slice of soap from each end of the cylinder to expose a clean cross section.
Expose the fragrant and colorful inner chaos that is soap!

29. Slice cylinder into ½ - to 1-inch pieces.
Give to a comrade as a gift, or hurl forcefully at your smelliest archnemesis.

SERVING SUGGESTIONS

Okay, so you've flung soap at your last fetid rival and now it's time to present some to your friends. Chances are they won't enjoy your pitching arm. Instead, try filling an empty Chinese take-out box with tape you've pulled out of old cassettes. You can get the take-out boxes at most party or restaurant supply stores, but I usually just go to a Chinese restaurant and ask them to sell me some— much cheaper. The magnetic tape from the cassettes acts kind of like Easter basket grass, but punk! You could substitute old report cards run through the shredder or anything that shows your general disregard for authority ("the Man") as packing material! Slap some band stickers on the outside and your gift of cleanliness is ready to rock.

Contact Info

You can reach Mary Jo via e-mail at Mjk789@mac.com. Even when she's on the road making rock 'n' roll manageable, she is still great with the whole communication thing. Laptops, you know?

Bead My Frankenstein

Victor Frankenstein was like any other overachieving nerd. As the story goes, he was obsessed with these outdated theories about what gives humans their "life spark." Something of an anatomical scrapbooker, Frankenstein scavenges human remains for the necessary body parts to make his "perfect human." Once he managed to bring the monster to life, he found it hideous, but somehow grave robbing and sewing together pieces of cadavers didn't bother him.

Anyway, he flees the monster because of its ugliness, and the monster is alone. Longing for companionship, it tries to befriend humans, but as you can probably guess, they weren't too thrilled with an undead quilt for a neighbor. The monster becomes afraid of humans but still observes them from a distance, learning just how different it is from them.

After even more rejection, the monster wants to take revenge on Victor Frankenstein, and sets out to find him. Along the way it kidnaps a boy to keep as a pet/friend, but 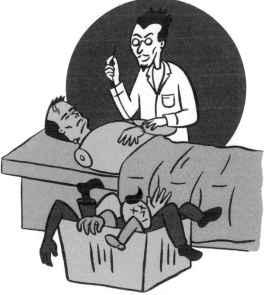 discovers that the boy is really Victor's younger brother, so it kills the kid, planting the boy's necklace on a beautiful girl who is later executed for the younger Frankenstein brother's murder.

Finally, Victor Frankenstein and the monster come face-to-face, and the monster demands that Victor create a female monster for its bride. Frankenstein, fearing for his family, agrees, but has a change of heart after looking back on the results of his last crafting project, so he destroys his work. The monster now vows even *more* revenge, scheduled to take place on Frankenstein's wedding night. Dr. and Mrs. Frankenstein basically elope and get ready for the groom's impending murder, but in a surprising twist, the monster kills Mrs. Frankenstein instead, whose father-in-law (Victor's dad) dies of grief over *her* death (Sheesh).

Victor finally vows to destroy the monster and begins following it to the North Pole, but dies from exposure before he can catch up with it. The monster makes an appearance at Frankenstein's deathbed to atone for the havoc it's caused, and then sets out on a dogsled to burn itself at the North Pole so that no one will ever know of its existence.

I see two important Bazaar Bizarre life lessons here: First, never underestimate yourself. You can accomplish a lot even if you're a patchwork of dead body parts. Second, though impromptu, no-rules crafting may be fun and can yield exciting, unexpected results, sometimes it really is better to *plan* your projects.

PRiNTMAKiNG
PROJECT: BiRD POSTCARDS
ARTIST: *Dana Berkowitz*

The term *printmaking* can sound like a really involved, technical skill, according to Dana, but there's no need to be intimidated. In fact, when Dana was teaching printmaking to kids, she realized that the class name was possibly keeping people away, so she changed it to printing and drawing, and attendance went right up.

I first encountered Dana's printed postcards at Bazaar Bizarre 2003 when she was kind enough to give me a set of red and pink glittery lovebird cards bundled in ribbon. They've definitely been too nice for me to even think of using as anything but an art piece until now. Now I (and you, dear reader) can feel free to mail these postcards with all the care and concern of Wendy O. Williams cuz Dana's taught me how she makes 'em. This project is so versatile. I wish I could say that about the men I meet, but you know what they say: French for "bottom." What Dana's given us is way more than just a set of postcards. This project is as much about a process as it is about aesthetics. Once you follow the steps, you'll be thinking of a zillion ways to use your mad printmaking skillz.

CRAFTER BIO

I did not know anything about Dana Berkowitz before her 2003 Bazaar Bizarre application materialized on my desktop, but I was instantly struck by her stylized images of birds. Now you have to understand that I have this thing about people looking like birds—especially indie and emo rockers, because they even seem to eat like birds. I mean, can I get you a suet bell? A chunky hipster haircut, maybe a faux hawk, angular features, and razorlike pelvic bones add up to a rather birdy profile, but in the words of Sophia Petrillo: "I digress."

Dana began her life as an artist in Bridgewater, New Jersey. As of fourth grade, she was already a drummer and accomplished unicorn portraitist. Her early work can still be seen on her father's refrigerator. She began studying ceramics in New Jersey and later studied at the prestigious School of the Museum of Fine Arts in Boston, where she graduated with a BFA in printmaking. After teaching printmaking to kids for five years, she moved to Los Angeles, where she was rejected from a dental assistant college program. Dana now divides her time between being a rock 'n' roll drummer and a rock 'n' roll crafter.

I share Dana's fascination with birds—not just cuz of the indie rocker thing, either. My seventh-grade science teacher, Mr. Hubley, would have us color these Audubon drawings in order to learn about bird species. On Fridays, there'd be a competition to see who could correctly identify the most birds in a row from his trays of slides. I became a classroom hero because I could go all the way until lunch, thereby sparing the rest of the students any actual class work.

During our interview I grew wide-eyed at the connections she drew between birds, teeth, and hearts. As a child, Dana had a lot of dental problems, and she explained to me that certain kinds of tooth damage can expand and lead straight to your heart, hence her obsession with teeth and hearts. One of her drawings of teeth looked like two birds on a wire, and she began to think about birds, too. Literally drawing connections between heartbeats and wing beats, she took off with the work that led her to Bazaar Bizarre.

What is the difference between an "art" and a "craft"?

I have been questioning the difference between art and craft for a long time and I still do not have a definite stance. I started my art career in a fine arts college, where the word craft was often used sarcastically. If a person considers himself or herself an artist, then they are making art. If a person considers himself or herself a crafter, then it is a craft. I think there is a fine line between art and craft. Personally, I consider myself an artist and a crafter.

What is your earliest crafting memory?

Well, I suppose the earliest memory I have making crafts is when I was maybe between the ages of eight and twelve. I remember making friendship pins and those knot bracelets that were all the rage. You could make the knot bracelets out of either some kind of vinyl material or cotton. I have also been a sticker collector since a very young age.

What was your best crafting moment (idea, inspiration, etc.)?

Hmmm . . . Maybe after completing my first raku ceramic piece. I felt very proud and accomplished. I am always inspired by and exchanging ideas with friends.

What was your worst crafting moment (a huge mess, project gone horribly wrong, etc.)?

Okay, well, the first thing that pops into my head would be this ridiculous incident: I was setting up for my student show at the Museum school, and I decided to paint a mural on one of the walls. I asked a friend to help me and we thought the fastest and best way would be to spray paint the image. Well, let me tell you that is probably the worst way to do it. We had to evacuate the building to let it air out. It was halfway finished, so the next morning I came in the building early and finished painting it with acrylic paint. In the end it looked pretty incredible, but a word of advice: Never, and I mean never, spray paint anything indoors. I guess we all have to learn our lessons some way or another.

What is your favorite craft you've ever seen?

I am constantly surprised and admiring new types of art/crafts. I can't think of one particular project that I have seen that is my favorite. There are too many.

Who made you the crafter you are (who introduced you to crafts, taught you crafts—whether or not it is the one you do now)?

I really can't remember who exactly introduced me to crafts. My family, friends, and teachers have always been 100 percent supportive and have also been a great resource for ideas and inspiration.

What are your crafting goals?

To continue making art/crafts every day. To continue meeting and being inspired by people involved with art/craft making. I am not sure where I ultimately want to end up. I make art because I love it and it is necessary in my life. I have been teaching after-school art classes, and, if I am lucky, I will be able to continue my life with a career where I am surrounded by art.

Kraft or Kraftwerk?

Kraftwerk seems to be the right answer for me, although I love Kraft macaroni and cheese.

Who is your fave crafty celeb?

I am not sure if I have one. At least I can't think of someone right now.

What is your fave craft resource (Web site, store, dumpster, etc.)?

Hmmm . . . where do I start??? I love any hardware or office supply store or any place with gadgets. Since participating in Bazaar Bizarre I have been exploring many Internet craft sites and one of my favorites that I check almost every day is craftster.org. I am also a fan of garage sales, antique stores, thrift stores, and garbage night is always a good time to find priceless objects on the street (especially if you live in a college town). People throw away all kinds of stuff that I would consider a treasure.

Global Techniques

Printmaking is one of the most versatile techniques around. It allows you to use your own drawings or found images, and makes them infinitely reproducible. There are a few different things you'll wanna keep in mind before you start.

BLOCK MEDIA

Making the actual printing apparatus, or block, is probably the most involved step. You have a number of choices when it comes to materials. There are superdurable materials like linoleum and wood, but keep in mind that these are literally, physically much harder substances than the rubber we use in this chapter, and may require a more expensive supporting cast of tools. At the extreme opposite end of the spectrum, you can use a potato. Of course I think this is the only block medium that will actually *rot* on you, but hey, you can get some cool, rough effects, it's a good way to get your feet wet, and it's supercheap.

We're using rubber for this project. It's very soft and easy to carve, allowing you to use less expensive, less hard-core tools. At the same time, however, rubber will hold up for a good long time—especially if you glue it to something sturdy like a piece of wood.

INK

There are many kinds of ink, including oil-based, rubber-based, powdered, and water-based. Water is definitely the best type of ink for home printing. You might want to hold off on using nonwater-based inks until you decide whether or not you want to get more seriously into printing. They require special chemicals to clean and work with, and aren't terribly kitchen sink friendly. By all accounts, Speedball water-based printing inks are the pigments of choice. Don't make the mistake, however, of buying something *watery* like India ink. It's got to be thick stuff in a tube.

SURFACES

What are you going to print onto? In this project we use paper, but you could really print on any number of porous surfaces—that is, surfaces that will absorb the water in the ink. There are many, many kinds of paper though, and not all are designed to soak up inks. Avoid ultrasmooth, glossy illustrators' papers like bristol board. Watercolor paper is definitely a safe bet, but don't hesitate to ask a salesperson at the art store for help when choosing a paper. They should be able to give you a range of appropriate options.

ONE FINAL NOTE: While researching this chapter, I found that you will have *much* better luck at an art supply store than a general craft chain like Michael's (which I love). If you have somewhere like a Pearl Paint in your town, that would be ideal. Try to find a store that has an actual printmaking section. I had a hard time finding all of the supplies for the project at a generalized craft supply store.

BiRD POSTCARDS   DiFFICULTY ✪✪✪✪✪

TiME LiNE I think, like a lot of us, Dana can kinda half watch and half listen to a movie or TV show while she works. And like me, at least, she seems to like to consume the same movies and music again and again. Seems like that way you can "watch it in your head." This project is mostly active time—about 3 hours. As far as passive time, you'll have a few half-hour chunks while you're waiting for glues and inks to dry.

Doves: *Lost Souls;* Radiohead: *The Bends;* Girls Against Boys: *Venus Luxure No. 1 Baby*

Some Kind of Wonderful; Say Anything . . . ; Pretty in Pink

SHOPPING LIST

THE CRAFT STORE

- **Carbon paper** You can find this at the hardware store, as well.
- **Watercolor paper or printing paper** Make sure it's a heavyweight paper—you don't want your card to buckle, wrinkle, or crack. Avoid nonporous papers like bristol board. Don't be afraid to ask for help! Describe your project to a salesperson, and they can help you choose the right materials. Alternatively you can print on cardstock, foam core, etc.
- **Tracing paper**
- **Kneaded gum eraser** Erase the carbon paper right off your hands! Plus it's stress relieving.
- **Rubber pad for your block print or stamp** You can find this in the printmaking aisle.
- **Carving tool** There are cheap "multitool" versions available with a handle and many interchangeable blades. Not the sturdiest but more than adequate for the soft rubber. Look in the printmaking or wood-block aisle.
- **Neutral ph adhesive** This is used mainly for bookbinding. It dries clear and won't cause your paper to buckle.
- **Brayer** This is a roller for applying your ink. They come in glass, wood, and metal, but rubber is the cheapest.
- **Water-soluble printmaking ink** Everyone I've talked to says Speedball is the best brand, without question. Ink comes in water-, oil-, and rubber-based varieties. Novelty inks (glitter, opalescent) are okay, but test to see how fast they dry. Water-based ink is best for working at home since there's no need for toxic solvents as with oil-based inks.
- **Stamp pad** Nowadays you can find really big ones. You can try this in addition to, or instead of, the brayer method.
- **Bone folder** For burnishing, creasing, and scoring.
- **Fine-tipped watercolor paintbrush**
- **Drawing pencil** The harder lead is easier to erase than a number 2 pencil.

- **Archival pen** Kinko's has these if the art store doesn't. Dana swears by this superpen: photo safe, acid free, waterproof, and fadeproof.
- **Workable fixative** Keeps things from getting messed up in the mail or sale.
- **Watercolor set** This is optional. Dana says Reeves is a decent, affordable brand.
- **Gouache—water soluble (optional)**
- **Water-soluble crayons or colored pencils** They let you color, and then brush with water for a painted look. Caran D'Ache is the brand Dana uses.
- **Toy store paint** Doesn't last long and dries up quick, but it is so cheap. Each little pot holds such a small amount that you're not wasting a bunch.

HARDWARE STORE

- **Spray bottle** For spritzing. We love to spritz.
- **Spray adhesive** You might find this as "spray mount" at the art store.
- **Block of wood** Use this for your print/stamp "handle." Make sure it's roughly the same size as your rubber pad.
- **Plexiglas (roughly 8½ x 11 inches is a good size)** They may have pieces precut at the art store, or they'll cut it for you at the hardware store.

YOUR VERY OWN CUPBOARDS:

- **Coloring books, colored paper, calendars, magazines, origami paper, tissue wrapping paper, etc.** Use stuff lying around the house for image and collage source material
- **A can of water**
- **A handy hand towel**
- **An old cutting board** You could use this instead of Plexiglas if you have a smooth plastic or glass one.
- **A spoon** Use the back of it for burnishing.

Step by Step

1. Xerox the bird skeleton image from page 49 of this book.
To make these projects, you can use any image you can think of. You can draw your own image; trace something from a magazine, whatever.

Bird skeleton image for print.

2. Transfer bird skeleton image onto the rubber pad, using carbon paper by tracing it with either a pencil or some kind of stylus (which is basically any pointy stick).

Tape the carbon paper onto the rubber pad, then tape the xeroxed bird image on top of the carbon paper. It's important to remember that the image will be reversed horizontally when printed, so make sure you orient your image opposite of how you actually want it on the page.

4. Once your image is transferred, use your carving tool to remove the negative space (the background).

Use a fine tip for outlining the image, and use the larger blades for subtracting negative or empty space. Remember that the rubber is very soft, so don't use too much pressure. For a different look you could also use a fine tip to strictly trace the lines of the image; this will give your print a "black" (inked) background and "white" (no ink) lines. If the rubber cracks, no problem—you can glue it using your neutral ph adhesive.

5. Glue the completed rubber carving to your wooden handle.

Choose a piece of wood the same size as the piece of rubber. A simple block will work. I don't think there is a handle section in the rubber stamp department at Michael's, but hey, you never know. You might be tempted to attach some kinda door-knobby, drawer-pull thing on top, but I recommend sticking with just a flat piece of wood. This is important so you can lay the stamp rubber side up for applying the ink.

6. If the whole brayer/Plexiglas/liquid ink combo seems a bit intimidating, you can use a large inkpad and proceed as you would with a traditional rubber stamp (which is what you've just made anyway).

Ink the stamp by pressing it onto the pad, and then make your print by pressing the stamp onto the card. If you choose this route, skip on ahead to step 13.

7. Apply your first color of ink to the Plexiglas, which will serve as your ink "station."

Lay down the ink you wish to use for the bird skeleton in a line near the edge rather than a blob in the center. This allows you to take ink as needed, rather than just squishing and pushing around a big puddle.

8. Using your brayer (remember that rolly thing you got?), pick up a small amount of the ink from the Plexiglas and roll it out.

Create a square ink reservoir by rolling your brayer both vertically and horizontally. Even coverage is your goal. Remember the line of ink you squeezed from the tube? Only dip in as much as you need. A little goes a long way.

9. Apply the ink to the rubber stamp with the brayer.

Lay your stamp on a flat surface, rubber side up. Several light rolls over the stamp

should do it. Make sure you get even coverage but don't mash it down. It'll
stick on its own.

**10. Optionally, you may want to spritz your paper with water for a more
uniform print. After spritzing and before stamping, blot dry with a paper towel.**
This can be really helpful if you are using something like watercolor paper, which is
ultraabsorbent.

**11. Lay the cardstock on the stamp and burnish (rub down like Presto Magix)
with a bone folder or the back of a spoon.**
Keep in mind that this setup is physically upside down from traditional stamping.
That is, we place the paper onto the upside-down stamp rather than stamping the
print onto the paper. Burnishing will assure that you get the most uniform print
without gaps or light areas. Of course, as with the spritzing of the paper, this can
also be an artistic choice, meaning you could choose to go for a rougher, more
random look to your prints. You could choose to use your wooden handle and stamp
the cardstock like a traditional rubber stamp, but this leaves more to chance in
terms of uniform application.

12. Make all your prints at once.
That is, if they are all going to be the same color of ink (which in this project they
are). We're making a series of four postcards, so it's not a major production to do all
the actual printing at the same time. If the ink on the Plexiglas begins to dry out,
spritz with a little water and rebray. Is bray an actual verb? I mean really, the thing
is called a brayer which must mean that it brays. Braying like a donkey might also be
a good stress-reliever at this point.

**13. While your prints are drying, wash off the rubber stamp so that the color
won't dry to the rubber and contaminate the color you use the next time you
make prints.**
The ink is water soluble, so it washes off pretty quickly, and the prints don't take
long to dry at all.

14. Fill in any unwanted gaps in your prints.
Use a damp fine-tipped watercolor paintbrush and some of the ink from the

Plexiglas to fill in light areas if desired. You can also use your Kinko's (archival) pen to get in the really small corners for a precision look.

BACKGROUND(S)

15. Choose and trace your background image.
Dana has supplied a couple of backgrounds for this project as well as a bird outline. They can be used separately or in conjunction. Trace the image using tracing paper (duh). If you are ever tracing directly from a book (especially this one), be careful not to press so hard that you tear through the paper and then mark up your precious book. You can always darken your lines away from the book after your initial light-touch tracing.

16. Prepare your card for transferring the background.
Tape your printed card to a table, desk, or whatever work surface you're using. Select the background image, and align it with your printed image, taping down only one edge. For instance, if you use the outline of the bird's body, make sure it's lined up around the printed bird skeleton. Lift up the tracing paper and lay your carbon paper between it and the print.

17. Transfer your background image by retracing it.
Here I might suggest using a stylus instead of a pencil since you don't actually need to make a mark on the tracing paper. This way, you avoid screwing things up too badly if you tear through the tracing paper. However, your kneaded eraser will work great for cleaning up any goofs if you do end up using a pencil. Remember to use more of a blotting than a smearing motion when you erase. If you need to fill in any gaps or add to your background, Dana recommends drawing pencils cuz they're easier to erase than number 2 pencils.

18. Repeat tracing and transfer process with the other backgrounds or background layers you want to use.
Remember that one print can have more than one background layer. For instance, you could transfer your bird outline and then transfer the leaves and branches image right over it. Dana's design has that in mind.

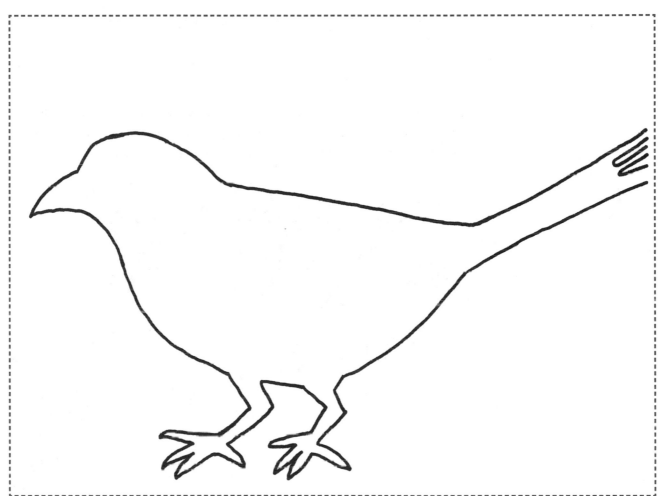

19. If you want a defined graphic look, use your archival pen to go over the line drawings.
You can skip this step if you do not want to have hard-edged lines (for instance if you wanted to paint or collage your background using the drawing only as a guide).

20. Now you're ready to fill in your background.
Once you have the basic outline of the background, you can use whatever you have on hand to embellish and fill it in. Dana used a variety of media for each print. For

one, she used cut-up pictures of feathers and gold paint, while for another she simply cut some flowers out of a magazine. Try origami paper, wrapping paper, magazines . . . anything you can think of will work. Another great variation is to use a hole punch or craft-paper punch to create collage elements.

21. Use spray adhesive, traditional glue, or a glue stick to attach collage pieces. Spray adhesive works well because you can spray the entire surface of the card and sprinkle something like glitter or confetti on top. You can also use tweezers to apply

Bird background images for tracing

elements more precisely. Remember to burnish collaged elements with your bone folder or spoon so that they really adhere.

22. Spray your cards with workable fixative before mailing or selling or handling. This will keep the images true. You don't want stuff coming off on hands or the image generally deteriorating. You can also use fixative in between process steps to finalize a layer before adding on.

SERVING SUGGESTIONS

Like I said, now that you've got a set of postcards, you'll want to mail them to your best friends. And since you are now a veritable one-punk print shop, why limit your missives to friends? Anyone can cut out letters from a magazine, but you can show that you're serious when you put a little love into a ransom note, and no more boring legal forms for your next subpoena. Here are just three of the ways Dana's craft inspired me:

- **Make your own envelope.** Cut up a brown paper sack, or teach that Starbucks gift bag a nasty lesson. Turn 'em inside out and fold 'em up! Not only will you protect the cards you're mailing (especially if you're sending a blank set as a gift), you can repeat your print theme on the packaging itself. Thorough!
- **Wrapping paper? Sho nuff!** Why spend your money on expensive glossy bourgeois packaging? I mean you stole it, right? Print your own gift wrap from a big, cheap roll of craft paper and save your ill-gotten booty for the gift itself.
- **Try printing on different surfaces.** I imagine it's best to stick with matte, absorbent materials. Show those fancy schmancy art and architecture mags with their heavy stock and understated design a thing or two by stamping a strictly déclassé icon on their smug pages. Maybe next time that Frank Gehry will think twice . . .

Contact Info

You can get in touch with Dana Berkowitz by e-mailing her at love13bird@yahoo.com. Or better yet, send her one of your postcards (you'll have to persuade her to hand over her mailing address).

Supplies Word Search

```
I H O L E P U N C H T G Y G X
N O D R I L L R M H U L S L A
T N H R A C E E I I N I S U W
E L E R U P N M Y O R T C E L
R O B E A B B E I D E T I G F
F Y R P R L B S P B A E S U D
A P I P E C L E A N E R S N R
C I C I B U S N R A Y I O S A
I G K Z M R D K F S B Z R K O
N M R E A A A A L L T A S C B
G E A T L E F Y E I O A R O D
B N C D L O M W E R S S M S R
I T K S D A E B Z R H A S P A
R H S U R B T N I A P T R E C
```

BEADS	GLUEGUN	RUBBERSTAMP
BRAYER	HOLEPUNCH	SCISSORS
CARDBOARD	INTERFACNG	SILKSCREEN
DRILL	MOLD	SOCKS
DYE	PAINTBRUSH	THIMBLE
EMULSION	PAPER	THREAD
FELT	PENCIL	TRIM
FLOSS	PIGMENT	WAX
FUSIBLEWEB	PIPECLEANERS	YARN
GLITTER	RICKRACK	ZIPPER

HAiR ACCESSORiES
PROJECT: CLiP-ON EXTENSiONS
ARTIST: *Stardust*

Golden living dreams and visions; mystic crystal revelations; and the mind's true liberation: This is the dawning of the age of the woman known only as Stardust (except to her parents, the DMV, IRS, USPS . . . even me, but I am sworn to secrecy). Before interviewing her for the book, I really didn't know anything about her except what her hair accessories looked like. I thought they were a great candidate for a BazBiz project since they are fairly simple, affordable, and removable. Just think of how expensive it is to get a weave or extensions "installed" at a salon (what *is* the proper verb for hairdos? "Done," I suppose). Plus, with those professional dos, you can't take them out, or change your whole look as the mood strikes you. Dress up and performance are abstract concepts I have long worked with in my academic career, so what could be a better manifestation of those concepts than totally glam hairpieces? Don't let the fact that these particular instructions will yield dreadlock extensions scare you off if that's not your taste. You can just as easily skip the dreading steps to end up with posh and polished instead of rough 'n' rocker.

BAZAAR BIZARRE
STARDUST
12730819
HAIRCLIPS

Stardust got started as a crafter when she worked doing extensions at a salon. She said she ended up with so many things tied into her hair that she felt naked without a buncha stuff up in there. She started saving her pieces when she would remove them. Facing the fact of reality and lifestyle and career restrictions placed on some of her friends, she began developing her removable extensions.

Stardust lives in a small cute guesthouse in Hollywood. When we met to do the interview, we sat outside to make her hair-clip extensions, while she told me about a distant dimension from whence she came (in another life, I guess). It seems that there were many planets orbiting a star, but unlike our solar system, there was life coexisting in harmony on all of them. One could easily travel between these worlds by stepping through portals usually located behind a rock or under a bush. (Kinda reminds me of "warp zones" in *Super Mario Bros.* and *Legend of Zelda*.) The star eventually did its whole supernova thing, expanding and collapsing; and in the process, killing all the living things on each world. All was not lost, however, as the inhabitants of the galaxy became part of the star itself: hence our crafter's name Stardust. I think this is what Ma and Pa Kettle think of when they think "Hollywood." It's called Bazaar *Bizarre* for a reason, folks.

However, Stardust is not without a sense of humor. Very much aware of the multiple connotations of being a star in this town, she's trying to bring a little celestial consciousness to a community that is very firmly rooted in the material. As cynical as I am, even I can't argue that that's a bad idea.

What is the difference between an "art" and a "craft"?
Art is a broader word that would encompass crafting. Art could be very abstract; a craft is something you could actually hold and possibly use.

What is your earliest crafting memory?
Those little sticks with yarn wrapped around them in pretty colorful patterns. They must have been some sort of dream catcher. [AUTHOR'S NOTE: These are called God's eyes.]

What was your best crafting moment (idea, inspiration, etc.)?
That would probably be the deer-skull headdress I made from an old deer skeleton I found when I was hunting for wood in the forest one day. It embodied the sweet deer spirit quite powerfully.

**What was your worst crafting moment
(a huge mess, project gone horribly wrong, etc.)?**
That would have to be when I was learning how to use the hot glue gun. The cat's tail ended up glued to my army boot with sparkles and pompoms and bells dangling from its paws—quite the rock opera when I started walking.

What is your favorite craft you've ever seen?
Wow. . . . Are you kidding? If I had to try and choose, feather mandala headdresses are pretty awesome.

Who made you the crafter you are (who introduced you to crafts, taught you crafts—whether or not it is the one you do now)?
That would be my long lost friend Suzanne. She was a huge inspiration and artistic mentor for me. She would channel from very magickal alien and Egyptian worlds and bring me right into them.

What are your crafting goals?
Make far-out hair accessories that inspire people to behave wild and crazy, proud and majestic, goofy and hysterical, elegant and sexy, and so on.

Kraft or Kraftwerk?

Die sind alle SuperGiel. Das es nur viel Spaß hat mussen. [AUTHOR'S NOTE: Google translation: "Those are all SuperGiel. It only much fun has mussen." Huh?]

Who is your fave crafty celeb?

Pippi Longstockings and Nina Hagen.

What is your fave craft resource (Web site, store, dumpster, etc.)?

Garage sales in the Hollywood hills.

Global Techniques

Except for a few basic guidelines, this is a very free-form project, and I think a lot more customizable than you might think.

HAIR

Human hair seems like it'd be best to use. It's more versatile than synthetic hair, if more expensive. There are some advantages that make it worth the price. Human hair is much more responsive to chemical processes like bleaching and dyeing than synthetic, and if you even want to think about curling or treatments that involve heat, synthetic hair can melt. I know burning human hair stinks, but I bet melting synthetic hair is smelly *and* toxic.

Stardust says it's easy to find bargain human hair on sale at salon supply shops. Her favorite is The Hair Shop on Wilshire Boulevard here in Los Angeles (http://www.hairpiece.com). You can use an entire weave as is, or you can cut it lengthwise into narrower extensions. Alternatively, you can use your own hair or a friend's hair if either of you is planning to make a big change. Store-bought hair has been chemically treated many times, and is generally very clean. If you are using donated hair, especially if it was dreads (which I think would be kinda gross), make sure you wash it thoroughly. Stardust recommends soaking it overnight in a bath of water, lavender oil, and a little bleach just to kill everything. Remember, if you are using loose hair, you'll have to make your own weave.

If you don't know where to find weaves in your town, I would do a local Google or Yahoo search. Why not go into a salon that does weaves and ask them where they get them or if they make their own? I love going directly to a source.

EMBELLISHMENTS

I like this project because you can incorporate almost anything you can think of from yarn to ribbon to wire to fake flowers to the rhinestones Stardust uses for her personal hair clips. Glitter is a great addition. I happen to love glitter on anything and everything, and, in this project, it adds a nice finishing touch. For instance, when you attach an embellishment with your E-6000 or glue gun or Aleene's Tacky Glue, there will be some gloppage sticking out. Sprinkle a little glitter on and ta-da! It's a feature, not a flaw. My own personal taste would dictate using ultrafine glitter that you can find at any craft store, but you can use larger, more standard glitter. Stardust advises that you make sure whatever glitter you choose is round. Some glitter is square, and those little tiny angles can irritate and even scratch your skin.

So now that you have a couple of basic guidelines to follow, try out Stardust's project. Straight or with dreads is up to you.

DREADLOCK HAIR CLIPS DIFFICULTY ✪✪✪✪✪

TIME LINE The hair clips can take anywhere from 30 minutes to 2 hours, depending on how elaborate you wanna get. You can add time to this if you process the hair (color, bleach, etc.). That's where the passive time comes in. Beauty cannot be rushed. As far as drying glue—give it a good 24 hours. You should check it after about 30 minutes to see if anything has slipped out of place, and, at that time, you can remove the clamp. During this time, you might want to channel the magick of an alien, or say Egyptian astral realm. I mean, couldn't hurt, right?

 Air: *Talkie Walkie,* ambient electronica on www.radioio.com (streaming Web radio), Magnatune.com's world music section

The Dark Crystal; Party Monster; 1970s–era Bugs Bunny cartoons (Stardust likes the episode when Bugs did the monster's hair.)

SHOPPING LIST

SALON SUPPLY SHOP

- **Hair**
- **Hair dye or bleach** This is optional if you plan on treating the hair before you make the clips.
- **Self-snapping weave clips.** They are comb clips and have holes for sewing on each end. Get as many as you will need to secure the width of your selected weave.
- **Rat-tail comb**

THE CRAFT STORE

- **Glitter**
- **E-6000**
- **Aleene's Tacky Glue**
- **Rhinestones**
- **Needle and thread** Use a natural fiber cotton thread—you want something strong. Choose a color that matches the hair—or color-treated hair—you will use for your weave.

Step by Step

1. Start with a weave.

I would actually start by renting the DVD of *B.A.P.* (which stands for "Black American Princesses") featuring Halle Berry and Martin Landau: A truly ghetto-fabulous—and surprisingly poignant—film. If making your own weave from loose hair, try gluing the hair along a small strip of fabric and then sewing a seam to kinda seal the whole thing. If not using a weave, skip to step 11

2. Color treat or process, if desired, and wash and brush.

This works best if you're using human hair. You can bleach it and color it or even perm it any way you want. Make sure it's clean, dry, and brushed.

3. Use a clip or clamp to anchor the weave—loose end toward you—to your pants or something.

Since there's no human head attached to the other end of the hair, you need *something* to keep it in place.

4. Back comb and twist with a rat-tail comb.

Just mess it up as if you were teasing it, but more severe. In this case you actually *want* tangles. Stardust leaves the ends loose.

5. Roll between your hands to shape.

Dreads can come out looking kinda chunky and frizzy. Rolling them between your hands will make everything cling to each other. This settling process will continue as you wear the hairpiece. I think it's like any other haircut in that it definitely looks new for a day and then settles in. Stardust claims that the pieces will take on your own energy, essence, and personality.

6. You can use a blow-dryer to tame the dreads a little bit.

Hold a towel behind the weave and just blow-dry. I am not exactly sure why this works. I think the heat relaxes the hair a bit. Be very careful if you're using synthetic hair—it could melt!

7. Place the clip on the back of the weave (the side that's going to go against your head), about 1/8 inch from the edge.

You don't want a big, loose flap of hair weave, but you also don't want the actual metal clip to be visible. Make sure the comb clip's teeth are pointed "down" toward the loose unwoven end of the weave.

8. Attach your weave clips using needle and thread.

Double up a length of thread, and thread loose ends through your needle, leaving a loop at the long end of the thread. Place the weave clip at the inside center of the weave, with the teeth of the comb pointing down. Starting on the inside of the weave, thread the needle through the hole, leaving a loop in the thread on the inside. Push the needle through the weave under the hole in the clip, then up through the loop in the thread.

If memories of my tenure in the Boy Scouts of America serve me correctly, I believe this is technically called a lark's head knot. Unfortunately, as a boy I didn't have the foresight to appreciate the relevance of knot-tying skills in wilderness male-bonding scenes, and consequently I wasn't paying too much attention. You hear all these stories about first sexual experiences in the Boy Scouts— experimentation and such. Lots of people seem to bring lawsuits against BSA for excluding homos, but I actually thought of suing because I never got any. Maybe if I had been paying closer attention I would have gleaned a special hidden message.

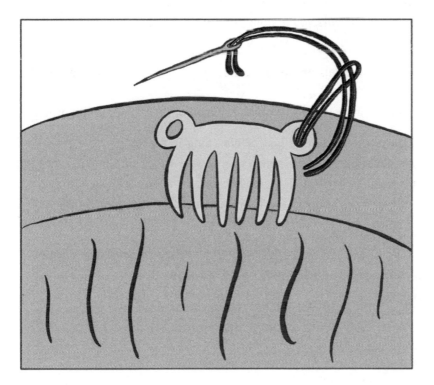

9. Repeat your knot a few times for added security.

Once you've made a few passes through the weave, trim the thread, but not too close to the clip. You don't want it to come loose. Dab a drop of superglue onto each knot and you know things will definitely stay put.

10. Repeat steps 8 and 9 for each necessary clip.

Don't leave more than ½ inch between comb clips along the width of your weave. Think security. You don't want gaps or something catching and ripping out—*that* would hurt.

11. Plot out your customized design.

Go to your craft basket and see what you've got. Stardust goes for the sparkle factor of her namesake: jewels and glitter. Once you've chosen your materials, I suggest trying a dry run *sans* glue just to be on the safe side. Position your jewels or whatever embellishments you're going to use on your hair clip. Get a feel for the overall amount of stuff you want to add.

13. Try matching jewels on opposite sides so it appears to go "through" the extension.

You don't want one finished side and a big blob of dried glue on the other.

14. Use hair clips or binder clips for clamping in place.

Check every 30 minutes over a period of a couple of hours to make sure things aren't shifting around. Once set, remove clamps. You can sprinkle glitter on blobbed-out glue before it dries so you don't have these plastic-looking chunks sticking out from your gems.

15. Leave your finished hair clips on a flat surface to dry for 24 hours.

Hanging will cause the embellishments to move due to gravity. It's a whole new detachable you!

SERVING SUGGESTIONS

Like I said earlier, I think there are limitless ways to modify this project. Choosing a theme is a great way to start. Animé, punk rocker, Bo Derek, superhero, woodland fairy . . . what's your taste? Personal appearance and style center around performance. Every day we dress up for the roles that we have to play: executive, delivery boy, dominatrix, author, craftsman, plumber, etc. When we come home at night, we switch roles, and switch again when we go out to socialize. The masquerade aspect of this project is what I think is so fun. On one hand, you may have a stuffy corporate job and glamming out in an otherworldly Ziggy Stardust hairstyle allows the "real you" to come out and play. On the other hand, you might actually feel more comfortable when conservative, and a detachable identity via hair might let you temporarily explore a new wild side.

To store your clips individually, you can lay them flat in a box. If they're dreads, it doesn't matter too much as long as the box doesn't crush. If you end up making loose, combable extensions, give them a rub with a little dab of leave-in hair conditioner, brush them out nice, and lay them flat in a box. I suggest placing a piece of felt in the bottom so they don't slide around when you move the box.

Another great way to store and, at the same time, actually display your clips is to get a mannequin head. If you get an actual plastic mannequin head, you may need to get a wig into which you can clip your extensions. If you buy a cheap Styrofoam one (which costs like two to three bucks) you can just pin the clips right into it. Either way, it's a lot of fun to decorate a dummy head, and it makes a great presentation in a hatbox if you want give these hair clips as a gift.

Contact Info

At http://stardustmagick.com you can buy some hair clips, and possibly be transported to Stardust's magickal galaxy, where we will all become one with a star . . . eventually, I assume. Her business phone number is (323) 769-5683.

"I feel like I just got the scraps beaten outta me."

Please don't misunderstand me, despite the rebel nature of BazBiz, I love moms. In fact, a couple of years ago, BazBiz knitting guru Simone Alpen and I, in the course of writing a New Year's Eve "what's in/what's out" list, rated *indie-rock-know-it-alls* as distinctly "out" and *moms* as "in." However, recently I saw the apocalyptic convergence of the two worst mom fads of my lifetime: baby-on-board meets scrapbooking. We are truly living in the end times. There I was in Michael's when I saw them: several horrible mutations of the Baby-on-Board windshield sign. Decals proclaiming Scrapbooker on Board and Honk If You Love Scrapbooking taunted me with their suction cups daring to drain the very love of crafts from my soul. I dug around for a Scrapbooker in Trunk placard, but I couldn't find one.

CRAFTOID

A lot of crafting's original imperatives and moral overtones centered around making use of what one already has, hence the idea of using leftovers, remnants, or scraps, tangible tidbits to document a lived experience. So what happened? I go to craft stores and they have all this scrapbooking . . . *crap:* from pretorn paper (for that authentic "torn-paper" look) to stickers printed with quotes you *should* have said at that perfect first birthday party you *should* have thrown. They should call it *crapbooking.*

Simone and Emily Arkin (expert playing-card maker) recently told me a story about how they were digging through a bin of variously themed little wooden trinkets for Memory Albums (a.k.a. crapbooks), when they found a tiny phone-bill charm. I can see me and my man, years from now: "Remember that time we paid the phone bill, sweetie? Those were good days."

BazBiz crafters zoom out from this practice to an abstract level by using cultural scraps—marginalized identities and representations—and recontextualizing them, making use of them in a crafty way. Reinserting abject images and social "scraps" into a historically domestic space and skill set serves to disrupt the value system that is thought to accompany traditional handicrafts.

A fitting example would be the refrigerator magnets I make from gay porn: Fagnets. We expect to see gay porn in seedy locales—adult bookstores, etc.—not the suburban household. When this "trashy" imagery makes its way onto the refrigerator—perhaps *the* defining symbol of the kitchen (center of the nuclear family)—we are forced to reevaluate who and what belongs on the icebox. What memories and experiences might we wish to honor alongside childhood drawings?

Also consider the work of our quilting contributor, Edith Abeyta. A literal instance of actual trash taking up residence in the home via another powerful symbol of tradition—the quilt—her craft highlights the conflict between a culture of disposable hyperconsumerism and a nostalgia for a bygone era of "values."

Perhaps the crafty relics of childhood are the work of future societal scraps. More important, perhaps, is how the insertion of cultural castoffs does the work of inclusion. Subjects that "don't fit" culturally may now reenter notions of family, history, and tradition.

SEWING WITH VINYL
PROJECT: HEART-SHAPED COIN PURSE

ARTIST: *Alison Simonian*

My father always told me to "spend up." That is, when you pay for something in cash, don't use your coins, but keep breaking bills and collecting the change, using it only for parking meters and vending machines and Ms. Pac-Man. At the end of the day you can dump your change into a jar. You'll be shocked at how quickly it adds up—not only in the jar but also in your pocket throughout the day. You're going to need somewhere to put all of this accumulated wealth. I love my wallet—don't get me wrong—but it has this dinky little zippered change pocket on the back. It barely holds anything, and coins are not very comfy to sit on. I used to be a loose-change-in-the-jeans-pocket person until I discovered the joys of a coin purse. As is my wont, I take any opportunity to aestheticize a utilitarian object, so when I was introduced to these amazing coin purses, I knew I'd found yet another cute necessity. These vinyl treasure holders are much sturdier and secure than those yonic rubber purses that one gets from the hardware store. Plus you'll avoid any Freudian castration anxieties that accompany accessories with an anatomical similarity.

CRAFTER BIO

BAZAAR BIZARRE
SIMONIAN, ALISON
19761209
VINYL COINPURSE

When I was introduced to Alison Simonian, I was like *"Parev, oriort!"* (which is the closest thing I came up with for "Hey, baby!" in Armenian). And her middle name is Satanig. How great is that? I'm certain it actually translates to something fairly normal like Janet or Susan, but I Googled it, yielding no useful translation results. Google kept asking me if I meant Satanic, which I thought was excellent. Interestingly enough, if you do a kind of pidgin English–Armenian translation, Satanig would mean "Little Satan" ("-ig" is an affectionate diminutive suffix for nouns in Armenian: for example, *shoon* translates to "dog," while *shoonig* means "little dog" or "puppy"). I wish my middle name was Little Satan, but it's actually Nazareth, which isn't bad considering that it's both a family name and a cheesy band that sang the truth about love hurting and messing with sons of bitches.

Alison's childhood education had a big influence on her craftiness. She attended several alternative elementary schools (think of the East Village school Patrick is sent to in *Auntie Mame*). There she engaged in lots of papermaking, crocheting, interpretive dance, and other crafty endeavors like building a tree house. Alison currently lives in Chicago and made the trip to Los Angeles for Bazaar Bizarre 2003. Her candy-colored vinyl accessories sold like crazy, and with good reason. They're not only glittery, their fabrication is rock solid thanks to Alison's mad skillz with an industrial sewing machine. I wonder if she uses a Juki. That's my favorite brand name for a sewing machine, and my favorite brand name for sewing notions is Dritz—just the *names*, mind you, not the brands. Try saying them aloud. I promise you'll agree.

What is the difference between an "art" and a "craft"?
I don't draw a distinction between the two. Art and craft go hand in hand in my book. I don't like the rigidity of defining what each is and is not.

What is your earliest crafting memory?
Crocheting a pink-and-yellow striped cozy for my recorder in kindergarten.

What was your best crafting moment (idea, inspiration, etc.)?
Anytime I'm in the zone, baby.

What was your worst crafting moment (a huge mess, project gone horribly wrong, etc.)?
I set my snaps by hand with a hammer and die set. It sucks real badly sometimes, because it often takes a lot of finger smashing in order to end up with a batch of nicely set be-snapped items.

What is your favorite craft you've ever seen?
I bought a huge, heavy, sand-filled, silk-screened earthworm stuffed animal last year at the Renegade Craft Fair that I'm in love with. I don't know that this is my favorite craft ever, but it's the thing I'm most enamored by currently. I'm also a big fan of the tall bikes and choppers the local bike nerds I know make out of thrown-away garbage, bicycles, and scrap.

Who made you the crafter you are (who introduced you to crafts, taught you crafts—whether or not it is the one you do now)?
My carpenter grandfather and dad. My seamstress grandmother. My painter ex-stepdad. My early elementary education by hippies. The kids in my public school classes who wouldn't be my friends and left me with abundant spare time for art projects. My crafty girlfriends and their ceaseless inspiration and support. I was taught to sew, embroider, and crochet early by my grandmother. Then in the alternative elementary schools I went to, we crocheted, made paper, built tree houses, painted, built playgrounds, learned to throw pottery on a wheel and visited metal forges regularly.

What are your crafting goals?

Right now I'm trying to figure out if making crafting my full-time job is my ultimate goal. There's a lot to consider still. I'm planning on working toward this while still investigating its viability.

Kraft or Kraftwerk?

No to processed cheese, yes to Kraut rock!

Who is your fave crafty celeb?

I dunno. I'm out of the loop on this one.

What is your fave craft resource (Web site, store, dumpster, etc.)?

Anywhere I can find new and exciting materials to work with, be it the hardware store, a craft emporium, eBay, or a dumpster.

Global Techniques

I think what makes this project fun, aside from its total adorability, is the adventure you might have to go on to get your materials. For this one I say, "Be brave." Find the industrial supply part of your city or town. If you live in a place with an actual "garment district," you're in for a treat. Take a day and walk around. In Los Angeles, for example, the downtown fashion district has dozens and dozens of specialty stores aimed at designers and resellers. Some carry everything you could ever think of for sewing on a small or large scale, while others feature hundreds of trims—and only trims.

When it comes to vinyl, you don't have to be too technical when making your choices. You can pick it out by look and feel. Jo-Ann's or another home sewing store *may* have one or two appropriate weight upholstery vinyl choices, but I speak from experience when I say this is largely a waste of time. If you live in a small town where there simply aren't big warehouse supply stores, you can often special order what you want either in a store or online. At these outlets, you're also gonna find a much wider range of options—in colors, materials, and lengths—when it comes to the zipper you'll use.

This purse is a fairly simple design and may only take you an afternoon, but I think the real "project" of this chapter is trying out some materials with which you may not have worked before, and doing a little Nancy Drew routine to find em.

HEART-SHAPED COiN PURSE DiFFiCULTY ✪✪✪✩✩

TiME LiNE This ultracute, heart-shaped zippered coin purse should take you about an hour to make. There's not exactly any passive time involved, but Alison suggests stopping halfway, laying another kind of needle on another type of vinyl, and being your own private dancer, a dancer for money (that you can put in your new coin purse). You'll do what *you* want you to do.

My Bloody Valentine: *Loveless;* Serge Gainsbourg: *Comic Strip;* The Sonics: *The Sonics: Boom;* Ween: *Quebec;* Kool Keith: *Black Elvis/Lost in Space*

Pee-wee's Big Adventure; Beyond the Valley of the Dolls; Little Shop of Horrors; Back to the Beach; and *Auntie Mame*

[**AUTHOR'S NOTE:** *Auntie Mame* is the Rosalind Russell version, *not* the dubious Lucille Ball screen adaptation of the stage musical *Mame* (a serious misstep on the part of director Gene Saks). Ms. Russell's film version of Auntie Mame is beyond perfection, and while *Mame,* the film version of the musical, blows serious chunks, it is worth a watch just to see the incomparable Bea Arthur reprising the role of Vera Charles, which she played on Broadway in the late 1960s, opposite Angela Lansbury as Mame Dennis. Both women won Tony awards for their roles, and the musical won a total of eight. *Please* don't think ill of the stage production because of the film. Don't even get me started on how a made-for-TV version is in the works.]

SHOPPING LIST

FABRIC STORE

- **Marine-weight industrial vinyl** This is what is used for restaurant upholstery and boat seats, and things like that. It comes in the most fun colors and glitter options.
- **#5, 5-inch, nonseparating metal zipper** Five-inch zippers are usually meant for pockets or doll clothes (sometimes they are referred to as dolls' zippers). They are available in different styles—metal teeth, coil, and molded plastic teeth. But I think metal looks best with this project. If you can't get your hands on a 5-inch zipper for some reason, buy a longer one and just cut it shorter from the top (be sure not to cut off the zipper pull). Then use a needle and thread to sew around each coil side to create a new stopping point for the zipper. Singe that cut cloth edge to prevent unraveling.
- **Needle and thread** You don't need a special needle or thread. Mercerized all-purpose thread will work fine. Make sure you use something at least *partially* synthetic, since 100 percent cotton thread is likely to break.
- **Thimble** I can't stress enough the importance of it for this project.

HARDWARE OR CRAFT STORE

- **Oaktag for pattern pieces** Oaktag usually comes in precut pieces. A letter-size piece will be too small, but the next size up (small poster board) will be more than sufficient.
- **Hem clips or small binder "bulldog" clips**
- **Scissors** Don't use your nice fabric scissors; you'll dull them. Use your general duty scissors you'd cut paper and cardboard with.

Step by Step

1. Xerox heart pattern images from page 78.
You will only need one basic outline shape from which to make your pattern pieces. You can use the pattern in the book or even draw your own. (The pattern will be printed actual size.)

2. Make two oaktag hearts.

Cut out your xeroxed heart, and trace around it onto the oaktag. You will need to do this twice, giving you 2 oaktag pattern pieces. One heart pattern will remain a solid heart shape and be used for the back and lining of the purse. The remaining front pattern piece will be cut more or less in half to create 2 pieces that will be joined by the zipper.

3. Trace the 2 parallel zipper guidelines from the xeroxed heart across the front oaktag heart piece. They should be about ½ inch apart.

Trace dotted lines across one of the oaktag pieces using the guidelines from the xerox of the heart image on page 78. You can also use your actual zipper as a guide by moving it around until it matches up with the edges of your heart in a way that you like. The zippers Alison uses are a standard size, and she based her pattern more or less to fit the zipper. It all works out rather nicely.

4. Cut along each of the 2 parallel lines on your front heart pattern piece.

This will leave you with 3 heart segments. You can chuck the middle one cuz that represents the zipper. Please keep in mind that simply cutting your front heart in half won't work. You actually have to subtract enough area to accommodate the zipper. Otherwise, the front and back of your purse won't line up correctly.

5. Trace your oaktag pattern pieces onto the reverse, nonshiny or "wrong" side of your vinyl. And cut them out.

You can just use a Sharpie here. It definitely won't bleed through and you won't see it later. Trace 2 of the solid pattern pieces, 1 for the back of the purse and 1 for the lining, onto the vinyl. Then trace the top and bottom front heart segments once each. Once cut, you should have 4 pieces of vinyl.

6. Keep that zipper zipped, and pin to wrong side of the front heart segments.
Most likely the zipper you bought will not come apart completely into 2 separate pieces, but even so, keep it zipped, pal!

7. Sew one side of the zipper to a front heart segment.
Alison recommends folding back the raw zipper end before you begin your stitches. This will give a more finished look and tack everything more firmly in place. Begin at the bottom of the zipper and push your needle through the zipper and the front heart segment. The cloth at the bottom end of the zipper may extend beyond the edge of the heart. You can use the lark's head knot mentioned in Stardust's hair clip project (page 65).

Stitch up through the zipper and vinyl, and then down only through the zipper. When you get to the end, fold the other raw zipper end under and knot into place. Trim the excess thread.

8. Repeat steps 6 and 7 for the remaining segment of the front heart.
You end up with basically 1 whole heart with a zipper stuck in the middle. This is exactly what you want.

9. Position the other 2 whole vinyl hearts wrong sides together.
These will become the back and lining of the purse.

10. Lay the zippered heart atop these (right/shiny side out) and clamp all three layers in place.
You can use actual hem clips, but binder clips are strong and work great.

11. Start sewing all layers together by making a lark's head knot (page 65).
Start your first stitch about ¼ inch from the outer edge of the heart. This is where you will *really* need your thimble to go through all 3 layers. Tie a knot.

cut along these dotted lines to remove zipper segment

12. Stitch all the way around the perimeter of your heart, removing the clips as you go.
To make your stitch, push the needle through all 3 layers, bring the thread around the outside, and begin your next stitch a maximum of ¼ inch from your previous stitch. The closer together you place your stitches, the stronger your seam will be. And remember, you don't want to try

Square Knot

to make your stitches too uniform. First, you won't be able to measure exactly by sight, and second, the random nature of the stitches adds a lot of Frankenstein charm to the project. Keep your stitches similar, however, in terms of how far in from the edge they are.

13. Once you have stitched all the way around the purse, finish by tying a knot between any two layers.
This will prevent a really obvious clunky ending knot. Make a few passes for added security.

SERVING SUGGESTIONS

There are several really simple variations on this basic design to get you started with customizing. Try using a contrasting color for the lining (interior) piece of vinyl. It's like a little surprise every time you go to feed the meter. You could also try using a different pattern shape like a star or an oval. Alison has made some that have an eyelet near the edge of one of the heart lobes. You can find an eyelet kit at the hardware store, and it'll be cheaper there than at the crafts store. You can run a ball chain through it or even a ribbon. It makes for a cute wrist dangler to go with the arm candy you've got on your other side when you hit the streets.

Contact Info

Yeah, she makes coin purses, that's how we fell in love, but you should see all the other way cool, glittery vinyl superfun purses, cuffs, and other necessities she makes at http://missalison.com. Or you can e-mail her at info@missalison.com.

Gepettophiles: *Beyond the Valley of the Dolls* Collectors

In my admittedly limited exposure to the world of doll pop culture, I've noticed a rather gendered division of consumption and production. Women seem to collect dolls while men seem to make them. However, both sexes seem to use dolls to fill some sort of psychic void.

For a startling example of how women do this, tune in very late at night to the Home Shopping Network for Doll Collecting hosted by Tina Berry (it's on about once or twice a month). As with most home-shopping shows, there are lots of call-in testimonials, but what makes the doll-collecting calls special is that they're more like call-in therapy sessions. It's heartbreaking, at times, to hear lonely stories of childlessness and premature death. Callers and host alike refer to their dolls as if they were living children. Add to this the aesthetic imperative to make these dolls ever more lifelike (which just ends up looking grotesque), and it really starts to get weird. But what do we make of the men who create these dolls?

Men's relationships with the dolls they make seem always to have some kind of sexual overtone. I suppose the most obvious example would be a blow-up doll. But in a subtler way, dolls seem to serve as prosthetic phalluses and agents for the men who make them. Movies like *Blood Dolls* (1999) and the *Puppet Master* series (1989) both center around socially impotent men who make dolls to exact revenge on those who've betrayed them.

Consider the story of Pinocchio: Gepetto (a single man) wants a child. Specifically, he wants a little boy. Why is there no would-be mom in the picture? Is Gepetto unable to marry? Does he not like girls? So he makes a boy puppet, and a *fairy* grants his wish for Pinocchio to be a real boy. Even this seemingly benign story has seen its horror movie permutations no doubt due to its seamier undertones. And then, of course, there's Pygmalion, but I suppose that's technically sculpture.

I'll willingly concede I am being totally cynical—maybe even sleazy—and painting with broad strokes, to say the least. Perhaps it's because I find humanoid dolls and puppets in general to be really creepy, and people's relationships with them even creepier. Maybe that says something even weirder about me—but I doubt it.

It seems like every hipster and her roommate makes handbags of some sort. I can't tell you how many Bazaar applications I receive for handbags. Each and every applicant describes her bags, purses, totes, or whatever as "unique" and/or "one of a kind." For the 2004 Bazaar, I actually received an application form that used the adjectives "unique" and "one of a kind" *in direct succession!* "Funky," "fabulous," "kooky," "fresh," and "interesting" are just some of the other frightening descriptors that immediately raise major red flags for me when it comes to homemade bag brokers—or anything really. Kinda like when you ask a friend or relative about your dress or haircut, and she says, "It's different."

Okay, so craft-tote designer Jenny is my friend, but I can testify under oath that hers was the *only* 2004 handbag application that did not make use of any of these crafting four-letter words. Ironically enough, that makes hers, well . . . unique. One of the outstanding qualities about Jenny's projects—and they're not limited to handbags—is how "finished" they are. During our collaboration on this chapter I found myself commenting repeatedly that I was impressed by the polished look and feel of her stuff. Her professional results truly speak to a lot of the issues this book tries to address.

Capitalism asks "why make when you can buy?" Its claim is that mass machine-produced products possess a consistency of appearance and quality as well as a technical precision that's missing from handmade goods. In fact, the very term *handmade* connotes a rustic, rough-hewn feel or a certain charming clumsiness. Jenny's bags are certainly a stylish rebuke to this ridiculous idea.

Jenny and I were introduced by BazBiz costar Emily Arkin last year at the Giant Robot gallery in West L.A. We briefly spoke that evening, but when we first met to discuss organizing a new L.A. branch of Bazaar Bizarre, we knew it was *bashert* (Hebrew for fated or destined). Since then it's been nothing but potty humor and *Reminisce* magazine.

When I left my job making fetish paraphernalia to write this book, I got Jenny to replace me and trained her for a couple of weeks. On the days the two of us worked together, the design department staff saw a whole new and frightening side of each of us that didn't quite shine through without the other. I think it was the nonstop monotone mantra of "Zbornak, Zbornak, Zbornak, Zbornak, Zbornak . . ." that actually got us separated—like as in *grade school* separated!

Mrs. Ryan writes, paints, sews, embroiders, and knits. She collects vintage crafting, how-to, and home improvement books and harbors an addiction to TiVo, Diet Cherry Coke, and knitting blogs. Married to cartoonist Johnny Ryan, Jenny lives in a candy-colored apartment in Silverlake with her two cats Kang and Kodos and way too many craft supplies.

What is the difference between an "art" and a "craft"?
There's a reason you hear the phrase "Arts and Crafts" bandied about, and it's because the two go hand in hand. Whether someone considers herself an artist or a craftsperson is a matter of personal perspective. I

see myself as both and certainly don't believe that one is superior to the other. If I knit a baby sweater using a pattern someone else drafted, I don't consider myself any less creative just because I didn't come up with the "recipe" myself. Sure, I'm very OCD and will usually tweak stitches like crazy, add embellishments, and get very particular about yarn textures and colors—but that's what adds a personal touch and elevates the sweater from off-the-rack crap to a one-of-a-kind keepsake. It's all relative . . . I mean, even paint-by-number unicorns are now sought-after pieces of "art." A lot of that may be ironic appreciation of a kitschy craft, but why wait for something to become "funny" or "hip" to enjoy it?

What is your earliest crafting memory?

Hmm. Probably making these weird little terrarium/diorama thingies out of glass bells, dried flowers, and seashells with my mom, or making Xmas ornaments with my dad. We used wooden clothespins, puffballs, toothpicks, and poster paints to make little Nutcrackers and clowns. I still have some of 'em to this day!

What is your best crafting moment (idea, inspiration, etc.)?

It's hard to pinpoint, but I'll always treasure the day knitting *finally* clicked for me. (Followed closely by the moment I first taught someone *else* to knit.)

What is your worst crafting moment (a huge mess, project gone horribly wrong, etc.)?

Know your adhesives! A few years ago I thought I was all cool and made a bunch of personalized wooden picture frames for my pals. They were raw wood, which I painted and decorated with all sorts of fun stuff—glitter, beaded letters, and toys. Sadly, I used a hot glue gun to affix a lot of these items together (it tends to dry very brittle, and I would use the almighty E-6000 if I made them again). Long story short, my oh-so-thoughtful gifts totally fell apart as people unwrapped them. There were piles of little plastic cowboys all over the place. I ruined Xmas! "Sob . . ."

What is your favorite craft you've ever seen?

I am a big fan of Jason Mecier, the guy who makes mosaic portraits out of candy, pencils, macaroni, and other sundry items. He's a perfect example of art *and* craft working together for the bemused enjoyment of all onlookers. My favorite piece of his is the *Showgirls* movie poster he made out of various beans. My best friend actually owns the piece, and whenever I look at it I'm in awe all over again.

Who made you the crafter you are (who introduced you to crafts, taught you crafts—whether or not it is the one you do now)?

I have a distant great-aunt-type person who made dolls, and it both creeped me out (she made dolls of my brother and me, which was eerie) and thrilled me. Another great-aunt helped me make a quilted pillow when I was around ten, and I was in awe of her mad sewing skillz. Yet another great-aunt crochets the most amazing afghans, and she's pretty much totally blind. I come from a long line of crafters!

What are your crafting goals?

I would love to sew an entire wardrobe of custom clothing for myself, but seeing as I've only ever made myself one skirt and a mermaid tail (don't ask), I don't think it will happen anytime soon. That being said, my main goal craftwise is to just plain have more time for it! (I need to finish that embroidered Morrissey portrait someday!)

Kraft or Kraftwerk?

As much as I love those Teutonic new-wavers, I gotta go with Kraft . . . if only because of their disgusting-yet-addictive mac and cheese, which fueled many a late-night craft session as a youth.

Who is your fave crafty celeb?

That's a tough one. I've read that William H. Macy makes pottery and has his own kiln, which is one celebrity rumor I *really* hope is true.

What is your fave craft resource (Web site, store, dumpster, etc.)?

Obviously eBay and thrift stores are great for one-of-a-kind fabrics—I'll cut up old dresses and line my purses with them—but don't underestimate the return bins in IKEA's "As-Is" section. It's an awesome place to snag upholstery fabric for cheap.

Global Techniques

In response to my praise for her craftsmanship, Jenny showed me that just a few simple techniques are what set her work apart from the crowd of bag makers. An item of note is that Jenny and Alison Simonian, our vinyl coin-purse artist, learned most of their sewing skills together. Despite the radical difference in materials and technique between the work of Alison to Jenny, you can definitely see and even touch a common standard that makes their work ethic tangible. So what are these simple things you can do to take your home-sewn projects from lumpy to luxurious? Here's a list:

- **Use interfacing:** This will add stability, body, and structure to almost any project. When making something that's going to take as much abuse as some sort of bag, this is vital. I think it's one of the differences between an item being "sewn" and "constructed."
- **Press your seams:** Just because something may not be visible does not mean it is hidden. Pressing your seams open and flat after you sew them is a simple step that Jenny says most people don't bother with. Don't skip it. It takes all of 2 seconds, and lends a much more professional quality to your work because you won't have bulky seams interrupting a uniform surface from underneath.
- **Plan:** Taking the time to plan your projects will actually make your project go quicker. You can make stylistic and technical decisions ahead of time that will keep you going in an efficient and focused linear way. This isn't because you wanna crank shit out, but because nothing is more frustrating than not knowing what to do next, stalling, and eventually putting away an unfinished project forever. And I promise you the Simplicity patterns from the bargain bin at Jo-Ann's don't always make that clear.
- **Hide flaws creatively:** An excellent example in this chapter would be the top reinforcement panels you'll be adding. Yes, they add a certain extra integrity of construction, and they make the finishing of the bag so much more forgiving. This goes back to the step of planning as well. You can also use trims and embellishments to mask mistakes. Use this trick sparingly, and it'll look like a feature instead of a flaw.
- **Use pinking shears:** Not only are the effects useful for decorative purposes, but

Jenny recommends pinking shears whenever you have to trim fabric in such a way that there will be a raw edge. The zigzag line of the shears prevents the fabric from fraying and shredding as much as it might with regular straight scissors.

- **Backtack:** Always, always, always. Backtacking is making a few stitches using the reverse setting at the beginning and end of a seam. This 2- to 3-second step can save you hours of work later by making your seams secure. It may not feel like an exact science, but it can make all the difference. The only thing that should be busting out is you!

- **Know your sewing machine:** Practice using your machine on scraps of paper just to see what different settings can do. Definitely consult your manual, but manuals aren't known for being particularly illustrative. If you know what features your machine has and how to use them, you'll not only make life easier but you'll also have a wider range of design options, and I definitely recommend a tune-up, re-tension, and lube once year.

CRAFT TOTE DIFFICULTY ✪✪✪✪✪

TIME LINE Jenny's awesome craft tote will take you about 3 to 4 hours to make, start to finish. There's no real passive time aside from the time you might be coming up with your ideas.

 One episode of the Phil Hendrie show on KFI 640 AM; several hours of LuxuriaMusic.com (Jenny's fave Web radio); The Misfits coffin-shaped boxed set; and Bob & Ray CDs.

 One DVD from a *Buffy the Vampire Slayer* boxed set; several episodes from *The Munsters* marathon on TV Land; and a viewing of the *Pee-wee Herman's Christmas Special* DVD, including all the extras.

SHOPPING LIST

FABRIC STORE

- **1 yard upholstery or other heavy fabric for the exterior of the bag (you will have lots left over)**
- **1 yard basic cotton fabrics for the lining and pockets** Prioritize prints and colors that you like rather than fretting about an appropriate weight or type of fabric. The great part of this design is that you don't need too much of any one fabric. You will use about a half a yard of one fabric for the lining of the bag and you can mix and match smaller pieces of fabric for the pockets.
- **1 yard medium weight fusible interfacing** Make sure it's only fusible on one side, which most fusible interfacing is. You won't need more than a yard or so. It's pretty wide off the bolt.
- **Fusible tape** Jenny buys 1-inch width, but it comes in different widths.
- **Oaktag, bristol board, or something similar for pattern pieces** In the instructions I will refer only to oaktag, but be aware that you could cut your pattern from any number of heavyweight papers.
- **Various trims, grosgrain ribbons, and rickrack to embellish your tote pockets** Nothing that'll melt cuz you'll be ironing them.
- **Strap turner** This is basically a tube and a stick, but I promise it's worth the two bucks.
- **Pinking shears** If you have 'em—don't go buy them just for this project unless you plan on sewing more in the future.
- **Sharp fabric scissors**
- **General all-purpose thread** Something strong. Color is a personal preference, but the patchwork nature of this project makes using contrast stitching look totally great. This way you can just stick with one color of thread that goes with the various fabric patterns and palettes. You'll save both money by buying less thread and time by not needing to constantly rethread your machine.
- **Disappearing ink pen—(mystically called in Spanish, *la tinta mágica*)**
- **Straight pins**

YOUR VERY OWN CUPBOARDS:

- Iron
- Ironing board
- Sewing machine

Step by Step

1. Measure out and draw all your pattern pieces (page 96) onto oaktag.

Use the images as a guide for your patterns. Since the shapes are so basic and numeric measurements are provided, there is no need to xerox or enlarge the actual image in the book. Just go ahead and measure out the shapes on your oaktag.

2. Cut out your 4 oaktag pattern pieces.

Some pieces will be used more than once, but you only need 1 pattern piece for each shape. The large trapezoid represents one-half each of the bag's outer body piece and lining. From now on I am going to call the outer body of the bag *the exterior* and the body of the lining *the lining.* Keep this in mind for when we cut the fabric.

3. Make a mark 3½ inches from the top (narrow end) on either side of the trapezoid pattern piece.

This will act as a guide for cutting out a top-lining reinforcement strip, which will add both strength and a finished look. It will also help hide any unevenness, bunching, or gathering where the exterior and lining come together.

4. Trace the trapezoid pattern piece twice onto the wrong (reverse) side of your upholstery or other heavy fabric and cut out.

Fold your upholstery fabric in half with the wrong side facing out. FYI: The printed side of the fabric is what we'll call the right side. Place the pattern piece on the fabric so that the bottom edge is flush against the fold of the fabric. For tracing, use your magical disappearing ink pen: *tinta mágica.* You will only cut along the top and side edges. This means that when you unfold the fabric you will have 1 piece that looks like 2 trapezoids with the fat ends stuck together. Technically, I guess this would be a sort of nonequilateral hexagon, but hey, I ain't no Euclid.

5. Trace the trapezoid pattern onto the wrong side of the cotton fabric and cut out.

Again, fold the fabric in half with the wrong side facing out. Place the pattern piece on the fabric so that the bottom edge is flush against the fold of the fabric. You will only cut along the top and side edges, so that you have 2 trapezoids joined at the bottom edge.

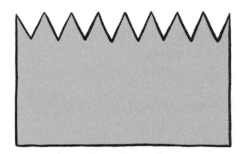

6. Trace the front pocket pattern 3 times and each of the back pocket patterns once onto the wrong side of your cotton fabric cutout.

Use leftover fabric from the lining or choose pieces of different colored and patterned fabrics. For each of the pocket pieces, Jenny recommends using pinking shears to cut the top edge. This will be the only visible edge once the bag is constructed, so it makes a nice built-in finish. This is optional, however. Two of the front pocket pieces will be used as interior pockets attached to the lining. One will be used on the exterior of the bag.

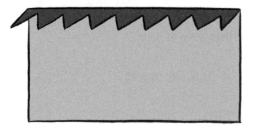

7. Cut a 34- x 5-inch strip of cotton fabric for the strap and apply interfacing.

There is no need to make a pattern piece for this. In fact, you can make your strap any size you'd like, but don't go narrower than 5 inches. Apply interfacing to wrong side of fabric. Straps are good places to use up interfacing scraps, but you definitely have to use interfacing throughout the entire strap.

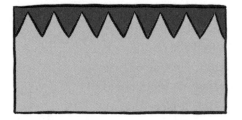

8. Trace the marks you made for the top lining reinforcement strips on the trapezoid pattern piece onto the wrong side of your exterior fabric. Cut 2 pieces.

These will be the reinforcement lining pieces for the top hem of the lining.

9. Use your iron to apply fusible interfacing to all project pieces *except* for the reinforcement pieces from step 7.

For the exterior and lining, you must be exact in matching the interfacing to the fabric. For the remaining pieces, you will be pressing a ½-inch hem along each edge, so there is room for error because none of it will be visible anyway.

10. On all pockets, press a ½-inch hem and attach with fusible web tape. This will leave you with a very finished look.

Fold edges of fabric over ½ inch all the way around the pocket and affix with straight pins. Press all hems without fusible web to get a strong crease. Remove the pins and insert fusible web inside the seam. Iron again until hem fuses. Trust me, you don't wanna gum up your iron with glue by trying to do 2 steps at once. If pinning seems like too much trouble, you can actually place a metal ruler ½ inch from the edge, and just fold over and iron.

11. Embellish your pockets with trims, rickrack, and ribbon.

Attach the trims with fusible web—no need to sew. Cut fusible web and trim for each embellishment longer than necessary so you can turn the ends and press them under and so there's no raw edge.

12. Press a lengthwise crease in each piece of reinforcement panel.

Fold the edges of the long end of the reinforcement fabric to make a ½-inch crease, wrong sides together. Press with an iron. This will act as your seam allowance, enabling you to stitch right along the crease.

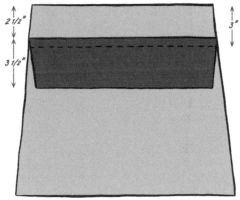

13. Attach both of the reinforcement panels to each end of the lining.

With right sides together, place the long edge of the reinforcement pieces 2½ inches from either edge of the lining. Pin in place and stitch along the crease you created in the last step (the actual crease will be 3 inches from the lining edge). Always backtack for security.

14. Turn reinforcement panels up and press flat, so that right side is now showing.

When you turn the stitched reinforcement right side up, its edges will be flush with those of the lining.

15. Attach interior pockets to lining.

Position interior pockets right side up on lining (eyeball this), pin in place, and sew 3 edges, leaving top open. On all pockets, use a smaller seam allowance by using the "right needle position" setting on your sewing machine. Keep pocket edges flush to the right edge of the presser foot. For corners, leave the needle down in the fabric, lift presser foot, and rotate the fabric. Lower foot, and continue sewing. Backtack your corners for extra strength. Sew a tiny bit above the top of the pocket and backtack. Roll up the rest of the lining fabric for ease of maneuvering while sewing.

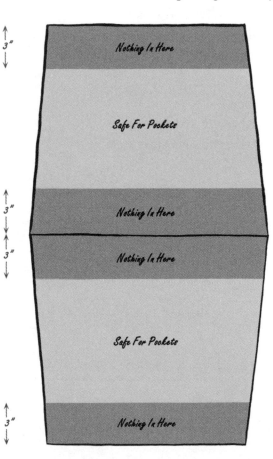

16. Segment the interior pockets (optional).

This is super easy. If you want to break your pocket into symmetrical or different-size compartments, just pick your width and stitch a straight line from bottom to top of the pocket. Each line of stitching creates a new segment.

17. Plot the position of your outside pockets.

Be sure to place the pockets a safe distance from the middle line of the exterior fabric piece—at least 3 inches from the bottom edge of each pocket. You can use tailor's chalk or your disappearing ink pen to mark this safety line and then eyeball the pocket placement. Just put the pockets anywhere you think they look good as long as they don't creep into the "danger zone."

18. Pin, and sew—just like the inside pockets.

Pin pockets to external fabric along 3 sides and sew. Use the right-needle-position setting, remember?

19. Fold the lining in half by joining the top edges together, right sides together, and sew the sides.

Move the needle back to the center position if it's still on right-needle position after the last step. Sew a ½ inch seam along each side (obviously you want to leave the top open—it's a bag). The end result should match the trapezoid pattern piece.

Clip the bottom corners, but be careful not to cut into stitches. This allows you to open the seam for pressing.

20. Slide the lining assemblage around your ironing board and press seams open and flat.

Fold either side of the raw edges of the seams away from each other and against the wrong side of the fabric. Press them with the iron into place. This is a really important step. Your bag will look much more finished and professional if you take the time to do this.

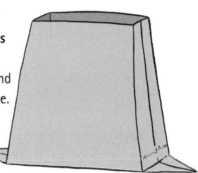

21. Press corner points flat and mark a line for your seam.

Once your seams have been pressed, you will notice that the bottom corners of the lining come to points. With a ruler, measure 1½ inches up the side seam from the tip of the corner. Flatten the corner so that it makes a small triangle and draw a 3-inch line perpendicular to the side seam. This is where the bag gets its bottom, or "feet."

22. Sew across each 3-inch corner line you've made.

Make sure you backtack for extra strength. This is especially important here because these are the main bottom corners of the bag. You don't want 'em busting out on ya.

23. Cut off the triangle "scrap" that's left outside your seam.

Jenny recommends pinking shears for this because they cause less shredding. You can turn the triangular scrap right side out to make pasties or a little elf bonnet.

24. Repeat steps 19 to 23 for the bag's exterior.

Lather. Rinse. Repeat.

25. Fold the strap in half lengthwise, right sides together, and press.

This will create a nice, crisp crease that'll make sewing the strap a lot easier.

26. Sew a seam along the strap with a ½-inch seam allowance.

Now you can see why you don't wanna go narrower than 5 inches for the original strap fabric piece.

27. Use your strap turner to turn the strap right side out.

Follow the instructions that came with it. It really is worth the two bucks it probably cost you.

28. Press your strap flat, making sure the sewn seam acts as an edge.

Roll the strap between your fingers to get the seam as far out as you can before pressing.

29. Topstitch the strap edges.

Again, use the right-needle position, and stitch all the way along each side of the strap. Now both sides of the strap are finished and secure.

30. "Puff out" the bag exterior (still wrong side out), flattening the bottom so the bag is open and will stand on its own.

The bag doesn't *need* to stand up, but you get the idea.

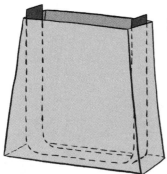

31. Lay your strap flat into the exterior assemblage, making sure it's not twisted.

Pin the strap ends to the side seams of the bag body, leaving ½ inch sticking out of the opening of the exterior fabric piece.

32. Turn the lining right side out and place inside the exterior (which should still be inside out).

Make sure to push it in around the seams and corners and get it as snug as you can. You can use a bone folder or chopstick for this.

33. Line up your center seams and top edges. Pin into place all the way around the top edge.

The extra bulk due to the strap inside will make flush edges tricky. Just make sure they are flush when pinned.

34. Sew almost all the way around the top edge of the bag, leaving a ½-inch seam allowance. Leave a 4- to 6-inch gap open in the stitching.
Remember to backtack a lot on this step. It needs the extra security when you turn the bag inside out. Take your time and leave the needle down in the fabric whenever you need to reposition. Remove pins as you go. You don't want to break your machine's needle by sewing through a pin. Don't forget to leave the gap in the stitching (right in the middle of one of the sides—not on the corner or seam) so you can turn the bag right side out.

35. Turn the entire bag right side out.
Stick your hand way down in the gap you left. Start by pulling out the strap. Be gentle so as not to bust any seams. Continue pulling at stuff until both the exterior and lining are sticking out. Now push the lining *back into* the exterior. Push out your corners and just kind of give everything a nice firm tuck.

36. Fold in and press the edges of the gap in the seam
Keep the edges consistent with the existing ½-inch seam. Insert a length of fusible web and press again to seal the gap.

37. Iron all the way around the top edge of the bag.
Again, roll the edges between your fingers to assure that the seam is as close to the edge of the stitching as possible.

38. Starting in the middle of the gap, topstitch all the way around the bag's opening.
Use the right-needle position and again keep the edge of the bag's opening flush with the right edge of the presser foot. Backtack and remember to leave the needle down when repositioning. The strap has to go under and around the presser foot, which will take some maneuvering, but you'll figure it out.

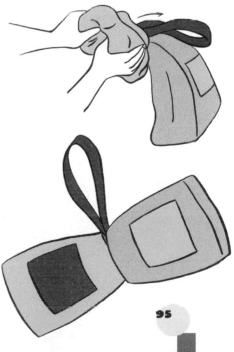

39. If necessary, you can hide any final opening edge flaws with trim.
Voilà! Your bag is complete.

Main pattern piece for the exterior and lining of your bag. Remember, you don't need to trace this, just measure your fabric according to the specs listed. Don't forget to mark the edge to line up to the fold and the notches 3½ inches from the top.

Main Pattern Piece

13" wide across top
14" high
15.75" wide across bottom

mark 3.5" down from top if adding reinforcements to lining,
cut two strips of outer material and affix to lining at notch marks

⟶ Place this edge on fold of fabric ⟶

Front Pocket

9.5" wide
9" high

Back Left Pocket

5" wide
7.5" high

Back Right Pocket

5.5" wide
8.75" high

Front pocket. While you'll only make one oaktag pattern piece from these measurements, you will be cutting out 3 pockets based on it—2 for the interior and 1 for the exterior.

Back pockets.
These pocket pieces are labeled "back pocket" but that's just to differentiate them from the "front pocket." I am not sure that this tote has an obvious front or back. That wild adventure is up to you. Cut out 1 of each.

SERVING SUGGESTIONS

This is one hell of a sturdy bag, and very utilitarian. However, depending on your taste and choice of materials, you could modify this bag into many styles. If you wanna use it as your day-to-day satchel, you can certainly add snaps or other closures for security.

Now that you've made a really pro-looking bag, you can start making your own designs simply by altering the dimensions of the various pattern pieces. For your first time, I would stick with the dimensions that Jenny provided. However, you can vary the pocket sizes and segment them to hold specific items such as scissors, pens, knitting needles, a cell phone, or anything. Also, depending on what craft it is that you do, you might need to make the bag bigger or smaller in order to accommodate your supplies. The tackle box I use to organize my cross-stitch supplies, for instance, would never fit into this bag. But hey, no problem. I can just modify the pattern's measurements to suit my equipment.

Contact Info

Jenny is all over the place online: live journals, blogs, you name it. She has her own Web store at http://www.sewdarncute.com where she sells her amazing handbags as well as knitting-needle cozies, pot holders, and tons of other stuff that really *is* sew darn cute! You can also e-mail her at jenny@sewdarncute.com.

"*Hester?!* I just *met* her!"

The Scarlet Letter, Nathaniel Hawthorne's novel about the societal consequences of promiscuity, is yet another great story about a vilified crafter. Well, I should say the plot is great—I actually thought the book itself was pretty boring, but I read it in high school, so who knows. Maybe I'd find it more thrilling now.

Hester Prynne was actually jailed for giving birth to an illegitimate daughter named Pearl. The crime, if I recall, was the sex rather than the birth. The story begins with her leaving prison to serve out her sentence: She must stand on display on the town scaffold for an hour, holding her three-month-old baby. In addition, she is ordered to wear a red letter *A,* to stand for Adulteress, on her chest (talk about the fashion police). In what I think is a totally punk-rock slap in the face to authority, she embroiders the letter with golden thread and intricate, beautiful detail, making her intended mark of shame a badge of pride (another sin I'm sure the elders weren't too fond of). True to the BazBiz credo, she takes something not only mundane but, in fact, oppressive and makes it her own through her skills. Hester and Pearl move to the edge of town, and Hester sews for a living. Apparently, the townspeople were willing to overlook her godless harlotry cuz she was handy with a needle.

So the story goes on, and there's a bunch of stuff about this long lost husband, Dr. Chillingsworth, and the ailing Boston pastor, Arthur Dimmesdale. Chillingsworth suspects that the good pastor is actually Pearl's father and is bent on revenge, so he takes Dimmesdale as a patient. The climax of the story takes place during some kind of swearing-in ceremony for town officials over which Dimmesdale presides. He's dying, and wants to confess his sin so Hester won't suffer alone, so he rips open his shirt to reveal a big letter *A* imprinted into his skin. It's unclear how the wound made its way onto his chest. Did he do it himself, was it the work of Chillingsworth's "medicine," or is it God's punishment for his sins? I like to think it was self-inflicted because that way it's like a colonial-era biker tattoo of your girlfriend's name or something. Plus, carving your own flesh is craftier than a pox from the Almighty.

After all the drama, Hester goes to Europe for a while, only to return without her daughter, Pearl. She lives the rest of her days counseling troubled townswomen and sewing these really opulent baby clothes that wouldn't be found in any Puritan New England home. Another illegitimate child in a faraway land perhaps? A BazBiz crafter to the end, she even displayed her letter on her gravestone. She was buried next to Dimmesdale under a tombstone engraved "On a Field, Sable, the Letter A, Gules." Keep on keepin' on, Hester.

GLASS MARBLE ACCESSORiES
PROJECT: MARBLE MAGNETS

ARTIST: *Leah Kramer*

Can you think of a more resonant symbol of home than the refrigerator? Not only does it hold our food and sustenance, but also it is often a center of household communication. Shopping lists, report cards, coupons, quizzes, and reminders have historically made their way onto this most major of appliances. And where would the fridge be without the magnet? Now you don't want to use a boring magnet to hold up these important social documents, do you? Unfortunately, every novelty magnet I have encountered is either grossly overpriced, too weak, or both. Free yourself from the chains of trendy department store housewares and lame novelty gift shops. In this chapter we learn how to make our own magnets—cheaply!

Leah Kramer is probably best known for her Web site Craftster.org, which has the tagline "no tea cozies without irony." It's been so successful that she's been able to leave the nine-to-five working world to work full-time on the forum where thousands of crafters make contact daily to break the rules.

Leah is a self-proclaimed crafting addict. Much to the chagrin of her parents, her love of making messes involving scraps of fabric, glitter, and glue began at an early age. Her crafty interests have ebbed and flowed, but lately she's thinking that she probably inhaled too much glue along the way because she's attracted to crafts that are ironic or kitschy or irreverent in some way. These are the qualities that made her an ideal candidate to get involved with Bazaar Bizarre. She joined up in 2003 and has been an integral part of the Boston edition's success. Her latest endeavor is Magpie on Huron, a vintage and handmade craft boutique in which she has collaborated with by BazBiz gals Emily Arkin and Simone Alpen.

My favorite thing about Leah is that I didn't think she liked me very much when we met. Her somewhat deadpan sense of humor takes a minute to key in on, but by the end of the day that I interviewed her for this book, I was latch-hooked.

What is the difference between an "art" and a "craft"?
I think that art tends to be more decorative, while crafts are more often functional. But having said that, I think that many, many crafts are also artful. Another big difference is that often times the

skills involved in fine art—such as painting and sculpting—take years and years to master. A majority of crafts, on the other hand, are easier to learn how to master, and then it's just a matter of doing really creative and unique things with those techniques.

What is your earliest crafting memory?

I think some time very early on my mother taught me how to sew a pillow, and as a young kid I was obsessed with making little pillows in every shape and every fabric. There's something kind of magical about how you sew it inside out and then when you turn it right side out all your stitching is hidden and you have an actual pillow! I was constantly sneaking into her sewing basket to use her good scissors and her pinking shears and whatever fabric I could get my hands on.

What was your best crafting moment (idea, inspiration, etc.)?

I'm always attracted to the beauty and irony of 1950s imagery in magazine ads, cook books, etc., and I can't help but snatch these things up when I see them in thrift stores and yard sales. One day I found a plastic box of 200 vintage Betty Crocker recipe cards at Goodwill. I pored over each beautiful card with their supersaturated photography of hotdog-bacon-cheese casseroles and Jell-O molds of every kind and wondered what I could do with all these individual gems. But it seemed blasphemous not to keep the whole box of cards intact. A few weeks later I was hopping from garage sale to garage sale, and I stumbled across two more complete sets of these cards in one day, and I was finally free to craft away with all of these extra sets! I experimented with zillions of ideas, and then finally I came up with the idea to make small notebooks where the cover of the notebook is the recipe card, with the photo on the front cover and the recipe on the flip side.

What was your worst crafting moment (a huge mess, project gone horribly wrong, etc.)?

Oh. Ouch. The first thing that comes to mind is when I was smart enough to try to wipe some goopy glue off my sharpest scissors by running my thumb across the blade. Even though this was two years ago, I still clutch my thumb in horror when I think about the pain and blood that ensued.

What is your favorite craft you've ever seen?

Oh, man—I envy anyone who can sew a sundress. On my Web site Craftster.org, one member posted a picture of a sundress that she made out of 1980s Smurf sheets she scored at a thrift store. She didn't even use a pattern. It's the most stylin' thing ever!

Who made you the crafter you are (who introduced you to crafts, taught you crafts—whether or not it is the one you do now)?

My mom taught me some basic crafty skills, but she didn't know how to do more complicated things like quilting and knitting. She is, however, a big do-it-yourself type of person. I guess that I attribute my craftiness to grade school when more of your time is spent doing artsy-crafty things. I can remember getting pats on the back and glowing comments about my work being so elaborate. Man, what I could do with a paper doily for Valentine's cards.

What are your crafting goals?

I would love to drop the "day gig" and find a way to make a living entirely from crafting. I think that some people fear doing what they love as a living because they are afraid that it won't be fun anymore. But for me an important part of enjoying crafting is enjoying the challenge of making it profitable. I love coming up with new ideas of things to make and sell. And I love the challenge of taking that idea and learning to make it in a way that's efficient and affordable so that I can hope to make enough of a profit when I sell it.

Kraft or Kraftwerk?

Heh. Cheese? Or cheesy keyboards? Tough choice. Luckily processed cheese food is *not* cheese and Kraftwerk is *not* cheesy. So Kraftwerk all the way baby! Besides, I *am* the operator with the pocket calculator.

Who is your fave crafty celeb?

My favorite celebrity in the world of crafting has got to be Liza Lou. For those who don't know her work, she basically covers three-dimensional settings in extremely *tiny* colorful glass beads. For example, she'll create a huge installation, which is a kitchen where every single thing in the kitchen is encrusted in carefully placed beads. It's so rich and complex. And sparkly . . . ooooooo sparkly.

What is your fave craft resource (Web site, store, dumpster, etc.)?
In Boston (well, Arlington, Massachusetts) we have a great, huge, mom-and-pop
craft store called Playtime Crafts. They have lots of modern craft supplies as well as
a huge selection of kitschy things like beaded-fruit materials, doll faces, chintzy
cake decorations, etc.

For fabric, I love the selection of printed cotton fabric at Repro Depot, which is
an online shop at http://www.reprodepot.com. Generally speaking, it seems like most
popular fabric manufacturers produce a majority of prints that are of the unicorns
and rainbows ilk. Repro Depot culls out just the coolest prints for you.

Thrift stores, flea markets, yard sales, surplus stores, and city streets on trash
night are sometimes a wealth of pleasant surprises.

Global Techniques

There's only one general guideline that could be considered global for this project
since it's so basic—but it's important since you can apply it to almost every project
in this book: Any time you have to buy supplies, it's important to consider where you
buy them. For instance, you will find the glass marbles at the craft store for sure,
but they're going to be more expensive. They know you want 'em and they're gonna
charge you. However, at a floral supply wholesaler (remember the industrial supply
district downtown?), you can find them much cheaper, because they sell them in
large quantities, and to them it's nothing special. So keep in mind that multipurpose
supplies like this can be found much cheaper at hardware stores or warehouse
supply stores as opposed to crafting stores.
Just keep this principle in mind whenever you buy supplies. Think of it: So much of
crafting is making stuff you *want* out of stuff you *already have* lying around. Now
whoever first used glass marbles to make magnets didn't find them in the "glass
marble magnet" aisle at Michael's.

MARBLE MAGNETS   DiFFiCULTY ✪✪✪✪✪

TiME LiNE   Like a lot of the projects in this book, you're going to be using stuff you have around the house, especially if you keep a crafting junk drawer filled with things you don't know what to do with, but know you might use someday. So finding and cutting out the images you will use for this project could occur over an indefinite amount of active time. Gluing the images to the marbles just takes a few minutes, while waiting for them to dry completely takes about 30 minutes. Leah clocks the gluing of the finished marble to a magnet or whatever you're gonna glue it to at exactly 12 seconds.

According to Leah, anything by "the masters of short songs: The Ramones, Minutemen, Descendents, and more."
[AUTHOR'S NOTE: You might wanna try Wire and by extension Elastica for short songs.]

Hervé Villechaize: *The E! True Hollywood Story; Strangers with Candy* DVD Set; *Best in Show*

SHOPPiNG LiST

HARDWARE/CRAFT/FLORAL SUPPLY

- **Clear glass marbles**   The type you'll want to use for this project are usually used for holding up flowers. You can find the smaller sizes at the department store in jars and bags. Larger sizes can be found at the craft store, floral supply store, or nursery. They come in a variety of colors and finishes. When you're picking yours out, make sure they are clear and colorless. Marbles with an iridescent finish will prevent you from being able to see the image through the glass.
- **Hole punch, circle cutter, or circle stencil and scissors**   I know they're scary, but check out the scrapbooking aisles at the craft store. Yeah, they're filled with hideous icons of suburbia and church, but you can find some very cool cutting tools. My number one recommendation for this or any other project where you'll

be cutting out circles is to try and find a large circular craft punch. Marvy Uchida seems to have the largest selection of sizes. Fiskars makes an adjustable circle cutter, but it's a little tricky for really small circles. The cheapest choice is probably to buy a plastic circle stencil/template and use a pair of scissors.

I think the main trick here is to buy the punch and/or template with the glass marbles in hand. That way you can match them up in size before you get home. The majority of the marbles are either ½ inch or 1 inch, and you can easily find a punch in these standard sizes.

- **Magnets** Make sure they are strong. The glass marbles—even the smallest ones—are surprisingly heavy. Definitely avoid any kind of cutable magnetic sheets or magnet tape. These won't even hold up the magnet, let alone any pictures to the fridge.
- **White craft glue (Elmer's, Aleene's Tacky Glue, etc.)** Leah says PVA (Polyvinyl acetates) is the adhesive genre you want. Just make sure it dries clear.

YOUR JUNK DRAWER

- **Image source material** Use whatever you have lying around. Catalogs, junk mail, greeting cards, etc. You also can print your own source material. Leah's had some success with matte photo paper.

Step by Step

1. Choose your image(s) from your source materials.
I always find this step tons of fun because it's one of those times when you really get to rummage through all the *crap* that you've saved up. If you're anything like me, you have folders, boxes, and bags full of printed material that you hung on to, waiting for a project just like this. Junk mail, catalogs, old magazines, cardboard packaging: All are great grist for your craft mill. It's like a knife through my heart to throw away a greeting card someone has given to me. I don't want it hanging around, but it's like you can't throw Aunt Mildred's get-well wishes in the trash—*especially* after the transplant. Leah's project is the perfect escape pod from Starship

Guilt. Take that albatross from around your neck and get out the scissors cuz:

1 Cards are usually nice heavy stock

2 They usually have iconic, very clippable images

3 You're not throwing away memories, you're giving them new life (*cue violins*)

2. Frame your image with and trace a circle.
If you are going to use scissors or an X-acto knife, you can use a circle stencil to "find" and draw your image borders. If you bought a large circle craft punch (about 1-inch diameter, although they do come bigger) from the Dreaded Land of Scrapbooking (I never said they didn't have cool tools, just bad taste), punch a plain piece of paper first. Now you have a little template to size up your target.

3. Cut out your circle with scissors or a hole punch.
You can also use a circle cutter. Fiskars makes a pretty cool one that's adjustable, but it might be a touch cumbersome for the smallest marbles. Keep in mind that your cutting does not have to be perfectly circular. The marbles themselves are usually a little oblong or at least wobbly edged. Cut your images to fit the flat surface of the bottom of the marble. The round edge will actually stick out beyond its diameter, masking most flaws.

4. Glue your image face up to the bottom of the marble.
Smooth it out with your fingers to remove air bubbles and to make sure you have a good seal between the image and the glass, with your glue going all the way to the edges. It will dry clear even though it looks kinda gunky when you turn it over to see the image through the glass.

5. Use an assembly-line approach if you plan on making a bunch of marbles in one sitting.
Instead of making each marble magnet start to finish, complete each step for every unit you plan to make. This way, by the time you finish gluing your last picture to your last marble, your first marble will be dry and ready to roll for the next step.

6. Glue a magnet to the back of the marble.
Leah used a hot glue gun when she demonstrated this project for me, but I might be

more inclined to try some sort of superglue. Hot glue seems to work best with more porous surfaces, but for the smaller pieces it won't make much difference. Now you just have to find some metal things and stick it to 'em!

SERVING SUGGESTIONS

These marble magnets make really great gifts. Like any handmade item, they say, "I love you, but I'm incredibly broke." When gift giving, it's easy to make 'em personal when it comes to the pictures you choose. You can make your selections based on the hobbies and collections of the recipient or even just use pictures of him.

Magnets aren't the only things you can make with Leah's picture marbles. You can find a ton of different templates to which you can glue your miniature masterpieces like thumbtacks, bracelets, earrings, barrettes, pins, and rings. Check out the Ornamental Resources Web site at http://www.ornabed.com. It's a specialty jewelry supply house where you can find almost anything you need in terms of "blanks" (plain metal jewelry findings meant for customizing with jewels and stuff). If you're going to glue your finished picture marbles to metal, you'll want to use trusty old E6000 industrial glue, which you should have handy anyway. Pick up a magnetic metal bulletin board at IKEA or Staples or somewhere. It's great for its intended purpose as an actual bulletin board, but you can use a tabletop easel to transform it into a sales display (for the next Bazaar). I just bought one for my Fagnets (the magnets I make outta jar lids).

Contact Info

Get in touch with Leah! She's a friendly gal, and is always willing to help out a fellow crafter. Or should I say craftster? E-mail her at leahkramer@craftster.org; visit http://craftster.org/; or take a trip down Huron Avenue in Cambridge to visit Magpie on Huron at 368 Huron Avenue, Cambridge, MA 02138. Dial (617) 661-1611 or click http://www.magpiestore.com.

Supplies Word Search

CRAFTOID

```
G N I T N I A P K L I S B W A
H C T I T S S S O R C Z A P B
T N I O P E L D E E N L R A O
Y S P I L C R I A H L I K G O
R S I L K S C R E E N I N G K
E Q F A A R T N T T B I I C B
D U S F I Y I E M Z K A T O I
I I W R U R I A N A R S T I N
O L O C H C K N M G E E I N D
R T L S R I D P G W A I N P I
B I L S N O A R I C T M G U N
M N I G H O C N O E A S I R G
E G P Z S Z G H L C E R R S O
S O C K M O N K E Y E F D E C
A M A R O I D R A T F R T S S
```

BOOKBINDING
COINPURSE
CROCHET
CROSSSTITCH
DIORAMA
EMBROIDERY
HAIRCLIPS
KNITTING

MAGNETS
NEEDLEPOINT
PILLOWS
PLAYINGCARDS
PRINTMAKING
QUILTING
RECORDCUFFS
SEWING

SHRINE
MILKPAINTING
SILKSCREENING
SOAPMAKING
SOCKMONKEY
WALLET

Most serious crafters have a signature medium in which they work. Mine, for instance, is cross-stitch. Getting to be an expert in any one skill, however, can eventually lead to familiarity and stagnation. One of the most fun aspects of crafting is discovering new materials to co-opt for your own devilish creative projects. Of course, you may not want to repeat the years you spent mastering your first love. When exploring new materials or crafts, I'd suggest getting your feet wet with something quick, cheap, and forgiving. That's where felt comes in.

Safety scissors and crusty paste in tiny Tupperware containers—that's what normally springs to mind when I think of felt. I'd always pitied felt as a somewhat inferior medium whose applications were limited strictly either to messy nursery school activities or really tacky Christmas ornaments. Thankfully, Hazel rescued me from my narrow felt perceptions by introducing me to her own nearly foolproof wallet project.

CRAFTER BIO

BAZAAR BIZARRE
MANDUJANO, HAZEL
19781002
FELT WALLET

Hazel is a wonderfully peculiar woman and talented artist. I'm still getting to know her, and it's kind of like poring over the card tables at a psychic yard sale. In requesting some biographical info from her, I received a bullet point list of Hazel factoids. Here are some of my favorites in Hazel's own words:

- My best friend calls me a little creep because she thinks I'm creepy.

- My favorite food is steamed rice.

- My favorite word is thunder.

- My last name is really Rodriguez.

- My favorite thing to do is visit the tide pools in San Pedro.

- I wish I had at least ten turtles.

- You wish you had seen the sixteen turtles I had.

- I also wish I had a bird that really liked me.

- I can't swim.

- I can't play the guitar.

This list probably presents more questions than it answers. Does she or doesn't she have sixteen turtles? Ten turtles? Does she have *any* turtles? I, too, wish I had a bird that really liked me (see Dana Berkowitz's chapter, page 41, to see more about my bird "thing"). Hazel and I have a lot in common, but unlike Ms. Mandujano, I *can* swim and play the guitar. There are an infinite number of abilities that any person does *not* possess. Why mention these in particular? Was she *expected* to do either? As I'm getting to know Hazel, I look forward to investigating more of her mystery. Like Pee-wee said, it's like "unraveling a giant sweater that someone keeps knitting, and knitting, and knitting . . ."

What is the difference between an "art" and a "craft"?
The difference is the intention and the audience; it's like masking tape vs. artist's tape.

What is your earliest crafting memory?
I remember making necklaces and bracelets out of dental floss for my friends in the neighborhood. I think I was five years old. The floss was green and sturdy.

What was your best crafting moment (idea, inspiration, etc.)?
I don't think I have one best crafting moment, yet. But, anytime I get to have a table at any convention and people like what I have is a great crafting moment.

What was your worst crafting moment (a huge mess, project gone horribly wrong, etc.)?
My worst crafting moment was the night before Alternative Press Expo. When the girl at the copy store cut my comic in the worst way she could have: She cut every page panel by panel, instead of the way I had asked (in strips). So, we had to recopy everything . . . sucky sucky sucky!

What is your favorite craft you've ever seen?
So far, my favorite crafts have been by two Japanese crafters, Jun Yokota and Mari Matsuo. Jun Yokota makes felt clocks, animals, and tapestry like pieces; and Mari Matsuo makes plush fruits with human faces on them. I like them because they're supercute, very well made, and reasonably priced.

Who made you the crafter you are (who introduced you to crafts, taught you crafts—whether or not it is the one you do now)?
My cousin Norma made me a crafter. It started one summer that I spent with her. She taught me how to embroider and sew to keep me from being bored.

What are your crafting goals?
My crafting goal is to teach people how to craft.

Kraft or Kraftwerk?
Kraft during Kraftwerk.

Who is your fave crafty celeb?
Martha Stewart. Yes, Martha Stewart.

What is your fave craft resource (Web site, store, dumpster, etc.)?
APE. Alternative Press Expo.

Global Techniques

You probably mastered the use of the materials for this project by your kindergarten graduation, but that doesn't mean you can't have some more grown-up fun. Besides what kindergartener carries a wallet? The real concept of a certain skill or technique for this one is more in the design than in the technique.

We're making a very simple tri-fold wallet. The challenge is how you can snaz up a really standard format through color and personality. Go to a department store, and I'm pretty certain you won't find any felt wallets. As with other designs in this book, we're making something out of materials you might not normally use. Instead of seeing this as a limitation, Hazel has taken it as an opportunity to make something really fun that you need to use every day anyhow. Plus, with a total cash output of *maybe* five bucks, you can have a different wallet for every outfit.

WALLET DiFFiCULTY ✪✪✪✪✪

TiME LiNE Hazel's cute felt wallets take about an hour to make start to finish. There are some short instances of passive time, waiting for the glue to dry on the Velcro, that sorta thing, but nothing major. Here are some of Hazel's faves to make you whistle while you work.

Björk: *Vespertine;* The Clash: *London Calling;* Peggy Honeywell: *Self-Titled*

Sixteen Candles; The Royal Tenenbaums; House Party

SHOPPiNG LiST

CRAFT STORE

- **2 felt squares** Okay, so maybe the last time you used these was with safety scissors and some tasty paste, but it's time to reacquaint yourself with felt squares. They come in more colors than the really huge pack of Crayolas and sometimes you can find them as cheap as ten for a buck! You buy them in squares, and if you use more than one color, you will need one square of each.
- **Aleene's Tacky Glue** By now you really should have a bottle of this stuff in your craft tackle box. In case you haven't noticed, it crops up in a bunch of projects in this book.
- **Nonadhesive Velcro** The Velcro sticky tape *could* work, but I don't think the adhesive is designed to stick to fabric, especially something as fuzzy as felt. And then if you have to use a needle and thread to tack it down, it gets all gummy. I recommend using the sew-on Velcro. You can additionally use tacky glue with this.
- **Embroidery floss** If you wanna embellish your wallet with embroidery, you'll need some good old DMC 6-strand embroidery floss. I imagine you could also use "craft thread" (they keep it right by the embroidery floss, and it comes in bags of

36 skeins). I wouldn't recommend using the decorative floss or craft thread for the actual constructive sewing. It's not going to be sturdy enough.

- **Needle and thread** Here I'd recommend good old Coates & Clark Dual Duty thread. In other words, what you get when you ask for thread at Michael's or some place where they don't have a zillion kinds of specialty thread. Make sure it has at least some synthetic material in it. This adds strength. When you sew with this, make sure to double it up. With this project you're not going to be turning any seams. The construction is very basic, and felt has no "wrong" side. Choose your thread by color, definitely. Make it part of the design.

- **Buttons or other embellishments** Totally optional, but buttons can make cute eyeballs. Of course you could use googly eyes or iron-on letters or whatever you want. But by now you know that a lot of the success of these projects rests on your initiative and imagination. I can't do *all* the work here.

YOUR OWN CUPBOARDS

- **Scissors** For cutting . . . duh.

Step by Step

1. Choose your felt colors.
Choose colors for your wallet. Keep in mind that there will be 4 wallet construction pieces, and then any optional felt you might use for appliqué. Your wallet elements do not have to be different colors from one another, but it's fun if they are. And variation doesn't mean crazy contrast, necessarily. Felt comes in a zillion colors, so you could use all shades of one color family, which might give you a more sophisticated look. Alternatively you could go for bright contrasting candy colors for something less Ralph Lauren and more Ralph Wiggum.

2. Cut out the wallet's exterior.
This is done by cutting a 12- x 4-inch piece of felt. When choosing your felt, keep in mind that this will be the color of the wallet. That is, when the wallet is closed, it will be the only color you see.

3. Divide wallet into 3 segments.

Hazel's design is for a traditional tri-fold wallet, so there needs to be 3 sections and 2 "hinges." Make 3 marks on the longer edge of the felt, each 4 inches apart. You can use tape or even a paper clip to make the marks. Make sure to use something removable and not a Sharpie since you'll be marking points that will remain visible on the completed piece.

4. If using appliqué, embroidery, or other exterior embellishments that require needle and thread, use them now.

For instance, when Hazel showed me how to make this project, she provided a few different examples, a couple of which involved hand sewing. If you're going to do anything like that that requires some amount of hand stitching, you need to do it before any of the other wallet elements are attached.

5. Create a closure for your wallet.

There are several ways to create a closure or fastener for your wallet. You could use a button, Velcro, or even a fancier closure you might find in the notions department at Jo-Ann's or the craft store. Hold the wallet exterior toward you and position the fastener (button, fuzzy side of the Velcro, or the latch for a hook and eye) just to the left of the left one-third division or hinge that you just drew. Sew into place. If using Velcro, make sure you buy the nonadhesive type. You can actually omit the fuzzy side of the Velcro since the bristly side will adhere to felt, but, over time, the bristly side will keep pulling at the felt, making it extra fuzzy where the Velcro attaches.

6. Cut out the large, primary pocket—for lack of a better word I'm calling it the billfold.

The billfold should cover the right two-thirds of the wallet's length, so you'll need to cut an 8-inch-wide felt piece. The height of this piece should be anywhere between $3^1/4$ inches and $3^3/4$ inches with an average height of $3^1/2$ inches. This sounds more confusing than it really is. If you are going to use a straight edge for the top of your billfold, then just go ahead and cut out an 8- x $3^1/2$-inch rectangle. However, Hazel showed me an example where the top edge was scalloped, and I thought it looked really nice. You could use pinking shears or even do something as simple as cutting a wavy line. Only the top edge should make use of a variation. The remaining 3 edges should be cut straight. If you decide to embellish the top edge, just keep any variations in the ½-inch zone so it maintains some uniformity.

7. Cut out 2 credit card pockets.

Cut two 3- x 1¾-inch rectangles. They can be the same color or different colors. Of course, my credit rating is a piece of shit, so I'll just be using these pockets for my Mensa, Costco, Subway Sub Club, and Southwest Rapid Rewards cards.

8. Before sewing anything, plot out your wallet.

Take a moment to sit back, relax, and enjoy a soothing cup of General Foods International coffees ("Jean Luc!"). Lay out all your wallet pieces starting with the exterior, then the billfold, and finally the card pockets on top. The pockets should be spaced on either end of the billfold, leaving a gutter between them. This will create a natural hinge for the wallet and keep it from being bulky and lumpy when closed.

9. Sew the card pockets to the billfold.

Remember your gutter. Stitch along the sides and bottom leaving the top open . . . duh, I mean that's what makes it a pocket and not a patch. Note that you are only sewing the pockets to the billfold, not to the exterior wallet piece (that's the next step).

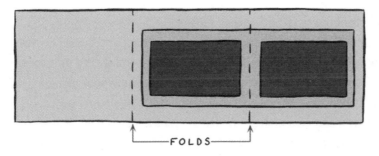

FOLDS

10. Sew your entire billfold assembly to the wallet exterior.

Align this entire billfold piece with the right edge of the wallet so that it occupies the eastern two-thirds of the wallet's entire length. Once you've sewn along the sides and bottom edges, the wallet is basically constructed. Remember—don't sew the top edge!

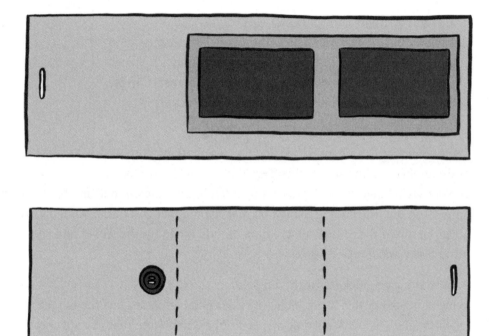

11. Sew the buttonhole or attach other closure.

To make a buttonhole, fold your wallet so that it is closed, and cut a slit near the edge of the wallet that is *not* covered by the billfold assembly. The buttonhole edge will be the left edge of the wallet when you're holding the wallet interior toward you. I'd suggest stitching each end of the buttonhole to avoid any potential rips, but it isn't essential. You can also choose to stitch a hair elastic into place where the buttonhole would go. If you choose to close your wallet with Velcro, apply the bristly side where you would put the buttonhole.

12. Apply any embellishments that require glue.

Felt is so great because it works really well with glue. This means you can add all kinds of additional felt appliqués to the outside of your wallet once it's all finished. In fact, if this is your first round making this project, I might stick with glue-on designs instead of sewing since it requires less planning. With the sew-on approach, if you miss a step, you're pretty much screwed, and you'll have to either start over or improvise some glue-oriented rescue anyway.

13. Stuff it with a grip of Benjamins, throw on your bling, and roll out of your crib with your fly new wallet.

SERVING SUGGESTIONS

Think of emblems that might work as embellishments to your wallet: hands clasped, a face with fangs, embroider your very own knockoff Vuitton logos all over it. After you master the tri-fold, think about making a wallet or pouch with a different orientation than the east-west one described in this chapter. How about a custom iPod holder or checkbook cover? Once you have the general idea of how to assemble the pockets and stuff, it's pretty easy. And hey, if you screw it up, it's no big deal since the supplies cost next to nothing.

Contact Info

Hazel's Web site is http://www.cakemountain.com. Write to her, and maybe she can enlighten you about her desires regarding turtles.

Watch Where You Put That Friggan Distaff!

I can scarcely think of a more resonant icon of "women's work" than the spinning wheel. In fact, the occupation of spinning has been so heavily associated with women historically that the word "distaff" (a long staff around which fibers were wound before being spun) is alternately defined as "of having to do with women." Spinning and the fruits of its labor are an important manifestation of the ideas of public and private spheres. In times when you had to spin your own thread to make your husband's clothes (we're talking the Dark Ages), his public personal appearance said a lot about his status and estate. It's here you can see that the behind-the-scenes role of women's work in the private sphere actually holds a lot of sway in the public. Being seen in poor-quality clothes could ruin a man's reputation. This power was somewhat jinxed, though, since if you attempted to besmirch your husband's good name through shoddy workmanship at the wheel, he'd probably either abandon you for a more skillful wife or just go ahead and kill you. I guess the secret lies always in knowing *how* to use your power. There is, however, no shortage of power associated with spinning historically.

Nearly every polytheistic religion has a goddess of spinning. Isis in Egypt, Athena in Greece, the Baltic Saule, Frau Holda in Germany, Japan's Amaterasu, and even the Virgin Mary are each associated with this particular handicraft. Frigga, the wife of big-cheese Norse god Odin (the all-father), was the goddess of the home and spinning, creating the clouds on her wheel and decked out in a girdle with house keys. The importance of spinning in the Norse culture is evidenced by its name for the constellation of Orion, known to the Vikings as Frigga's Distaff. The processes of spinning are often used as a metaphor for fate, and it was Frigga who was thought to know the fate of men (which she kept to herself). Frigga was always spinning, measuring, and cutting the threads of life.

In the human realm, the distaff carries with it a dual meaning of both subservience and domination. This binary was particularly ominous for the man of the house. The tools of spinning could be seen as a ball and chain, a means of control, keeping the housewife tethered to the hearth and kitchen, working for the good of the family and primarily the husband. However, its power was pulsing just below the surface. In addition to the figurative intangible power of reputation possessed by women through spinning, the most recognizable (in its day) tool of this art—the distaff—was often employed as a very literal weapon. Like the latter-day rolling pin, frying pan, broomstick, and even purse, this one-time implement of female subservience was used to beat the crap out of a cheating or lazy husband. Even the devil can be seen encouraging the housewife to wield her domestic weapons in ancient illustrations. This imagery was often used as a threatening reminder of the importance of male authority since female dominance signaled a world turned on its head.

It is precisely this inversion of power that *Bazaar Bizarre* champions. We as crafters can figuratively and literally cut the ties that bind us to the notion that crafts are quiet or weak. The predictably precious imagery of commercialized decorative crafting only fosters the lame sexist ideas surrounding traditional handicrafts and their worth in a culture that wants to keep crafts in a very specific devalued pocket of representation. I suggest we take hold of the distaff of appropriation and beat the husband of dominant aesthetics.

BOOKBiNDiNG
PROJECT: CROSSED-STRUCTURE BiNDiNG BOOK

ARTIST: *Stacie Dolin*

always wanted to be a journaler. I remember when I was young, I saw a TV ad for a girl's diary set that included a pen concealed as a bottle of nail polish. I will never forget the perfectly feminine penmanship of the girl in the commercial as she crossed the *t* in the word "math." I am not sure I understand the functionality of hiding a pen in the guise of nail polish, but there it was. I used to practice writing script before I even understood what cursive was. I would just draw line after line of squiggles, with the occasional *t* thrown in (the only letter I actually knew how to form due to the nail polish pen ad).

So how come I never managed to get myself in the habit of journaling? Somehow I couldn't bring myself to actually mark up a nice blank expensive book—it seemed wrong and, therefore, I never pursued it. That same brand of material conservatism instilled in me, for instance, the pointlessness of buying cut flowers since they're just going to die anyway. How depressing is that? A friend told me that this is a uniquely masculine trait (does this mean I'm butch?). Stacie's project has saved me from this dark fate. I mean, how much sleep can you lose over writing a book that you made for mere pennies? I now feel free to chronicle my secret crushes and deepest desires, because now I can make my own fancy blank books and be just like that girl in the commercial. Does anyone have a nail polish pen?

CRAFTER BIO

Stacie is another one of those wacky Somerville ladies I met during my two-year furlough in Massachusetts. At the time she was working at a self-described "women's sexuality boutique" and a comic book shop. Interesting combo, since at that point in my life I hadn't encountered any comic fans that were sexually informed, let alone well adjusted, but then again, my only real reference was Comic Book Guy from the Simpsons (well . . . him and me, but that's really for another book).

The first interesting thing I remember learning about Stacie was her love of New Jersey. There is a Bazaar Bizarre tradition known as the Rabbblerousers calendar, for which twelve participants each illustrate one month's page. I, for instance, chose Joan Collins and Morrissey that year (both of whom I share a birthday with). Stacie, though, in a brilliant shift of paradigms, chose the state of New Jersey. I suppose New Jersey *has* roused its share of rabble over the years. You can find out more by tracking down a 2001 calendar, or asking Stacie herself. She is always happy to expound on the virtues of the Garden State.

These days Stacie teaches bookbinding at the North Bennet Street School in Boston and teams up with Simone Alpen, our knitting contributor, at times to make their vintage material matching apron-and-eye-patch sets under the name of Fancy Lady Housewares.

What is the difference between an "art" and a "craft"?
Art goes on your wall. Art rhymes with fart; craft rhymes with daft.

What is your earliest crafting memory?
I mean . . . uh, there's a framed picture that I drew when I was three or so of a birthday party—my mom has it in her living room. I always traveled with many crafts in my satchel. . . .

What was your best crafting moment (idea, inspiration, etc.)?
Best crafting moment is when you realize that you *totally* get it, and you can do anything with that knowledge. And if you are able to teach it to others, you *really* get it.

**What was your worst crafting moment
(a huge mess, project gone horribly wrong, etc.)?**
I can always nitpick the problems with any craft that I create.

What is your favorite craft you've ever seen?
Anything useful and multitask, like a rubber band. It must be useful, and if it makes something useful more beautiful, all the better.

Who made you the crafter you are (who introduced you to crafts, taught you crafts—whether or not it is the one you do now)?
My grandma: Ruth Julie Dolin. She was an art teacher. And both my parents are artsy-fartsy types.

What are your crafting goals?
Make more stuff, find time to get through the stash of crap that I have for future projects. Ideally, I would list my projects and work my way down, but I know that's not going to happen.

Kraft or Kraftwerk?
I don't understand the question.

Who is your fave crafty celeb?
N/A

What is your fave craft resource (Web site, store, dumpster, etc.)?
Friends and their input. I look to books sometimes to master technique, but mostly asking my friends questions incessantly.

Global Techniques

Stacie's project makes use of what's known in the book universe as a crossed-structure binding. I won't go into too much detail here because we'll be covering it in the step by step, but there are a couple of terms you should know:

- **Folio:** A folio is a piece of paper folded in half. The result is four pages. Each front and each back of the paper counts as one page. So an unfolded piece of paper is two pages. For this project we're gonna keep it simple and use 8½- x 11-inch paper. What type of paper you use is up to you.
- **Section:** A section (sometimes called a signature) is a number of folios gathered together inside one another. The number of folios per section depends on the thickness of the paper. For this project you'll want to limit your sections to three or four folios.
- **Landscape:** When paper is laid out so that it is wider than it is long.
- **Portrait:** When paper is laid out lengthwise.

CROSSED-STRUCTURE BINDING BOOK DIFFICULTY ✪✪✪✪✪

TIME LINE The book that Stacie made while I interviewed her took about 1½ hours. There isn't any passive time in this project except as a result of some optional gluing. While investigating what stimulates her craft libido, I made the shocking discovery that Stacie *hates* movies. I have never met anyone who hates the actual cinematic experience—not just a certain genre or something—until I met Stacie. There is *one* movie I know she likes, but it's based on a TV show, and her former job at a women's sex boutique gave her a taste for porn. However, I think we can all agree when I say that porn isn't what we immediately think of when we're invited over to a friend's house "for a movie."

 The Avalanches: *Since I Left You;* Built to Spill: *There's Nothing Wrong with Love;* The Rapture: *Out of the Races and Onto the Tracks*

 The Uncle Floyd Show DVD; *Jackass: The Movie;* Major League Baseball

SHOPPiNG LiST

CRAFT STORE

- **Olfa knife** It's kind of like an X-acto but has a straight edge with snap-off blades. It's good because with a lot of projects you're gonna wear down your blades quickly.
- **Paper for pages** For this project we're gonna stick with any paper that comes in 8½- x 11-inch sheets. Just choose something that makes you smile.
- **Needle and thread** There are lots of choices here. A traditional bookbinding thread is waxed linen, but you could use wire, dental floss, or just about anything of decent strength. You can even wax your plain old regular thread by dragging it back and forth across a candle.
- **Bone folder** Sharp creases are superimportant for bookbinding.

YOUR OWN HOME

- **Cover material** You can use cardstock, cardboard, salami, lox. Something thick and delicious—wait—I meant sturdy.
- **Ruler (preferably metal)**
- **Cutting surface** You'll need a general work surface on which to cut but you'll also need something a little smaller and more portable like a piece of cardboard.

ANARCHY SOAP

BiRD POSTCARDS

CLIP-ON EXTENSIONS

page 58

HEART-SHAPED COIN PURSE

page 70

CRAFT TOTE

MARBLE MAGNETS

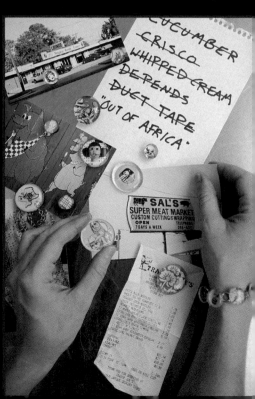

WALLET

page 110

TRASHY QUILT

page 134

PLAYiNG CARDS

CAP

SILK-PAINTED PATCH

page 219

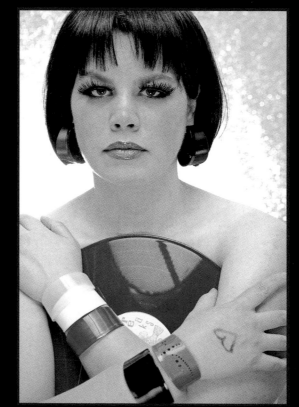

VINYL CUFFS

page 233

Step by Step

1. Make your 8½- x 5½-inch folios and gather as many sections as you'd like for your book.

To make your folios, you will fold 8½- x 11-inch paper in half lengthwise so that they are 8½ x 5½ inches. Remember that sections are made from groups of folios, and each section should be made up of the same number of folios. For this project, we are limiting the sections to three or four folios. The more sections you use, obviously, the more pages your book will have.

2. Outline your folio size on a piece of scrap paper.

Lay one folio landscapewise across the middle of a scrap piece of portrait-oriented paper. Trace a line across the top and bottom edges of the folio. This will give you an 8½-inch column in the middle of your scrap paper.

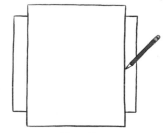

Step 2

3. Make a mark ¾ inch inside either end of the column.

Just a little mark at the edge of the paper is fine. This will designate a space 7 inches wide.

4. Mark every inch inside the 7-inch space.

You should have seven 1-inch spaces marked. With me so far?

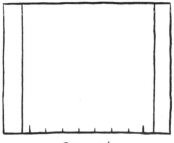

Steps 3/4

5. Stack your sections (folded edge toward you) and place the marked scrap paper on top of your stack.

Align the 8½-inch space on your scrap paper to your sections. Your inch markers should line up across the folds of the sections. Make sure the sections are stacked up very precisely cuz we're about to slice into em. You should have what looks like a number of tiny books on top of each other.

6. Using your Olfa knife, slice downward into the section folds at each inch mark.

Make a ⅛-inch slash through the fold at each mark. Here you're basically creating slits through which to sew—just deep enough to make a small

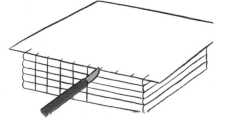

hole in the innermost folio—no more than $1/8$ inch. Use enough force so that you're sure to pierce the innermost folio of each section. You don't wanna end up with big slashes though. Once cut, you can set your sections aside for the moment.

7. Measure and cut 2 pieces of cover stock.
Cut 2 pieces that are $8^1/2$ inches high and at least 12 inches wide. You will trim the width later on so that it matches the pages. Stacie suggests using contrasting colors or patterns for the front and back covers. It will make things easier to keep track of later when you weave the covers together. (NOTE: The finished, closed book will be $8^1/2$ inches high by $5^1/2$ inches wide.)

8. Fold cardstock pieces in half lengthwise with a bone folder.
Lengthwise means that the crease should be along the $8^1/2$-inch dimension. You must use the bone folder because sharp creases are essential.

9. Transfer the 1-inch markings from the scrap paper to the crease of both pieces of cover stock.
These are gonna be cut.

10. On one piece of cardstock, cut perpendicular lines from the crease to the edge across one side of cover stock at each mark.
You are only cutting through one side cover. You can use a triangle, protractor, or similar tool to make sure that the lines are perpendicular to the crease and parallel to one another. Repeat for the remaining piece of cover stock.

11. Cut off each end strip at the crease.
The end strips are the ones ¾ inch wide (on the top and bottom). This will leave you with 7-inch-wide strips or "flaps."

12. Fold in every second flap and cut off the flaps that are sticking out.
Be careful *not* to cut the flaps that are folded.

13. Repeat steps 10 through 12, cutting the opposite flaps.
You will end up with two "opposite" pieces of cardstock that will fit together.

14. Lay one section of your pages on top of the uncut/whole side of the cover.
Choose the cover that has outer flaps that are farther in from the top and bottom edges and lay it flat. Put one section of inner folios on top. The flaps will be loose, but you'll sew them up in a minute.

15. Start sewing (snug but not too tight) through the slits of the first section.
Start at the outermost slit and push the needle through from outside to inside. Leave the end of the thread loose for the moment, but leave plenty of thread for a knot later.

16. Sew from the inside to the outside at next slit, around the cover flap, and back into the section.

17. Repeat until you get to the end of the binding.
The flaps will now be bound to the beginnings of the book

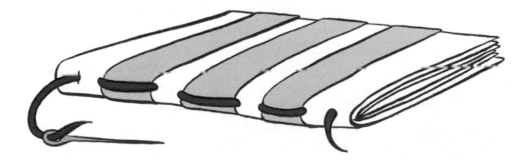

18. Add another section on top of the pages you've sewed and under the flaps. Repeat sewing in the opposite direction.

Starting at the top (where you ended up) repeat the process of sewing in and out around your cover flaps.

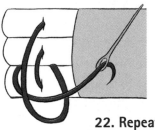

19. When you get back to the bottom make a square knot.

Take your two thread ends and cross left over right and then right (which was just the left) over left (which was just the right).

20. Add another section.

Repeat steps 15 through 17.

21. This time when you get to the top, make a kettle stitch.

You are on your third section, so you draw your needle in between sections 1 and 2, starting on one side of the stitch that joins them and coming out on the other side. Bring the needle through the slack thread and pull tight to make a stitch.

22. Repeat in/out sewing along binding, and kettle stitch again when you get to the bottom.

By now you should be getting the hang of how this all works. You can just keep repeating this whole process of adding sections until your book has as many pages as you'd like.

23. While sewing your last section, loop around the long thread segments on the outside of the binding to pull them together (optional).

This pulls 'em together like a little bow. It's purely decorative and optional.

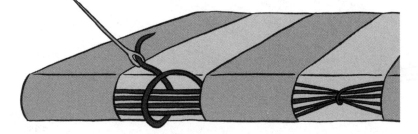

24. When all your sections are sewn, make 2 kettle stitches at the edge.

This will help to finish everything off securely.

25. Place the remaining, "opposite" cover on the uncovered side of your book.

The uncovered side of your book should be the one already facing up. You'll notice how the flaps interlock when you set the remaining cover in place.

26. Flip your book over.

Now the already-attached cover should be on top.

27. Mark weaving slots along the uncut cover.

Using the flaps of your unattached cover as a guide, mark (just a dot will do) where you would like to make slits though which to weave each flap through the uncut cover. Mark where you would like to make your cuts on both sides of the flaps so that you will know how wide to make your cuts. Uniform spacing is not important—it's an aesthetic choice. In fact, unevenly spaced cuts can add visual interest. An even number of slits will leave the ends of the flaps on the outside and an odd number will have the ends hidden inside. Strictly your preference.

28. Fold the flaps back off the cover and insert a cutting surface directly underneath.

This will protect the book pages when you make your cuts in the next step. You can use an actual cutting mat, but you can use a thin piece of wood or the back of a pad of paper, anything that will keep the Olfa blade from screwing up your book pages.

29. Cut slots through which you can weave the opposite cover's flaps.

Just go ahead and connect the dots, as it were, with your Olfa blade.

30. Weave the flaps in and out of the slots you just cut.

Start by going down through the closest slot, up through the next, and so on until you've gone through all the slots.

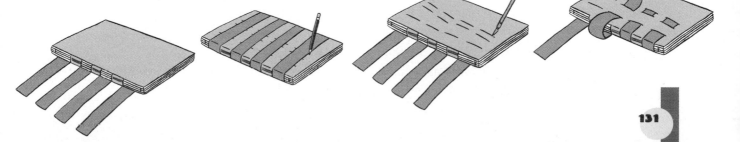

31. Weave flaps of the other cover.
Flip over your book again and repeat steps 27 through 30. You can affix the end of the woven flaps if you don't like them loose. Stitch, glue, staple, etc. Again this is purely aesthetic; the book isn't going to fall apart or anything if you don't do it.

32. Ta da! Now you just have to start writing down all the dirty little secrets you've been collecting about your friends.

SERVING SUGGESTIONS

This project is so versatile. You can make a book out of almost anything. Even if you use plain old paper for the pages, you could cut up album covers for the cover and use unwound cassette tape for the thread. Keep in mind that your book doesn't have to be a blank journal. You could use printed materials like origami paper or magazine pages. Maybe stick on some of those photo album corners and fill it with dirty pictures. It doesn't even have to be functional . . . it can be strictly for looking at. One idea that really stuck out was using envelopes instead of sections so that you end up with a book of pockets. Just use the crease of the envelope's flap instead of the crease of a book section. Save up the letters you get in the mail and make 'em into an epistolary masterpiece—that is, if anyone even bothers to write to you. I know *I* certainly have enough fan mail for an encyclopedia-size set.

Contact Info

The extremely busy Ms. Dolin can be reached via e-mail at staciedolin@hotmail.com. However, you gotta catch her between Red Sox games; play station, and a never-ending parade of projects.

'Tis a far far better craft I do . . .

Okay, so maybe those weren't the exact final words of Charles Dickens's classic *A Tale of Two Cities,* but I thought it made a catchy (and relevant) title. Dickens's novel about the French revolution featured the ultimate punk-rock crafter: Madame Defarge. A woman who had seen her entire family murdered by a corrupt government channeled her rage into a *craft.* Using some kind of self-taught knit-purl code, she stitched an entire revolutionary hit list into a freaking afghan-of-death! I mean, honestly, were I the object of a death warrant, I'd rather have it signed in *yarn* than in blood. And as far as a way to go, what's sexier than *le guillotine?*

Now I am not suggesting by any means that we use our crafty powers for evil or violence, but I think Madame Defarge is a great example of how you can really shake things up when it comes to a time-honored skill.

She appropriated a symbol of home and hearth, a sign of her duties and (subservient) place in the domestic sphere and was able to lead a revolution—with knitting needles! Yes, she may have been a little overzealous, but hey, she's not even a real person.

Her creator, Charles Dickens, is undeniably a man. He does afford her a measure of sympathy due to her oppression, and even raises some relevant questions about marginalized persons becoming oppressors themselves, just as their victims will continue that series of oppression. Dickens, however, seems typically susceptible to male fantasies about women, blood, hysteria, and rage. But I still love Madame Defarge.

CRAFT

QUILTING

PROJECT: **TRASHY QUILT**

ARTIST: *Edith Abeyta*

What I think is so interesting about quilting, and Edith's work in particular, is its relationship to what I've termed "social scrapbooking." That is, her quilts are a document and tell their stories using the literal scraps of Los Angeles—the dregs of cultural production, communication, consumption, and representation: *trash.*

One of the themes not only of this book but also Bazaar Bizarre as a generalized *mode d'être* is a hesitant, critical consumerism. Sure, we have to participate in capital-for-commodity exchange as artists—I mean, it's kinda hard to harvest glue, for instance, from mother earth. What I mean is that, yes, we have to buy things, but a Bazaar Bizarre crafter like Edith knows how to appropriate our lifestyle disposables and turn them into sculpture; quilts; and extensive, community-based collaborations. She exposes the ugly side of abundance in the beautiful objects she makes.

BAZAAR BIZARRE
ABEYTA,EDITH
19660311
QUILTING

What can you say about a woman who chose to look more or less like Sonny Bono with a hormone problem in her artist portrait? I would kill to be able to grow that mustache, by the way. Edith Abeyta is a pack rat after my own heart, scavenging the streets and dumpsters of Echo Park in search of treasure. After seeing her work at Bazaar Bizarre 2003, I was excited to invite her to be part of this book. Her quilts, like traditional quilts, tell a story. The story that they tell, however, is a far different one than that of agricultural country life or some concept one might normally associate with the term *quilting*.

What is the difference between an "art" and a "craft"?

I am interested in blurring the distinction between art and craft. Combining crafting techniques that were historically viewed as women's work with conceptually based processes allows me to challenge both worlds. If an artist asks me what I do and I tell her that I make quilts, I am quickly dismissed; but the same is true for individuals exclusively interested in craft. Once they find out I only know a few stitches and have only learned enough of the craft to complete a project, they become disinterested. By subverting the notion of the expert of which I think craft heavily focuses on and utilizing methods such as quilting, crocheting, and embroidering, I hope to open up new possibilities.

What is your earliest crafting memory?

I have blotted out a large amount of my history so I will latch onto a memory I saw in another's artist work—the water-based, marker-colored macaroni necklace. The dried noodle is the quintessential source material along with the paper plate and dried beans for young crafters.

What was your best crafting moment (idea, inspiration, etc.)?

Like for any creative pursuit, the best moment is when the epiphany occurs. The solution comes to you, sometimes inexplicably or maybe after a lot of thought, discussion, and research—or maybe by chance—and the piece gets resolved.

What was your worst crafting moment (a huge mess, project gone horribly wrong, etc.)?

I have numerous creative disasters that were all heartbreaking in their own way, but the most dangerous was when part of one of my installations caught on fire in the basement of a bank. I had another project where I handcrafted boats out of empty plastic water bottles with a tea light inside, attached paper sails, and tried to float them on the lake at Echo Park. I had done some test runs in my bathtub. The boats balanced and floated like the seaworthy crafts I thought they were. Braving the wind and the rain on a Christmas day, others and I launched the vessels only to see them all immediately capsize and sink just like the *Titanic*.

What is your favorite craft you've ever seen?

A cozy that was knitted for a tank.

Who made you the crafter you are (who introduced you to crafts, taught you crafts—whether or not it is the one you do now)?

Hmmm, I don't have an answer. I became really inspired by women's crafts when I lived in Portland, Oregon. There was an abundance of artists embracing and celebrating women's work.

What are your crafting goals?

I am currently working on a project titled *Shade with Materials & Applications,* an architectural exhibition space in Silverlake. Myself and the crafting group I am part of, the Los Angeles Needle Exchange, have been hosting workshops at M&A since the end of May, teaching people how to crochet and inviting experienced crafters to help crochet a sunscreen out of plastic bags. We are hoping to complete the project before the summer ends.

Kraft or Kraftwerk?
The Model is eating macaroni and cheese.

Who is your fave crafty celeb?
I realize I live in Los Angeles, but I don't know anything about celebrities. I just recently found out what craft service is.

What is your fave craft resource (Web site, store, dumpster, etc.)?
The street is the best resource for materials. Anything and anyone can be found there. It is much more accessible than a mall and more convenient than mail order. You don't need to use up limited resources, financial and otherwise, to retrieve the goods. You need only to open your door and walk outside.

Global Techniques

Yes, this chapter is about how to make a pinwheel quilt, but in a general sense, it's more about scavenging and found objects as they relate to a craft. Here are some general tips about scavenging. For more in-depth knowledge of quilting, you might want to consult the library.

- Keep your eyes peeled for interesting trash: Gum wrappers, for instance, can make for a fun and colorful quilt.
- Base your quilt's theme on what you find or look for stuff based on a chosen theme.
- The needle, thread, and a thimble method works great—no need for a sewing machine. You want to keep it simple. Hand sewing, in this case, is both thematic and practical.
- Use what's on hand—this is what makes it such a BazBiz craft. Using what you have, making art from trash.
- Salvaging is not for everyone. Wash your stuff! It's an adventure though. Stains show

use and wear, many found objects can tell a story through the wear and tear they've already endured.

- You don't have to scavenge from the garbage. Try library book sales, remnant bins, your garage, yard sales, etc.
- E-mail all your friends or post online asking for old shirts, books, blankets, etc. This makes a project collaborative as well as creative. You may have to take the bad with the good though. Beggars can't be choosers. Just say thank you and toss what you don't need.
- IKEA has tons of damaged furniture and upholstery fabric scraps—and they're clean!

TRASHY QUiLT DiFFiCULTY ✪✪✪✩✩

TiME LiNE According to Edith, scavenging for materials for this project (scavenging being the central theme) can take days, weeks, months, or years. The assembly will take about 5 hours all told, and the drying time for the medium is a minimum of 8 hours to overnight. Here are some suggestions from Edith to help you pass the time.

The Big Boys: *The Fat Elvis;* Szeki Kurva: *Music for Joyriders;* Caroliner aka Caroliner Rainbow aka numerous monikers: Any album is a scavenger's dream.

The Gleaners and I (Great inspiration for heading out onto the streets and scavenging—watch this before you start the project); *My Best Friend.* This should inspire you to watch more Herzog films starring Klaus Kinski. I highly recommend *Fitzcarraldo*—a great uphill battle for both director and actor. Lesson to be learned from the film: Obsessive and compulsive desires can result in beautiful art. *Love is in the Devil.* (The story of Francis Bacon and his lumpen lover. The film is beautifully lit and has an exquisite score by Ryuichi Sakamoto.)

SHOPPING LIST

CRAFT STORE

- **Gel medium** This comes in matte or gloss. You can achieve different effects depending on the material to which it is applied. It might make colors run, or shift them. You can also tint the gel or add some glitter.
- **Needle, thread, thimble** All-purpose thread is fine, but make sure it's strong. You don't wanna cut corners here. You'll be doubling it up to sew. Make sure you have a thimble handy since you'll be sewing through quite a bit of material at some points.
- **Scissors or X-acto knife**
- **Ruler, straight edge, or triangle**
- **Cutting surface** You can use a fancy self-healing cutting mat or plain old cardboard.
- **Fusible interfacing**
- **Bone folder (optional)**

RIGHT IN YOUR OWN HOME

- **Quilt material** Trash, found objects: papers, letters, postcards, record sleeves, lotto scratchers.
- **Border material** Fabric scraps, old towels, found objects to use for the quilt boarder.
- **Backing material** Use an old mattress top since it already has a quilted surface. Or use any fabric or other material you have lying around.
- **Batting and/or stuffing** You will need to add batting between the quilt and backing material if you don't use a mattress top for your backing. You will also need to stuff your pocket pillows.

    Found materials would be in keeping with the theme of the project. Make sure you *wash* found stuff that might contain bugs or something. Edith has used intentionally stinky materials at times. It can be a "statement." Poly-fil is cheap if you're worried about germs or smells, and is available at craft and fabric stores.
- **3 old button-up shirts for pocket panels**
- **Wooden clothes pins or binder clips**

Step by Step

1. Decide on materials for your quilt. You could come up with a concept theme for quilt material (try letters and envelopes, take-out menus, magazine covers, or whatever you can think of).
Edith uses a lot of miscellaneous paper for her quilts.

2. Make some editing choices.
Edith, when cutting up her source materials, reads any text and selects her pattern pieces to include textual bits of interest.

3. Cut your source material into thirty-six 3-inch squares.
Try to use something like a T square or grid ruler. Having accurate angles will make things go a lot smoother putting the pieces together. You will want at least two contrasting materials to make an attractive pinwheel pattern—for the purposes of instruction, I will call your materials A and B (although you may have many more than just two).

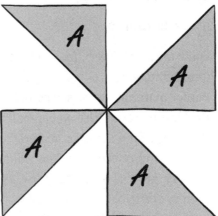

4. Cut each square diagonally into 2 triangles (for pinwheel pattern).
Edith just eyeballs it. When your 3-inch squares are accurate to begin with, it's pretty simple to bisect the squares corner to corner.

5. Layout your A triangles corner to corner in a pinwheel pattern.

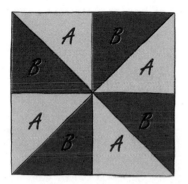

6. Layout the B triangles in between the A triangles to complete the pinwheel square.
Laying these out, even if you're only going to take them up piece by piece to assemble, will help you maintain your pattern.

7. Stitch together 1 A triangle and 1 B triangle, using needle and thread or sewing machine.
For the remainder of these instructions, when I say "sew," you can assume either needle and thread or a machine. Edith uses needle and thread because it's simpler when working with nontraditional materials (like paper instead of fabric). Allow a ¼-inch or less seam allowance. It's not necessary to backtack with the sewing on this project since you'll be attaching sewn segments to each other.

8. No need to press seams flat—just fold.
When using unusual materials, getting involved with an iron is way unnecessary.

9. Continue adding alternating A and B triangles until you have made a complete, approximately 5-inch pinwheel square.

10. Repeat steps 7 through 9 until you have made 9 pinwheel squares.

11. Lay out pinwheel squares into entire pinwheel quilt panel.
This panel will be 3 pinwheels high by 3 pinwheels wide. Allowing for the seam allowances, you'll end up with a pinwheel quilt panel about 15 x 15 inches.

12. Cut two 4- x 15-inch strips and one 23- x 4-inch strip of fabric for the borders.
Your border can be comprised of strips of one type of fabric. Alternatively, you can join fabric segments of equal width (for this project we're going to say 4 inches wide) but varying lengths together until they add up to the length of one edge of the pinwheel panel. Consider using materials of similar weights. You can make either square or mitered corners. You will only be creating a border around three sides of the quilt panel.

13. Make your border by attaching a segment of border material to the top, left side, and bottom of the quilt.

Pin into place and then sew with a ¼-inch seam allowance. You can sew the corners of the border together by either creating a diagonal seam that aligns with the diagonal seam of the adjacent 3-inch square, or you can create a horizontal seam.

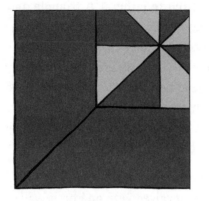 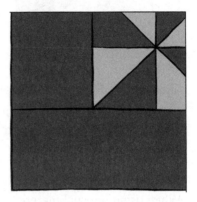

14. Once the border is attached to three sides, cover the front of the entire assembly with gel medium.

This adds flexibility and strength, and a certain sheen that looks cool. Gel medium— even when dry—can gum up a sewing machine. This is why Edith hand sews this entire project.

15. Attach fusible interfacing on the back to make it one solid piece, especially if using delicate materials (optional).

If mixing fabric and paper, test a separate scrap with gel before coating your whole panel to make sure your quilt and borders don't melt when the iron is applied and to be sure the interfacing will stick.

16. Cut 7½- x 7½-inch panels out of 3 button-up shirts.

Be sure to include the front pocket of the shirt when cutting out the panels. Iron a design onto the pockets if you want. Or embroider. Or whatever. Of course, you can just leave the pockets unembellished.

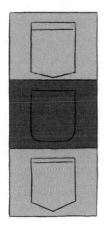

17. Sew your shirt panels together so that the pocket openings are facing the top. You will have one 7½- x 21½-inch panel

18. Sew your shirt panel to the quilt along the side without the border.
Your shirt panel should be at least equal, up to 1 inch longer than the quilt panel. So you may need to trim ½-inch off the top and bottom of the shirt panel.

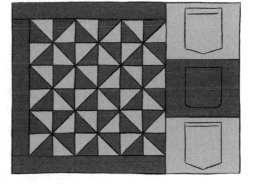

19. Choose a paper image or shape for the pillows you will put in your shirt pockets.
Each pillow can use a different image or you can make them similar (Edith, for instance, uses color xeroxes of her hand). Just make sure your image is sized to fit into the shirt pocket.

20. Pin together your pillow image and a piece of fabric (for the backing), wrong sides together.
Cut out the shape of the pillow through both layers. Unpin the two cut pieces and coat the paper piece with gel medium and let it dry.

21. Hand stitch the cutout paper image to the fabric backing.
Embroidery floss is great for a contrast stitching look. Don't bother trying to sew the right sides together and then turning inside out. We're working with trash, remember? It looks cooler all "unfinished" anyway.

22. Stuff your pillows.
Cutting up old pillows makes for good stuffing.

23. Choose a material for the quilt backing.
A mattress makes a perfect quilt backing because it's a big piece of fabric, already quilted with batting. And it most likely has a pattern—probably a really hideous one. If you don't have an old mattress lying around, you can use any fabric or material for backing. Lay your quilt onto the mattress or backing material and cut it roughly the same size, leaving about an inch or two all the way around to fold under.

If using a mattress, you will need to cut the padded part out and separate it from the springs. If you would like a more raw finish, you can cut the backing material to the exact size of the quilt and sew with no folded seam.

24. Clip the quilt front to the backing material.
If not using a mattress or some kind of prepadded material for your backing, place a layer of batting between the quilt and the backing material. Use clothespins or binder clips to hold the layers together. Just beware that if you plan to leave it clamped for a while, binder clips will end up sticking to the gel medium. If you sew it right away, it's no problem. Wooden clothespins, however, will not stick and can be left overnight if needed.

25. Hand stitch the quilt top to the backing.
This is really *way* too thick for a machine. Use an all-purpose duty 50/50 thread doubled up. You could also try embroidery floss or quilting thread. Sew opposite sides of the quilt first (both long sides, then both short sides). Fold under the "rough" backing edges and stitch. Corners that are too bulky can be avoided by snipping a square out of the corner.

26. Tie off your quilt.
Use embroidery floss to tie off your quilt by sewing a knot to secure the layers together throughout the surface of the quilt. This will lend a tufted appearance and security. Starting at the back of the quilt, make one stitch at the center of each pinwheel square, leaving plenty of loose thread on the underside. Tie the two ends of the thread together. Don't pull too tight or you'll tear the quilted paper. Sewing buttons on the back of the quilt instead of tying knots can help you avoid tearing. Make one knot per quilt square. Since this project is made of a somewhat random mix of materials, use your judgment to decide where to add extra tie-offs for extra security.

27. If you like, tie your little pillows at this point.
Using embroidery floss, you can tie them to each other, or knot them through the quilt inside the shirt pockets. It's mostly an artistic preference. It may not be terribly soft and cuddly, but you just made a quilt!

SERVING SUGGESTIONS

To hang, use bamboo if you can find it, or a stick, or a dowel. Not *every* element of your quilt has to be scavenged. You can also use those little plastic loops that come separately or sometimes are prefastened to a strip of fabric.

Gel medium is wipable with a damp towel. To clean, just basically dust it with a soft brush to keep excess dirt off. Or don't—dirtiness can end up being part of the charm (for the quilt, that is). I promise no one will find you more charming if you're dirty.

Be careful when bending or folding the quilt when you have to move it, pack it up, or anything. If you have to ship it, pack it flat if at all possible. Gel medium will stick to itself, so wrap it up with some fabric so that gel-covered surfaces do not come into contact with one another.

Contact Info

Edith's e-mail is edith@suprememundane.com and her Web site is http://www.suprememundane.com. I'm sure she'd be happy if you could hook her up with some junk for her quilts.

Girls on Film

There are so many totally excellent crafters in the magical world of make-believe that I just had to stop to mention a few.

- **A-Team** These guys were a real team of talents. Sure they could build bombs and all that, but they were also masters of disguise.
- **Blanche Devereaux** In a *Golden Girls* episode entitled "Like the Beep Beep Beep of the Tom-Tom," Blanche gives up sex due to anxiety over her new pacemaker. To fill the void she takes up Popsicle stick crafts.
- **Bobby Hill** Perhaps the most endearing animated adolescent sissy in TV history has had many hobbies, including gardening and mural painting.
- **Boo Radley** He's one shut-in who makes you open your heart. His signature craft was soap dolls that he made for Jem and Scout Finch.
- **Bree Van De Camp** Wisteria Lane's first lady of etiquette can be seen cross-stitching in more than one episode of *Desperate Housewives.*
- **Denise Huxtable** Gordon Gartrell would have been proud of her efforts to knock off his shirt design for Theo's big date on a memorable *Cosby Show.*
- **Elly Kedward** Okay, so she might have tortured and killed all the Birkittsville, Maryland, children, but witchcraft wasn't the Blair witch's only hobby. She was also known for some very cute, rustic dolls made of sticks and twine.
- **Holly Golightly** She's a champagne lady with upscale tastes, but she'll use her dubious knitting skills to hang on to her Brazilian rancher.
- **Karen Richards** Looking smart in a smock, she plots Margo Channing's comeuppance while painting an interstate-motel-quality still life. Celeste Holm's character might have known *All About Eve,* but she didn't know too much about art. Just tell yourself she's being ironic.
- **Kramer** Jerry Seinfeld's lovable oddball neighbor proves he is master of macaroni when he makes a ministatue of Jerry out of fusilli

- **Louise Hovick** Ladylike stitches are the hallmark of this stripper's handicraft. She may be a Gypsy, but she sews like a housewife.
- **Lieutenant Ellen Ripley** In *Aliens* she duct-tapes a flamethrower to a machine gun. To know her is to know true love.
- **MacGyver** Despite his government affiliations, he refuses to buy into their fancy selection of gadgets (unlike that bourgeois James Bond). He can make his own jetpack, thank you, from the gum wrappers in his pocket and dog feces on the ground.
- **Mame Dennis Burnside** Weaving, sculpture, leather craft—what hasn't Auntie Mame tried? For her latest endeavor, check out the Marie Antoinette room at #3 Beekman Place.
- **Marge Simpson** From creative cheese and cracker arrangements to memorial Lenny Leonard needlepoint to the Vincent Price egg-painting kit, "versatility" is the buzzword for Mrs. Simpson's craft repertoire.
- **Molly Jensen** She made pottery and frumpy overalls *almost* sexy in *Ghost*.
- **Nancy Downs** First of all, the movie was called *The Craft*. Fairuza Balk's character may have gotten a little carried away, but I think she was on the right track with the rule breaking. Just be careful with your soul, girl!
- **Sophia Petrillo** That bamboo handbag holds a lot of secrets, not the least of which is that gigantic amorphous crochet project that surfaces from time to time on *Golden Girls.*
- **Sylvia Fowler** She's a catty one, all right, and she loves to play with yarn. Rosalind Russell makes another appearance on our list, this time in *The Women,* knitting as fast and furiously as she gossips.
- **Uncle Jesse Duke** Was there a finer whittler in Hazzard County? With the stars and bars atop the General Lee, do you think those Dukes of Hazzard might have been related to David Duke?
- **Witches of Eastwick** Demi Moore should take a hint from Cher if she wants overalls to be sexy. Susan Sarandon and Michelle Pfeiffer and Mrs. Sonny Bono actually defeat Satan through crafts when they make a voodoo doll out of soap (that'll be in the next book).

CRAFT

DiORAMA
PROJECT: MiNiSHRiNES

ARTIST: *Josh Yeager*

As a Bazaar Bizarre crafter, you have a statement to make, but sometimes mere words aren't enough. In the world of diorama, however, you can stage your own personal psychodramas. Catharsis is just a glue stick and a Q-tip away when you set out to construct microcosmic scenes of conflict, love, hatred, and glamour. Who needs therapy when you can work out your problems in magazine cutouts and construction paper?

CRAFTER BIO

78"

6 ft.   6 ft.

66"   66"

BAZAAR BIZARRE
YEAGER, JOSH
19710524
MINI - SHRINES

5 ft.

I will never forget the night that I met Josh. I couldn't really tell you what time of year it was, but I was enjoying a libation at the gay old 119 in Boston (RIP) when I saw him: tall, dark, handsome, and thick. Our eyes locked, and by the end of the evening he was telling me all about how he wanted to sit around with me in our jammies painting each other's toenails whilst listening to Sleater-Kinney records. Oh, how I thought I'd hit the jackpot with a huge hairy, burly man who was as big a lesbian as me. Alas, our romance was not to be, but we've been the best of girlfriends ever since Mom helped me sort things out after a rather unexpected heart-to-heart about the dangers of, shall we say, "married" men. A swing and a miss, but I have no regrets.

It was right around the time that I was scrambling to organize Bazaar Bizarre 2001 when I learned that Ms. Yeager was also a crafty sorta cinderfella. His tiny, tiny shrines made from the odds and ends he calls divine detritus are some of the most beautiful—and most thoughtful—art objects I have encountered. Josh had this to say about his original inspiration:

I was inspired by a postcard from the 1800s picturing a church altar in Germany. The altar was multileveled, symmetrical, and completely enshrined with statues of saints, carved woodwork, and candles. I picked an old fridge door out of the trash and brought it home with the idea of enshrining it like the altar, but completely out of plastics and junked materials. I saw a parallel between the different levels and compartments of the fridge door, and the triple realms in Christian beliefs: heavenly realm, earthly realm, and the underworld. I enshrined the door with plastic baubles; game pieces; buttons; used gift wrap; playing cards; plastic king cake-babies from New Orleans; religious medallions from unwanted direct mail solicitations; old greeting cards; plastic animals; motel ashtrays; miniature automobiles, houses, trees, and people from an old train set I'd trash-picked; parts of old nativity scenes and crèches; junked Xmas ornaments; coins; plastic baubles from gumball machines; material scraps and fringe from my grandmother's sewing kit; wire caps, washers, nuts, and bolts pilfered from my dad's workshop; and flea market finds. The centerpiece of the shrine was an embalmed cat's paw from a high school biology class. The fridge door was illuminated with junked Xmas window display candles and was topped with a motorized tick-tocking baby Jesus, rocking to and fro between two old funerary cardboard fans displaying the seasons and representing the balance of nature. It was flanked by two smaller shrines I made out of old

Twizzler containers. This was my largest and most off-the-wall piece to date. I worked on it on and off for five years.

Despite his artistic anxiety about their potential reception at the Bazaar due to Boston's Catholic population, the shrines were a smash and ended up being stocked by Cambridge boutique Otro Lado. You'll soon see Josh's work at Magpie on Huron (Simone, Emily, and Leah's store).

What is the difference between an "art" and a "craft"?

In my opinion, the only difference between an art and a craft is perspective. This harks back to the old modicum of "one man's trash is another man's treasure." If you truly adore the kitschy paint-by-numbers portrait of doe-eyed, encephalitic children nuzzling a baby deer that hangs in your grandmother's den, then to you, that's art. Beauty is in the eye of the beholder, and I think each person's relationship with art is completely experiential and uniquely tied to their own context and worldview.

What is your earliest crafting memory?

In many ways, my earliest childhood experiences were tinged by the tail end of a dying era in U.S. history—that of the nuclear 1950s household, complete with Mom, Dad, and dog. In elementary school we had wooden desks with inkwells. I walked home from school at lunchtime and then back again for afternoon session, without the luxury or security of a minivan pool. And most important, my mother made our family's meals, desserts, holiday decorations, and even Halloween costumes—from scratch! So my earliest crafting memories consist of sitting at the kitchen table with Mom, armed with an arsenal of scissors, glue, and felt, and making our own holiday decorations. There were thirty or so jack-o-lantern window clings, caringly crafted and individually detailed in felt. There was the snowman/woman couple born of quart glass milk bottles, cotton balls, and again, more felt! And Mom made kick-ass Easter dioramas using colored string soaked in sugar water, wrapped around a balloon and set aside to cure and dry. Once thoroughly dried, the balloons were popped and we had bright, pastel Easter egg dioramas to fill with fake grass and bunny rabbit families.

Today, in our Wal-Mart laden era of mass consumerism, I don't think that parents have the ability or time to create these types of things with their kids. The memories I hold so deeply now were forged as lovingly as those felt decorations, way back when.

What was your best crafting moment (idea, inspiration, etc.)?
The day I realized that a magnetic saint figurine I'd picked up in New Orleans fit perfectly inside of one of the many empty Altoid tins I'd been hoarding. Voilà— instant shrine!

What was your worst crafting moment (a huge mess, project gone horribly wrong, etc.)?
I don't think I've ever had a bad crafting moment. Crafting is all about having fun and not setting stringent ideals and goals for yourself. Enjoy what you're doing, and don't be upset if you topple a bottle of glue on your jeans. It's all about enjoying yourself and the results of your efforts!

What is your favorite craft you've ever seen?
Sheesh. I'm pretty partial here, because I love my shrines and PopKomps. [AUTHOR'S NOTE: These are another line of shadow-box art pieces Josh makes.] However, I have to give accolades to women I met in Boston who make lamps out of anything and everything. At the second Bazaar Bizarre, I purchased a lamp made from an old Tupperware juice pitcher. I adore it, and it's in my living room as I write this!

Who made you the crafter you are (who introduced you to crafts, taught you crafts—whether or not it is the one you do now)?
Although my dad is quite adept with power tools and woodworking, the person from whom I harvested the majority of my knack is definitely my mother. She is the hot glue maven of Houston, and I garnered all of my abilities, skills, and creativity from her. She's the one who taught me "the way of the hot glue gun," and how to commune with and understand its dynamically fluid nature.

What are your crafting goals?
I craft for fun. When I feel the urge to be creative, I either rearrange my furniture or

hunker down into a hot glue trance. There exists a finite limit to the number of ways I can reassign my digs, but give me some baubles, hot glue, and shiny objects and I can craft for days on end. The best part is that no two shrines are alike, and no two crafting experiences result in the same exact finished product.

Kraft or Kraftwerk?

While I am known to partake in the many delights of cheese, I have a bit of a bent toward those that are naturally created like Emmenthaler or Gouda. Velveeta doesn't really cut it for me, as it's too "produced." However, when it comes to electronic music, I completely appreciate layer upon layer of synthetic production. So in my book, Kraftwerk really does make the grade.

Who is your fave crafty celeb?

There isn't just one crafty celeb whom I like, rather thousands of them who are all celebrities in their own right. I am talking about drag queens. Every drag queen I've ever met has been indubitably crafty, with a keen eye for creating and a wit and talent to match. Drag, in and unto itself, is all about crafting; creating a personality, a look and a flawless artifice of feminine reality. Most drag queens look better than your average woman on any given day, and that's no easy task, considering the bizarre beauty regimens and socially imposed ideals we place on women in Western culture. So to all the drag queens in the world, especially those who tailor their own gowns/outfits and construct peerless personae from everyday drudgery—a nod of my fez to you!

What is your fave craft resource (Web site, store, dumpster, etc.)?

While I do need to expend a certain amount of money for supplies (like hot glue, shadow boxes, or what have you), the best source for supplies are friends and family. If you tell them you're going to build it, they will come—in droves! Before the 2002 Bazaar Bizarre, I told everyone I knew, either by word of mouth, or via e-mail, that I was on the hunt for supplies, including Altoid tins, shoe/cigar boxes, old scraps of wrapping paper, ribbon, beads, and baubles, etc. I was amazed and delighted by the resulting *anschluss* of stuff that people had been hoarding in their homes and were willing to donate to me. Every day I went into work and my co-workers had boxes, beads, and bracelets for me. Packages came in the mail filled with old jewelry, leftover holiday decor, and abandoned ephemera. I collected more than I could store, and I was happy to bring the constructed pieces to the Bazaar and free up my kitchen for cookery! So even though you can spend all the money your budget will allow in Michael's or Jo-Ann Fabrics, I say that "community is the best policy" and my best source of goods/raw materials.

Global Techniques

There are three main elements to any shrine: the stage, the backdrop, and the figurine. The stage is gonna be your vessel or housing. You can try using a shadow box, cigar box, or various tins. Don't go out and buy something. Recycle! I bet you have plenty of usable stuff around the house. For this project, we'll be using an Altoid tin. The best backdrops are recycled from scraps, cardboard coasters, wrapping paper, postcards, photos, and packaging. You can really use anything that you think would look cool, whether it's due to its color and composition or an ironic juxtaposition of its content to the figurine, for instance. Save the cardboard when you buy underwear or T-shirts—it's really useful for turning something that would normally be too flexible into a suitable stiff backdrop.

As for your figurine, the choices are limitless. An old GI Joe, or any kind of action figure, and model train supplies make great players for your tiny scene. Catholic supply stores are treasure troves of religious-themed figures. Churches in some tourist locales will have gift shops. Josh found a buncha stuff at a voodoo shop in New Orleans. Look to your friends. According to Josh, his Catholic relatives won't throw out any religious icons. It's a bit morbid, but if you know of a death in a friend's family, ask what they've got. Chances are your bereaved pal will feel a lot better knowing that Granny's old salt shakers are going to be reincarnated rather than thrown out. Once you start asking around, your friends will begin setting stuff aside for you of their own initiative. Christmas is a great season for gathering ephemera, because there is such an abundance of trinkets, ornaments, and disposable decorations floating around.

THE MiNiSHRiNE DiFFiCULTY ✪✪✩✩✩

TiME LiNE On average, it takes between 2 and 3 hours from start to finish for a tiny Altoid tin shrine, sometimes longer for a larger piece made from a cigar box, or something larger (with more surface area to cover). Bigger is *always* better for a size-queen like me.

Komeda: *What Makes It Go?* (Pure Swedish pop pleasure!); Bulgarian Women's Choir: *Le Mystère des Voix Bulgares* (A moving religious experience!); Cibo Matto: *Viva! La Woman* (Makes Josh feel "hyper and funky!")

Moulin Rouge (Such glittery costumes and sets—a veritable visual feast!); *Pink Flamingos* (Dirty, dirty!); *Björk: Volumen* DVD (especially the videos directed by Michel Gondry)

SHOPPiNG LiST

CRAFT STORE

- **Glue gun and glue sticks** Use a low-temp glue gun for this project. The high-temp guns can cause the glue to come out too liquid and make it difficult to control.
- **Craft foam or florist foam (dense Styrofoam)** Look for this in the floral deptartment of the craft store. It's usually an ugly green. Do *not* use oasis (the softer foam meant for soaking up water in the bottom of a vase). It's way too squishy.
- **Glue stick or spray adhesive** This works much better for gluing flat things like paper to cardboard. Hot glue would not be at all appropriate for thin, flat materials.
- **Trims, ribbons, beads, flowers, et al.** You're on your own for this one. Be creative. Look for stuff you already have lying around the house. I can't tell you how to decorate your shrine—that's what makes it personal. Just go where the mood takes you. Keep in mind embellishments that might be useful for hiding flaws.

YOUR VERY OWN CUPBOARDS

- **Staging** Find a material that can cover the ugly, green florist's foam. You could use something that has an adhesive side (like contact paper), felt, or even a heavier special paper.
- **Tools for cutting** You'll need several for this project: scissors, X-acto knife, and a regular kitchen knife. You'll figure out what you need as the occasion arises. Nothing terribly fancy.
- **Needle-nose pliers, tweezers** It's useful to have a couple of tools to help manipulate and position small objects, especially when you have big caveman hands like mine.
- **An old magazine** This is perfect for a glue gun rest and for wiping off excess glue from the tip. When the page you are using gets too messy, just fold it up, tear it off, and pitch it. Voilà! A brand-new clean surface.
- **Q-tips, chopsticks, or thin dowels** You'll use these as stabilizers. You may need heavy kitchen shears or pliers to cut a dowel.

Step by Step

1. Preheat your glue gun.
Plug it in before you get started on anything else. That way it's waiting for you and not the other way around. Remember to rest it on your old magazine so you don't mess up your work surface.

2. Cut your foam base.
You will be cutting a piece of foam to fit inside the Altoid tin. Press the tin into the foam first to make an impression of the shape to help guide you while cutting the foam. Use a kitchen knife to cut the foam along the impression lines. Don't worry if it's too big at the corners, because you can just squish it in, which will make it more secure anyway.

3. Glue your foam into the tin.
Shoot a few big globs along the bottom of the inside of the empty tin and then

squish your foam into it. The excess glue will go up into the foam. If the foam is sticking up above the tin "horizon," you can just shave it off with the kitchen knife you used to cut it.

4. Trace your tin onto the back of your staging material.
Place the tin right side up on the backside of your material, if it has one (felt, for instance, does not have a "back" side). Trace around the tin.

5. Cut out your staging.
Use scissors for this. Make your lines neat and round the corners as best you can. If you want to get real high-tech, you could use a corner punch made for scrapbooking, but unless you already have one I wouldn't bother. Minor flaws will be covered up later.

6. Place and affix your staging.
Use hot glue if you choose something that doesn't already have a sticky back. Even if it is adhesive, you may want to glue it anyway since foam is not the most stable material.

7. Stabilize the tin's hinge.
This is done by hot-gluing a Q-tip or dowel segment into the crook created when you hold the tin lid open at a 90-degree angle. You may have to hold this in place for it to set, but since we're using low-temp glue it'll just take a few seconds. Once set, Josh recommends a second application of glue to coat it for extra stability.

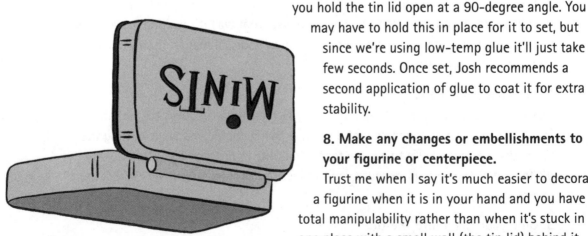

8. Make any changes or embellishments to your figurine or centerpiece.
Trust me when I say it's much easier to decorate a figurine when it is in your hand and you have total manipulability rather than when it's stuck in one place with a small wall (the tin lid) behind it.

9. Prepare your backdrop.

If you are using a flimsy material such as wrapping paper for your backdrop, you will need to glue it to cardboard before affixing it to your shrine. Make sure you glue all the way to the edges of your paper with your glue stick to avoid peeling. You can also wrap paper around the edges of the cardboard for a finished look.

10. Fill in hollow of the tin lid with bits of dowel or Q-tips.

You don't want to skip this step. The dowel pieces or Q-tips will give the lid more surface area upon which to glue the backdrop. Doing this will also prevent the backdrop from sinking in or bloating out because of a weather change. Hey, it can happen.

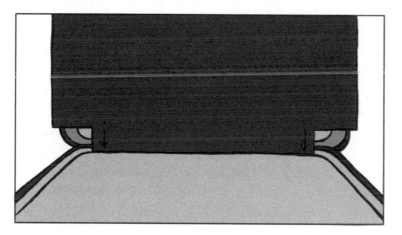

11. Glue backdrop in place.

You can create a tab by leaving a little extra cardboard on the bottom edge of your backdrop. This will allow you to wedge it in between the foam and the tin bottom. It's an optional step, but it can add stability.

12. Deck out your tin with ribbon, beads, and trims.

Decorating the tin is good for hiding any dried glue globs as well as packaging logos or printing that might interfere with your design. When affixing flexible materials like ribbon or strings of beads, begin by placing glue in the center of the back of the material and use extra glue around corners. This anchors the trim so you can pull it taut around the tin once it's set in place.

13. Now that the stage is set, glue your figurine in place.
If you like the scene as is, great. If you want to get more elaborate, just glue more crap on as you see fit. Little cherubs, birthday candles, sequins—whatever you can think of. Don't be shy. Part of the charm of these pieces, and part of the majesty of real-life religious shrines, is their somewhat over-the-top presentation. The more there is, the more there is to look at and contemplate. Now just sit back and say a little prayer to whatever strange new crafty deity you've summoned.

SERVING SUGGESTIONS

I think variations are inherent in the very technique of this project, but I can think of a couple of specific recommendations for you. One is to try inverting a large jar: Use the lid as your stage and the jar itself as an enclosure. The other is to be sure to personalize a shrine if you plan to give it as a gift. Pick out figurines that resemble the recipient, or try to re-create a familiar scene, warped by your Bazaar Bizarre imagination.

Contact Info

You can e-mail josh at josh.yeager@gmail.com

Alterknit Spaces

The division of labor within the American family has always been entrenched in gender. Expressions such as "women's work"—no matter how outmoded we might like to consider them—are a persistent part of the American lexicon. We all know what women's work includes. Cultural creations like *Mr. Mom, Who's the Boss?, Mr. Nanny, Mrs. Doubtfire,* even 2005's Vin Diesel vehicle *The Pacifier* serve to reinforce "natural" gender roles by showing how freaking hilarious it is when a man does something like wear an apron or change a diaper—things culture dictates should obviously be done by a woman. There is an upside to this, however. One of the cool things about cultures that are markedly divided into public and private spheres is that just because women are "on paper," for lack of a better term, kept at home it doesn't mean that they do not participate in the exchange of power. In Iran, the country of my birth, for example, the divide between public and private is much more strictly observed than it is here in the States. At first blush, we tend to think of veils, silence, and submission when we think of Middle Eastern women, but in the private sphere of home and family, it is these apparently disenfranchised women who steer the course of events.

The isolated administration of the domestic economy by women could be considered drudgery. Those confined to the home, however, found their own ways of congregating. Sewing circles and quilting bees served as spaces where women could socialize as a group while doing what might normally be solitary (and lonely) work. These gatherings could certainly be considered professional organizations wherein ladies could share skills and supplies, if not protofeminist spaces in which familial and social values are reoriented to a woman's point of view. They are a place not only for artistic expression, but—by function if not design—a political space where the leaders of the domestic sphere could share their experiences, problems, and solutions. Each woman takes with her a tool in the form of narrative. These shared experiences fortify a sense of solidarity and a confidence in knowing that problems—and solutions—are not unique.

You need only to look at the resurrection of knitting clubs, to name one example, to see that these social traditions have been rekindled in a more self-conscious way, as crafting has again taken its place in the menu of American leisure. This incarnation, however, is born less of occupational isolation than a nod to an art form's social origins.

If I had to hazard a guess, I'd go out on a limb and say that most readers of this book are not confined to the home due to an adherence—on their part or the part of a spouse—to traditional values and family gender roles. Those people are probably reading some other book, or not reading at all! The readers of *Bazaar Bizarre* are interested in exploring new approaches to traditional handicrafts and the value systems that once surrounded them. By engaging in reenactments of social rituals associated with crafts, group crafters celebrate the value of labor once known only as women's work.

Now if we could only get more men involved. They look so cute in little aprons, behind sewing machines, and using glitter.

Children and adults have enjoyed sock monkeys for more than a hundred years. According to supersockmonkey.com, the original crafter who created this lasting icon is unknown, but the creativity behind this wonderful doll has brought joy to millions. The Red Heel socks used to give sock monkeys their signature look were first manufactured in 1890 by the Nelson Knitting Mills in Rockford, Illinois. These quality socks were intended and used as work socks, but in the 1900s mothers started crafting them into monkeys and other animals for their children. In 1920 Nelson Knitting Mills started to include the directions for the sock monkeys with every pair of Red Heel socks. Nelson Knitting Mills was purchased by Fox River Mills in 1992, and now Fox River Mills continues the tradition and includes the original directions with the modern-day Red Heel socks.

I like sock monkeys so much because they are a reminder of the expansion of industrialization and the aestheticization of crafting. I mean, here are these ladies who are used to making their own socks and then whammo! There's some machine in a factory doing it. So now what do they do with their sock-making prowess? Like any pool of laborers set out to pasture by mechanized capital, the newly obsolescent throwbacks are left with wasted skills. Unless, that is, they invent new uses for them, like our beloved sock monkeys.

Shawnee describes herself as a "Desk jockey by day; artist, crafter, singer of silly songs, and Queen of the Sock Monkeys the rest of the time." After interviewing her in her Tustin, California, apartment, I'd have to say that's a pretty accurate description. I don't usually indulge in sentiment when it comes to inanimate objects, but her monkeys are pretty special, a fact supported by the countless orders she gets for sock monkeys from all over the world. Really . . . like *Singapore* and places like that. Sometimes it can be kind of sad because lately Shawnee's orders have included several monkeys for children with serious illnesses. I think mostly happiness, however, surrounds the podiatric primates. Shawnee made a big impression at Bazaar Bizarre 2003 in Los Angeles. Mary Jo Kaczka, in fact, missed out on her monkey of choice just by running to the ATM. You'll have to be quick on the draw to snag a new friend from her table.

What is the difference between an "art" and a "craft"?

First off, the selling price for the finished piece! It seems to be a highly subjective distinction. Lots of folks think of crafts as something their elderly aunts do, like tole painting or macramé. Not a lot of people realize the artistry that goes into what is traditionally considered to be craft. Do they think that painting, which is usually considered an art, is any more challenging than knitting, which is traditionally considered a craft? The great thing is that more and more people are discovering that there is art in craft, and there is craft in art. This blurs the lines of distinction.

What is your earliest crafting memory?

Drawing a happy-faced flower on a rock in preschool. The teacher shellacked it and I gave it to my mom (she still has it!). I also recall building houses with my Playskool Bricks (similar to Legos) back then with my mom.

What is your best crafting moment (idea, inspiration, etc.)?

I've met so many people over the past ten years who've inspired me with their own creativity. It's amazing to me that there is *so* much talent in the world. Most of it unrecognized beyond the immediate peer group.

What was your worst crafting moment (a huge mess, project gone horribly wrong, etc.)?

Lots of little incidents (seams sewn wrong, paint spilled on the carpet, pricey fabric cut in pieces that were too small), but nothing too horrible. Or maybe I'm just repressing.

What was your favorite craft you've ever seen?

Seeing Niki de Saint Phalle's crazy giant sculptures in San Diego at the Craft and Folk Art Museum was a big inspiration, and an eye-opener about the grace, beauty, and importance of folk/outsider/primitive art.

Who made you the crafter you are (who introduced you to crafts, taught you crafts—whether or not it is the one you do now)?

My mom made me, fed me, raised me, and nurtured my creativity. So it's all her fault! Mom always made sure my sister and I had plenty of art/craft supplies on hand: scissors, glue, crayons, blank paper, bits of fabric, needles and thread. I remember her teaching me how to sketch a person's face while we were at a restaurant waiting for breakfast. Mom always allowed our creativity to flow, and taught us skills beyond drawing and collage and sewing. She taught me how to use a hammer, how to saw wood properly. And even though she was on a supertight budget, we wanted for nothing. And how happy was I when she brought home a big roll of leftover blueprints for me to draw on? Very.

What are your crafting goals?

To learn how to do *everything*. Or more immediately, how to knit in the round.

Kraft or Kraftwerk?

I'll have to go with the latter, because I'm not so much into the pasteurized process cheese "food."

Who is your fave crafty celeb?

Gosh, I don't know any celebrities! Are we talking crafty folk who are popular in the crafting world, or famous folk who do crafty stuff?

What is your fave craft resource (Web site, store, dumpster, etc.)?

- Sterling Art Supply in Irvine
- American Science and Surplus
- Leah's for Quilters (fabric store) in Orange
- Target (for socks!)
- Jo-Ann's and Michael's for basic craft supplies
- Used book shops
- Thrift stores
- Ethnic markets

Global Techniques

The odd thing about this chapter is how lengthy and specific the instructions are, especially considering what a homespun, rustic craft sock monkeys are. I think it's probably because the mothers and children who originally enjoyed these cuties already possessed a common repertoire of domestic tools. I mean you or I may not immediately recognize the term *whipstitch*, for instance, but in the early twentieth century, mom and the kids would be using these basic skills all the time.

WHIPSTITCH

With the edges of fabric together, thread your needle up from side B of one piece of fabric, over the open seam, and then down through to side B of the second piece of fabric. Pull the thread across the open seam to side B of the first piece; then, placing the needle in front of where you made your first stitch, push back up to side A. Pull snug and repeat.

SHAWNEE'S INVISIBLE STITCH

Stitch down and immediately back up through side A on first piece of fabric, over the open seam at a slight diagonal toward next stitch position. Thread needle through to side B of the second piece of fabric and immediately back up, making a nearly invisible stitch on side B. Thread needle back across the open seam, pull tight, and repeat. Note that the stitch will be invisible on side B of this fabric, and kind of messy looking on side A. Side A should be the underside, or unexposed part, of your project.

BACKSTITCH

Backstitching is used for creating a continuing line of stitches, like "drawing" a line on fabric with floss. For this project, we'll be using backstitching to create the eyes, nose, and smile of your monkey. Other potential uses include decorative embellishments on other parts of the monkey (not unlike a T-shirt insignia). It can also be used to "sign" your piece by stitching your initials. Depending on the context of its use, you might or might not begin by making a knot and starting from the backside of the cloth. Push your needle up through the fabric. Make a stitch a short distance behind the point where the needle came up through the fabric back down through to the underside. Place your needle a short distance in front of the point of the original stitch and come back up through the fabric. Backstitch again down into the same hole created by your very first stitch. Repeat this process until your line is as long as you

The "visible" side of the invisible stitch. The stitches will not be detectable on the reverse side of the fabric.

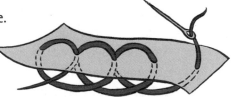

want. Be careful not to pull too tight, or you'll end up with a dotted line and have small gathered gaps in your fabric. Backstitching is also used for outlining in cross-stitch, operating on the same technique but through a grid layout.

THE SOCK MONKEY DiFFiCULTY ♣ ♣ ♣ ♣ ♣

TiME LiNE You could "give birth" as it were, to one of Shawnee's sock monkeys in about 2 hours. Hey, that beats 9 months, and you, too, will have that special glow—especially if you sit *really* close to the TV while making it.

Talking Heads: *Sand in the Vaseline;* Throwing Muses: *In a Doghouse; Jesus Christ Superstar* Soundtrack (Original London Cast)

Frida; Animal House; Monty Python's The Meaning of Life

SHOPPiNG LiST

RIGHT IN YOUR OWN HOME

- **One pair of socks** Socks for this project must be calf length or longer. If using baby socks, the leg and foot segments have to be at least of equal length. Make sure to use high-quality socks made with natural fibers (no less than 50 percent cotton) and a tight knit. If shopping for new socks, Target has *the* best selection of socks ever.
- **Sewing machine**
- **Fray Check (available at craft stores)**
- **Clear nail polish**

CRAFT STORE

- **Needle, thread, and thimble** This project requires hand sewing as well as machine sewing. For the actual constructional sewing thread, you want to pick a color that will match, blend, and disappear into your sock. Get both general dual duty thread.
- **DMC 6-strand embroidery floss** Choose bright, bold colors that will stand out. The floss is for decorative purposes, so contrast is good.
- **Marking gizmo** Disappearing ink fabric pen (ah, *tinta mágica*), tailor's chalk, pencil, etc.
- **Ruler** A wide, clear, plastic one works nice.
- **Larger needle for embroidery** You'll need one with an eye big enough to fit DMC floss—all 6 strands.
- **Fiberfil (the brand Shawnee recommends)** Make sure to use a softer stuffing that has long fibers. Cheaper stuffing with shorter fibers ends up all over the place. Don't be cheap on the stuffing—it comes in huge bags and it's worth the extra buck to get the good stuff.

Step by Step

PREP YOUR SOCKS

1. Pick out a pair of socks and turn each one inside out.

Separate the pair and turn each one inside out. You'll use one sock to make the head, trunk, and legs—we'll call this the body sock. The other sock will be your arms, tail, mouth, and ears. I don't have some technical name for this so I will call it the limb sock.

2. Flatten out the body sock.

Lay the sock on your work surface with the toes pointing up so that it's straight when it lies flat. If these are brand-new socks from the store, there may be a crease. This crease will end up in the center of the flat sock and will be useful later for gauging certain measurements. The heel pocket will be sticking up. Just fold it flat up toward the toe.

Body sock

3. Draw a line across the width of the body sock 1½ inches below the heel.

There will be a "line" where you folded the heel pocket. Measure 1½ inches from this line toward the sock opening and draw your line.

4. Draw a line lengthwise down the center of the body sock.

Mark the midpoint of the line you just made in step 3. Draw a line from that point all the way down the center lengthwise to the open end of the sock. Use a ruler to make sure it is straight all the way down. There may already be a crease at the midpoint that you can draw right onto.

5. Flatten out the limb sock.

Lay it out so that you see the profile of the foot (curved) as opposed to straight like the flattened body sock. This is much easier than the body sock because even though it's inside out, it'll be pretty much flat the way it was in the packaging. Make sure you match the seams at the toe.

6. Draw a line across the limb sock just above the heel.

By "above" I mean toward the sock opening, not toward the toe. This line should pretty much divide the sock in half if you are using calf-length socks, which have roughly equal foot and leg segments. If you're using longer socks, you'll have to fudge the halfway point and make your line there. You can do this by folding the sock in half lengthwise, or doing a quick and dirty measure with a ruler. Please don't waste your time trying to be unnecessarily precise.

7. Draw a line lengthwise down the center of the limb sock.

Just like in step 4, you'll start at the midpoint of your horizontal line and draw the line to the sock opening.

8. Draw a line for your monkey's tail.

The tail will be an inch wide. Draw a line 1 inch from the top of the foot section, from the horizontal line to the toe. You can eyeball this or be OCD and measure.

9. Draw the monkey's mouthpiece.

You will be cutting out the heel cup for the mouth. The heel cup on a fun, colorful sock is usually a contrasting color and is clearly visible. Draw a line creating a 1/2-inch seam allowance around it.

10. Draw 2 semicircles for ears.
Use the unoccupied space between the toe and heel, with the creased edge of the sock comprising the flat sides of the semicircles. Ears can be as big or as small as you want—even charmingly nonuniform. Bigger ears might be easier for your first monkey.

SEWING THE BODY SOCK

11. Sew one monkey leg in the body sock.
Position the presser foot so that its edge is flush with the long line you made down the center of the sock and place the needle 1½ inches from the heel. It does not matter which side you start on. You will be sewing the opposite side of the line in the same fashion. For clarity's sake, let's just arbitrarily say we'll start with the left edge of the presser foot flush with the center line. Your stitches should be pretty small: No less than 10 stitches per inch. This will ensure stronger seams. As with all sewing, make sure you backtack at the beginning and end of your seams. Knit socks have a lot of stretch, so you'll want to stretch the sock slightly as you feed it through the machine. When you get to the open end of the body sock, curve away from the center to the edge for a rounded "foot."

Limb sock

12. Sew the other monkey leg
Repeat step 11, this time with the presser foot's right edge flush with the center line. Mirrored, see?

SEWING THE LIMB SOCK

13. Sew one of your monkey's arms in the limb sock.
Again, align the presser foot edge flush with the lengthwise line you drew (refer to the limb sock illustration). Sew until you reach the open end of the sock, and

curve around for a closed "hand" when you get to the sock opening (just like you did with the feet).

14. Sew your monkey's other arm.
Basically repeat step 13, mirrored.

15. Sew your monkey's tail.
This time we're actually sewing *on* the line we drew (refer to limb sock illustration). Position the needle on the tail line. You can use the guide on your machine's needle plate for a 1-inch seam allowance in addition to the eyeballed 1-inch line you drew. Sew *on* the line and remember to backtack and curve around when you get to the end.

16. Sew your monkey's ears.
For the ears, sew right on the ear outlines you drew.

CUTTING THE BODY SOCK
17. Cut along the center line (step 4) to separate your monkey's legs.
The line you drew down the center lengthwise is now the line you cut (refer to body sock illustration). Convenient, eh? Ah, the pragmatic simplicity of rustic crafts. Cut to about 1 inch above (toward the heel) the original horizontal line.

18. Secure your monkey's crotch.
Hand sew a couple of stitches at the end of the line you cut, or use a few drops of Fray Check. If you skip this step, the entire sock will run when you start stuffing it. I like the old clear nail polish run-in-your-nylons trick. I am sure we all have some clear nail polish lying around.

19. Turn legs and body right side out.
Start with the legs—the body will just kinda do itself while you're working the legs. You could use a long hook made from a coat hanger or a chopstick or a strap turner. Of course your hands are probably the cheapest and most versatile tools for the job. Extra fingers? So much the better.

CUTTING THE LiMB SOCK

20. Cut your monkey's arms.

Cut along the horizontal line (refer to limb sock illustration), right along the top edge of the sewing, being careful not to actually cut the stitches, and then cut down the lengthwise center line.

21. Cut your monkey's tail.

Cut right alongside your stitching. Keep your seam allowance very small ($1/8$–$1/4$ inch) to leave enough room for your mouth and ears. Turn right side out.

22. Cut out the mouth piece.

Cut along the line you made in step 9, $1/2$ inch from the heel well.

23. Cut out the ears.

Cut close to your stitching as you did with the tail. Snip the fold open and just turn inside out. They should pretty much look like pasties or something at this point.

24. Trim all the loose threads hanging about.

STUFFING YOUR MONKEY

25. Stuff the body sock.

Use very small bits of stuffing at a time—like a *pinch*. Pieces of Fiberfil that are too large will cause your monkey to be lumpy, not luscious. This takes a long time cuz the sock material keeps stretching, but keep going. You really want it well stuffed because it will hold its shape much longer if It's stuffed fully. To stuff the legs and any other part that might be hard to get your meat hooks down into, use a chopstick.

26. Stuff your monkey's crotch.

A tricky area on so many levels.

27. Stuff the your monkey's arms and tail.

Again, use a chopstick to shove the pieces way down into the end. It's gonna get good and fat like a nice sausage. Remember to use mere fingerfuls of Fiberfil and stuff thoroughly.

ASSEMBLiNG YOUR MONKEY

28. Sew up your monkey's crotch.

"*Plug it up! Plug it up!*" Cut a length of thread, double it up, and tie a knot at the end. Start from the end of the machine stitching (overlap a little) and stitch across the crotch toward the beginning of the machine stitching on the other leg. A simple whipstitch is fine. Push your stuffing in as you go across. When you reach the midpoint of the crotch, you'll notice that the knit begins to unravel with wide gaps. In

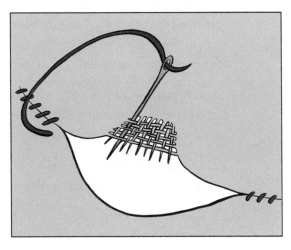

order to keep your entire monkey from unraveling from his crotch, sew through the horizontal threads that run parallel to your seam. Do this on both sides of the crotch opening—in the words of Salt-N-Pepa: "very necessary."

29. Trim your monkey's crotch.

Fiberfil tends to get caught up in the stitches, leaving your monkey with quite a need for a bikini wax.

30. Make a knot at the end of your stitching.

Run the tip of your needle in and out through the fabric, wrapping the thread around it a couple of times and then pulling through. You can use you finger to anchor the closing loop so that it doesn't "travel" up the thread away from the fabric. Make a couple of passes for extra security. Run it around the knot and under the fabric. Trim the loose end (it'll pull itself back inside the monkey and stay hidden).

31. Attach your monkey's tail.

Make a knot and baste around the open end of the tail to gather it. Then pin the tail to the money's rear end (make sure it's the *rear* end unless you want a freaky John

Holmes sock monkey). "Catch a piece of tail" with your needle and whipstitch around the base. As in step 30, make a knot at the end.

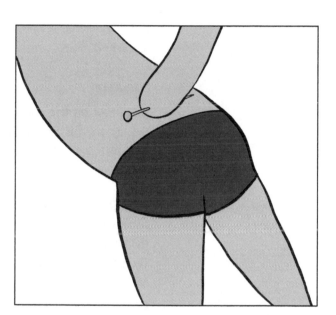

32. Attach your monkey's arms.

Baste the opening of the arms like you did with the tail. Position the arms roughly halfway (a few inches) between the top of your monkey's head and its butt. This will help dictate your monkey's mouth placement. Pin in place and stitch just like the tail.

33. Attach your monkey's mouth.

Stuff the heel cup that you've cut out for the mouth piece. Pin down the sides to anchor. Fold under the raw edges of the fabric along the top and bottom. Make your first stitch on the body just below the mouth using the lark's head knot trick (page 65) to anchor. Sew around the perimeter of the mouth piece as you did with the arms and tail. Keeping the fabric folded under as you go. Leave a small gap at the end and add more Fiberfil to really stuff the mouth before you make your knot and finish it off.

34. Attach the ears.

Knot the end of your thread and make a stitch attaching the ear to the head at eye level (the monkey's, not yours). Set aside the needle for a sec and pin the ear to the head so that it's flat against the head, with the opening facing backward. Starting at the top, whipstitch the back/inner layer of the ear.

35. Secure the ears with invisible stitching.

When you get to the bottom, instead of whipstitching the other layer, revisit the invisible stitch (page 165). This both folds the seam under and hides the stitch in one fell swoop. When you are finished stitching your way to the top (of the ear— not "to the top"), make a knot and run the needle under the fabric to hide the loose end. Snip.

EMBROIDERY

36. Draw on the mouth with chalk.

Smiles, frowns, fangs, lips, jagged line, etc. No one said your monkey had to be cheerful. Hell, you've been shoving a needle in and out of its crotch for the last twenty minutes. I'm not sure I'd be smiling.

37. Backstitch your monkey's mouth.

Stick your needle right into the side of the head beside the mouth piece, and pull it back up through the fabric no more than ¼ inch in from where you want the end of the smile to be. Leave a few inches of loose floss hanging out at the entry point. Now backstitch across the line(s) you've drawn for the mouth. At the end of the line, so to speak, you'll want to replicate the starting point, running the needle through the head and out the other side. Trim each loose end of the embroidery floss close to the fabric, and it will pull back inside the monkey. Remember, make your stitches snug but not too tight. Pulling too hard will leave your monkey with a puckered granny mouth and create small gaps in the fabric. You'll end up with a dotted-line look instead of even coverage. This could be what you're going for, but I doubt it.

With this and all the other embroidery you'll use on this project, there is no real way to anchor the embroidery with a knot. At the end points of your embroidery, use a few drops of Fray Check or clear nail polish for a touch of added security.

38. Repeat steps 36 and 37 for each facial feature.

Mouth, eyes, hair, nostrils, a monogram—whatever you want.

SERVING SUGGESTIONS

There are zillions of zany directions in which to steer this project. Make a monkey that is decked out in the trappings of the recipient's profession. Make the Village People out of sock monkeys—perfect for that special cowboy, Indian chief, or leather . . . person on your gift list. One of Shawnee's most requested monkeys is the pirate monkey, complete with peg leg. There are technical variations you can make as well. Experiment with appliqué instead of, or in conjunction with, embroidery. Use up those felt square scraps from Hazel's wallet project. Add buttons, little clothes, perhaps monkey offspring. You'll notice in Shawnee's color glamour shot that she's made one monkey from long adult socks, and another from a pair of adorable toddler socks. She tacked 'em together and put a needle in the hand of the biggun so that he's actually *sewing* the baby sock monkey. I wonder if that's how sock monkeys reproduce. And what about the alternative universe where lost laundry socks go? We always say that a lone sock is missing "its mate." If one sock monkey is made of two socks, then do they even need a mate? Or are they already one with themselves? Sheesh—sock monkeys are a lot more self-actualized than I am. I should really get a refund on all that therapy.

Contact Info

Wanna adopt your own Kornely original? Shawnee's wild world of sock monkeys can be visited by pointing and clicking your way to http://www.geocities.com/mysockmonkey.

Handicraft History 101: Quick and Dirty!

Ever wonder how we got to where we are with the whole crafting thing? Here is a superbrief history of some changes the role of crafts has undergone in American culture.

- **Mid–Late-Nineteenth Century** Male-identified socialist artisans, architects, and designers such as William Morris staged a reclamation of design and architecture. Opposed aesthetically and philosophically to Victorian decadence and ornamentality, they espoused functionality, simplicity, and clean lines. There was a focus on pride in the quality of one's work as opposed to a sumptuous or baroque style. Gothic arches seemed to be a real sore spot for these guys.
- **Preindustrial Society** Just as it depended on the male figure of the farmer for its survival, preindustrial agrarian America was dependent upon women's work that involved productivity at home. You can find a lot of great books about how to run a household and make items of necessity (the old sock example). Did you know some stitches were considered proper while others were thought of as sloppy and whorish? Every young girl was expected to know overstitch, hemming, running, felling, backstitch, buttonhole stitch, chain stitch, whipping, darning, gathering, and—my favorite—the cross-stitch.
- **Industrial Revolution** Innovations like Samuel Crompton's steam-powered "mule" combined James Hargreaves and Richard Arkwright's automated warp and weft machines, fully automating the weaving process. Jane American, left with neither warp nor weft to call her own, is set upon by the industrial age. Suddenly an array of domestic skills is rendered obsolete by massified commodity production. Female home economists migrate gradually toward decorative crafts in the

growing absence of the need for functional domestic handicrafts. Dad now has all the socks and hankies he could ever need, so Mom has some free time to explore her creative side.

- **World War II** As depressed economic situations settle in and the Axis threat grows, more women are forced into the workplace to keep the American war machine running at top speed. Crafts become largely aestheticized as a bourgeois symbol of leisure time for ladies of social status who can afford not to work.

- **Postwar** The postwar exodus of women from factories plays witness to a new generation of crafter with a bright future in her eyes and a Jell-O mold on her table. Soon it's owls, owls everywhere as the macramé-crazed 1960s and 1970s empower women to burn their bras and, with a few simple knots, turn anything into a planter.

- **Present Day** Today there is an entire generation of crafters who have taken a look back at some of the skills learned in childhood. We've uncovered and, through our own craftiness, added meaning to the skills and arts Mom and Grandma taught us. Whether we choose to simply follow the directions or to chuck it all and make something brand new, craftiness is back on the cultural map. Viva *Bazaar Bizarre!*

Everyone is familiar with playing cards—we play with them all the time. Maybe you even know that there is some lore attached to playing cards and that their origins and applications are as varied as the games you can play with them. The names of certain court cards (often called face cards) are bandied about in poker games when calling what's wild: "black whores and red fours" or "suicide kings and one-eyed jacks," and other things of that nature. I was intrigued to learn some different requirements for the design of playing cards. Did you know that the queen of clubs is known as the Good Flower Queen and that her flower is always standing straight up and down? Jokers are similar to The Fool in the tarot deck: a court jester figure often portrayed as evil (like how clowns are scary). See Batman's nemesis if you need further clarification.

There are some more mysterious and multilayered aspects of playing card lore, though. The suits may represent the four elements and the four humors (blood, yellow bile, black bile, and phlegm—*yummy*). Check out http://www.wsu.edu:8080/~hanly/chaucer/coursematerials/humours.html for a little more information on that score. Some historians claim that court cards have been based on actual rulers such as Mary Queen of Scots. Emily says that her subconscious peeks out through her homemade deck, and friends claim to see themselves portrayed in the court cards. She even concedes that her queen of hearts might be an unintentional self-portrait. My queen of hearts, however, shall always be Juice Newton.

Besides the traditional deck we will be making for this project, another of Emily's playing card passions is the transformation deck: cards that are more pictorial. Emily described one example of a deck that uses beetles with the different suits worked into the backs of their shells. Some decks—like those featuring pinups—have only the number and suit in the corner and no relational image whatsoever. I have a deck of gay porno playing cards I got from the adult bookstore in Bloomington, Indiana. Talk about transformational . . .

Craft historywise, playing cards were originally handmade until woodblock engraving and printmaking made them more affordable. So in a sense, Emily is really taking us back to a time before they were mass-produced—with a little help from modern technology, of course.

CRAFTER BIO

I met Emily Arkin through fellow Armenian rocker Stephanie Melikian. While my band Prettypony was touring in what I vaguely recollect as 1999 (damn that loud punk rock), Steph and I met online and managed to book a show with their band, The Operators, at the Milky Way Lounge and Lanes in the Jamaica Plain neighborhood of Boston. It was this very magic moment of rock 'n' roll kismet that ultimately led to Bazaar Bizarre. In meeting The Operators and their zany circle of Somerville friends (including Bazaaros Stacie Dolin, Simone Alpen, and Leah Kramer),

I met the folks that would help me start the Bazaar Bizarre odyssey—of which Emily was one of the original conspirators.

Emily describes herself as a scholarly publisher (Web manager for the prestigious Harvard University Press) by day; and a guitarist, animator, playing-card designer, knitter, and WMFO deejay by night. So when does she sleep? Founding member of the Handstand Command music collective and board member of the Somerville Arts Council; no one I know does more stuff than Emily, and now she's part owner of the vintage handmade collectibles boutique Magpie (along with Leah Kramer and Simone Alpen). I'm glad someone has the energy.

What is the difference between an "art" and a "craft"?

My first thought is that crafts are something you make multiple copies of and art is a unique *objet,* but I guess that definition totally breaks down in the age of mechanical (and digital) reproduction. The most important difference is probably that crafts are supposed to serve a function and be decorative, while art is for its own sake. But to some extent, I think it has just become a convention—oil paint denotes art while fabric must be craft . . . never mind that something made out of fabric may be more beautiful or thought provoking. It also seems like the term craft has often been used to put down art that's made by women. In any case, the important thing to me is usually whether a work is original and good and not what medium it's in or whether it has some kind of fine art imprimatur. I do believe in fine art, but I think it's a spectrum, not a dichotomy. And I'd be happy to see the definition between arts and crafts break down more (mostly, see the crafts get more arty and see arty crafts get their due as art).

What is your earliest crafting memory?

In preschool, when I was about four, we made a giant papier-mâché dragon, painted it green, and rode it through town in a parade, singing *Puff the Magic Dragon* (and I think also *John Jacob Jingleheimer Schmidt,* which makes less sense). It was fun and messy. Earliest professional crafting memory: I used to draw these crazy abstract designs (I was exposed to a lot of Paul Klee and other modern art at a tender age) on paper plates and a friend of mine and I set up something like a lemonade stand to sell them one weekend when I was about seven. I think a few passersby took pity on us, but in retrospect I feel silly thinking about trying to sell my weird doodles. I guess it was a good lesson in putting myself out in the world as an artist (how embarrassing it can be! but also how strongly you want your work to connect with people). I think twenty-three years later I'm still basically trying to sell my weird doodles and it still feels silly.

What was your best crafting moment (idea, inspiration, etc.)?

A Kodak moment on the balcony of a villa in the hills near Rome at sunset, where I was hanging out drawing with my best friend since high school, Jessie. The design for my playing card tattoo, which I'd been working on for a year, suddenly gelled and I realized I should carry through the idea and make a full playing-card deck design. Soon afterward, the laundry drying rack out on the balcony tipped to one side, dumping all my underwear and bras into a nearby cactus, which left them riddled with teeny, invisible needles. My worst laundry moment still didn't completely dampen my best crafting moment. But it did earn me the nickname Prickle Tits for the rest of the trip.

What was your worst crafting moment (a huge mess, project gone horribly wrong, etc.)?

I once designed and hand made a gift for a friend I was on the outs with, to try to make amends, show how much I cared, etc. But I believe it was taken as one-upmanship, like: I always make things, aren't I so great, and in fact, better than you? It was a huge amount of labor and care, so I felt bad and resentful when my efforts weren't appreciated. Things were actually worse between us after the gift than before. I guess it's kind of like the stupid sweater curse (which states that if a lady starts knitting a sweater for her man, they will definitely have broken up by the time it's finished). For a cynic, I guess the moral is don't make anything for anyone, ever, if you never want to be disappointed. But I personally still think one of the better feelings in life is when you've made something unique for someone and they do love it.

What is your favorite craft you've ever seen?

An impossible question. I do really treasure the spray-paint-and-macaroni recreation of a Mission of Burma album cover that my friend TD made. It's ironic on many levels (I think he was kinda making fun of the idea of a punk-rock craft fair, but in a good-natured way) and it reminds me of one my favorite records.

Who made you the crafter you are (who introduced you to crafts, taught you crafts—whether or not it is the one you do now)?

I was a latchkey kid and also very nerdy, so I attended a lot of after-school classes (Shakespeare club, embroidery, etc.). My after-school calligraphy teacher, Penny, inspired a great love of the carefully handmade in me. We did some illuminated manuscripts, traditional nib calligraphy, and Chinese calligraphy. She was a fairly prim and proper German Catholic lady, and her motto was that calligraphy is the very opposite of cursive writing: slow and deliberate, with lots of stops and starts. This ethic always annoyed me, even though I loved my teacher and her classes. Penny's strong sense of care and attention to detail helped me focus, but I rebelled against it at the time (and—who am I kidding?—still do now). I think I needed both spontaneity and discipline to do good work, and I learned a lot about the latter from her.

What are your crafting goals?

I would like to make at least one totally new thing per year that I didn't foresee— a new design, a new medium, something that just surprises me.

Kraft or Kraftwerk?

Definitely Kraftwerk. And/or Can.

Who is your fave crafty celeb?

Queen Bee's Rebecca Pearcy. Does she count as a celeb? Her handbag and guitar strap designs are really swell and she still finds time to be a musician in addition to crafting and running a business! Plus, she very patiently taught me to sew at LadyFest in Olympia.

What is your fave craft resource (Web site, store, dumpster, etc.)?

The old paper factory in my neighborhood has stacks and stacks of different colored paper. Going in there is kind of like the Easter egg warehouse at the end of The Country Bunny and the Little Gold Shoes.

Global Techniques

This project, while detailing a specifically xerographic process, does make use of some more universal reproductive concepts. Composites and separations, for instance, are a cornerstone of single-ink reproduction, be it silkscreening, Xerox, or something else. Any multicolored image requires its color elements to be divided into different templates before they can be reproduced. If an image is red and black like our playing cards, there will need to be one original that represents only the red parts of the image and then a second that represents only its black components. Then each color element must be reproduced individually. When you lay these on top of one another, the result it a single composite image that has both red and black elements. From this, keep in mind that for this project you'll need to create composite images by xeroxing right on top of an image you already xeroxed (specifically, for the face cards). So don't be alarmed when you find yourself loading the copier with pages onto which you have already printed.

Emily says that reading about all the card designers and the production recommendations for making your own deck really gave her the confidence to go through with the idea. Here's a resource list from Emily:

- **World of Playing Cards (http://www.wopc.co.uk)** See especially: the history of playing cards (http://www.wopc.co.uk/history), the meaning of court cards (http://www.wopc.co.uk/cards/courts.html), production methods for small-batch cards (http://www.wopc.co.uk/otc/production.html), and the gallery of card designers (http://www.wopc.co.uk/otc/)
- *Antique Playing Cards: A Pictorial History* **(Dover Publications, 1996)**
- **Playing Cards in the Victoria & Albert Museum**
  http://www.wopc.co.uk/bibliography/index.html

Here are some other helpful tips from Emily:

- **When designing your cards, use a method that allows you to reproduce easily.** Designing cards involves lots of repetition, which is why Emily uses a computer. If you don't go digital, use a stamp, graph paper, or cut and paste with xeroxes. There are lots of ways.

- **Find your local, small copy shop that knows local artists and is supportive of their projects.** Try to find a nerd who likes a challenge.
- **Use white as your design and color as your background.** This seems to make the cards look less cheap. Your copy nerd may balk at large, solid expanses of toner and ask you to come back with a halftone (where dots make a solid tint—like a comic strip or Lichtenstein painting). The enthusiastic copy nerd is definitely a double-edged sword.
- **Use a copier that allows you to swap in color toner cartridges like the Kodak ImageSource 110.** If you can find one of these dinosaurs, it's really an amazing tool. If you plan on doing a lot of xerographic projects, try to find some people to pool resources—like a collective. Buy a copier before they become cool like Print Gocco, the little Japanese screen printer that's become the trucker hat of the art world.

PLAYiNG CARDS   DiFFiCULTY ✪✪✪✩✩

TiME LiNE Emily breaks down the time lines like this: If you use a predesigned image for the deck (like hers in the book) it's gonna take about an hour to produce. Designing a deck from scratch is gonna take you anywhere from 4 hours (drawing) to 4 years (you know, conceptualization and all that). The copying should take about 30 minutes, but the people at the copy place may make you leave the project there and go home, so it could be overnight. Cutting, collating, and making the box/sleeve will take you all of 30 minutes.

 The Shaggs: *Philosophy of the World;* Kleenex/*Liliput;* The Raincoats: *The Raincoats*

 Ladies and Gentlemen, The Fabulous Stains; The Heroic Trio; Desperately Seeking Susan

SHOPPING LIST

There's actually not much shopping to be done for this project unless you are going to start designing your own deck from scratch instead of using Emily's designs.

THE COPY STORE

- **Cardstock paper** Just pick from the selection at the copy shop.
- **Copy machine with color toner (NOT a color copier)** Kinko's *never* has the right kind of copier for this project. You need one with color toner—they will just try to sell you *color copies,* which are NOT what you need. Many Staples locations will have a machine with red toner, but they seem to be getting fewer and fewer. Your best bet is to call around to smaller copy shops. See if you can find one with a friendly nerd working who is really into xerography. Sometimes asking for a machine that does "spot color" helps.
- **Any special heavy stock paper out of which to make your box/sleeve for the deck**

FABRIC/CRAFT STORE

- **Pinking Shears**

Step-by-Step

1. Xerox or scan the pattern images on pages 189–197, enlarging each.
When xeroxing or scanning from this book, enlarge to 125 percent. Emily's pattern is designed perfectly for the 8 ½ x 11-inch laser printer office paper. You should ultimately end up with 9 pattern pages: 1 page of the back pattern, 1 page of each suit (a total of 4 pages) and 4 pages of court cards (2 red outline, 2 black).

2. Go to the copy shop and find the right contact.
Get a copy nerd to help you. Definitely find someone who will take the time to help you get your project done right. Don't be too pushy—listen to his/her advice, but remember, it's a copy shop employee's job to help you make the copies *you* want.

3. Choose your cardstock.

I suggest choosing from the selection at the copy shop. That way you just buy what you need, not some whole big package. If you have cardstock at home and you bring it in, they may let you use that. You will need 6 printed pattern sheets per deck, but you may want to make extra copies in case of error.

4. Print your back pattern pages.

You will need 6 pages of back pattern pages to make one deck of cards, but you may want to print more in case you mess up. Emily's are printed in green. Choose any color you like, but remember that your cards will be red and black, so you might want to choose something other than red or black. Remember that you cannot use a color copier, because your original is black, and you want the copier to reproduce in your chosen color. Now you have your printed pattern blanks on which to print your cards. This is really the only straightforward xeroxing step. It gets a little trickier from here.

5. Load your printed pattern blanks into the copier.

Use either the feed tray or the actual paper-loading drawer. Your copy nerd will most likely make this decision since it's unlikely that you'd be able to self-serve on a machine like this. The blanks only have the deck back pattern on them, so you will need to position them so that the card numbers or face patterns will print on the blank side.

6. Make your first round of copies: red suits and courts.

Copy all 4 of the red pages. This means Hearts, Diamonds, Court 1 red, and Court 2 red. There's not too much to mess up here as long as the paper is loaded correctly so that what's copied in this step is on the *opposite* side of the paper from the green pattern backing.

7. Make your second round of copies: black suits.

Print the two black suits: 1 page for Clubs and 1 for Spades. Do not print the black court outlines yet.

8. Print Court 1 black outline on top of your printed Court 1 red.

Position your printed Court 1 red cards in the input tray. You are printing black outlines onto both the Hearts court and the Spades court in this step. In order to ascertain the proper input and output paper orientation, I strongly suggest doing a few test copies of both the backs and fronts on plain, cheapo paper. Your copy nerd will probably do this anyway. If not, insist on it before going ahead with the expensive stock.

This and the next step are by far the most mindbending. Positioning the original on the glass and correctly loading the paper can break your brain. You'll go bonkers like James Stewart in *Vertigo* and your disembodied head will fly through a hyperspace vortex of changing colors and your hair will get messed up and you'll land in a sanitarium. Is that what you really want?

9. Print Court 2 black outline on top of your printed Court 2 red.

Position your printed Court 2 red cards in the input tray. You are printing black outlines onto the Diamonds court and the Clubs court in this step. See warnings in step 8.

10. Say hello to your multitoner spot-color xeroxed card deck.

Hopefully, they are more or less lined up. Limited control means registration is a crapshoot with xerox, but whatever minor deviations may result will be charming. You'll minimize variation by doing all your copying at once.

11. Cut 'em out.

Using pinking shears will obliterate the dotted guidelines and circumvent the need for impossibly unattainable uniform edges. Besides a nice handmade look, it adds an unexpected functionality in that you can't mark your cards or tell one card from another across the table, even though no two are sized exactly alike.

Advanced: Optional steps if you plan on trying to design your own deck

1. Design a basic theme for your deck.

Do some rough sketches for basic design and layout with paper and pencil—or use a stamp—and graph paper.

2. Reproduce designs on computer.

There's lots of repetition in this project, which makes the computer ideal for at least automation if not design. Lay out your designs on a template using a specific layout application like Quark or Illustrator to import and arrange your images. Reproduce each suit and court set based on your layout template. Lay out all the black cards together and all the red cards together. Make your color separations and then export the whole shebang to Photoshop. You might wanna use Emily's patterns as a guide for layout but use your own designs.

The thing about this computer stuff is that it might not seem so "handmade," but like all Bazaar Bizarre crafters you're kinda subverting the tools of your exploitation—the tools of labor. Chances are your job sucks and you're chained to a computer all day anyway. Viva Bazaar Bizarre! Turn that to your advantage and learn some creative software. Adobe's *Classroom in a Book* series is excellent, but there are certainly many other really helpful books out there. I love Macromedia's *Training from the Source* series, myself.

3. Design and print everything on 100 percent black.

The color comes in when you xerox. You can make colored documents for design testing purposes, but not for the actual printing.

4. Print out your deck.

You should end up with 4 suit pages and 4 court separations as well as 1 page for the back pattern. Print these all in black to bring to your copy shop.

5. Follow steps 3 through 11 above.

Back of Deck.
Enlarge to 163%
when you reproduce.
You'll need 6 per deck.
Print green

Hearts.
Enlarge to 163%
when you reproduce.
Print red.

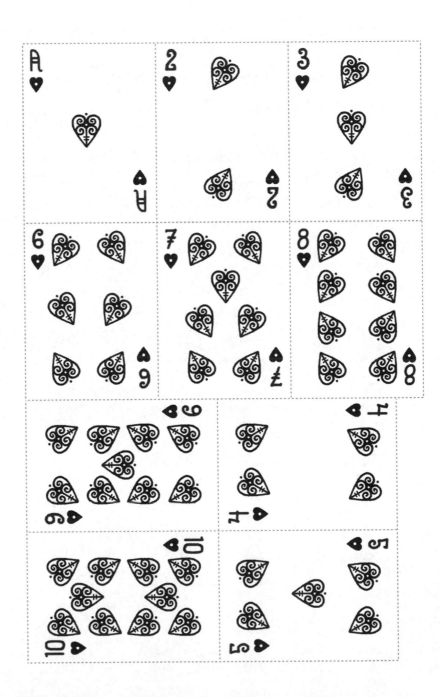

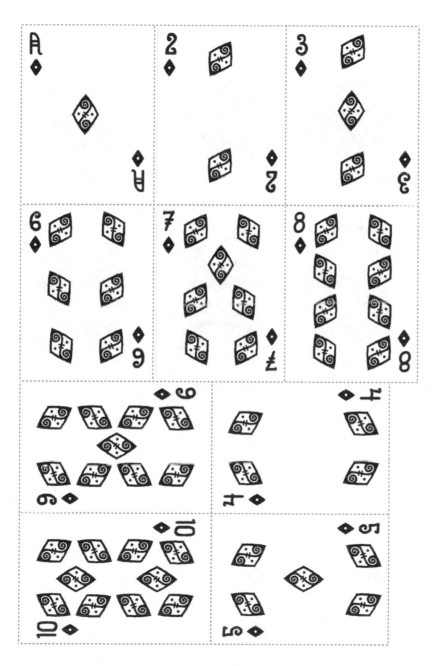

Diamonds.
Enlarge to 163%
when you reproduce.
Print red.

Court 1 Red.
Enlarge to 163%
when you reproduce.
Print red.

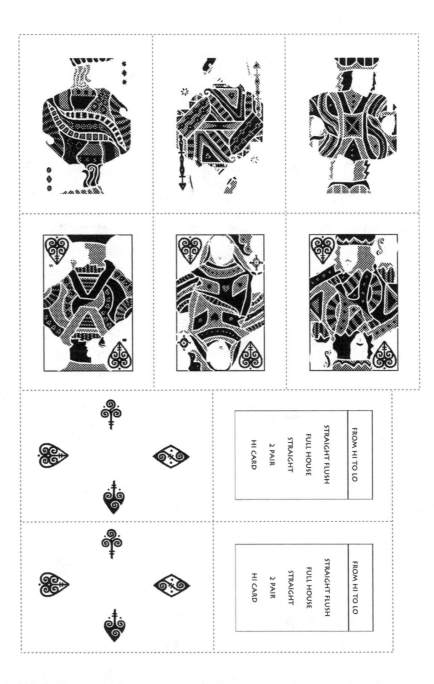

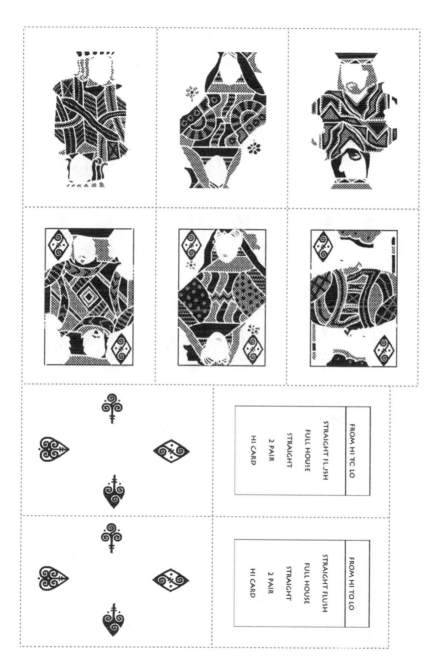

Court 2 Red.
Enlarge to 163%
when you reproduce.
Print red.

Clubs.
Enlarge to 163%
when you reproduce.
Print black.

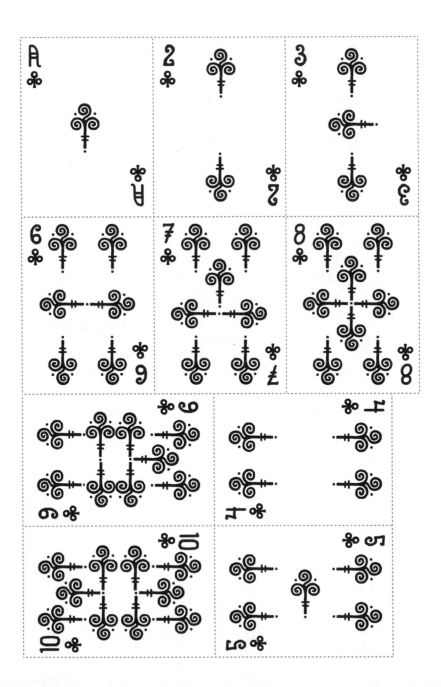

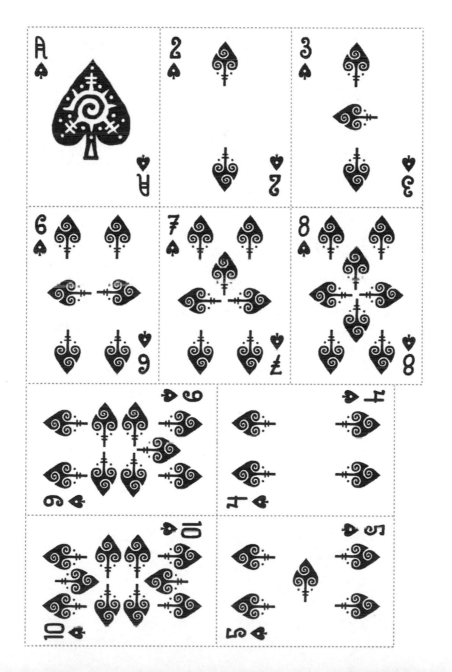

Spades.
Enlarge to 163%
when you reproduce.
Print black.

*Court 1 Black Outline.
Enlarge to 163%
when you reproduce.
Print black on top of
Court 1 Red.*

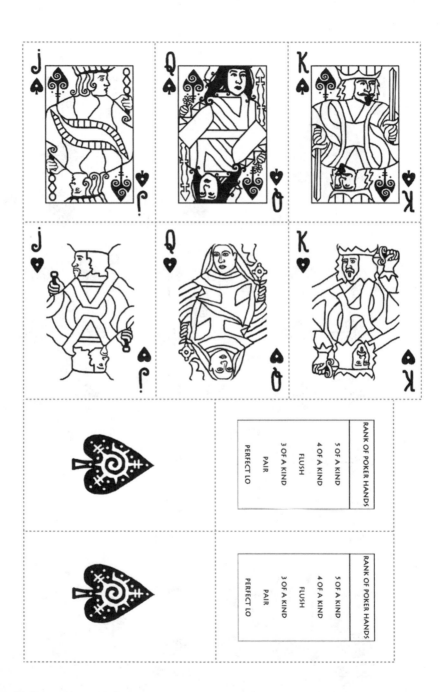

Court 2 Black Outline.
Enlarge to 163%
when you reproduce.
Print black on top of
Court 2 Black.

SERVING SUGGESTIONS

Try using the cast of your favorite TV show for the basis of your court cards. I know I'm gonna make a *Golden Girls* deck, and Bea Arthur is definitely King. *Match Game 75? The Nanny? Charles in Charge? Dynasty?*

Now that you have mastered the traditional deck of playing cards, why not try making your own design for a different card game? There's lots of 'em out there. How about your own UNO deck, for example? If you are really adventurous, you might wanna try making your own tarot deck, but be aware that this is a lot of work as far as design goes. If you thought there were a lot of specific requirements for playing cards, try reading up on all of the particular design elements of a tarot deck.

Contact Info

Emily Arkin, along with Simone Alpen and Leah Kramer, is a co-owner of Magpie, a boutique specializing in handmade goods. You can check their Web site at http://www.magpie-store.com/. She can be reached via e-mail at emily@the-operators.com or visit her very own Web site: http://www.emilyarkin.com.

Rumplestiltskin:
Say My Name, Say My Name!

I think there are some interesting connections you can
infer between the domestic arts (or "crafts") and the craft of magic
(sometimes called "witchcraft"). Witchcraft is overwhelmingly
characterized as feminine and—in many of our cultural
depictions—appears as a perversion of the traditional domestic skill
set that threatens to disrupt the home and family unit. Cauldrons,
witches brews, lists of strange ingredients, gingerbread houses,
and the like suggest reexamination of the culinary arts. Cooking is
not the only domestic skill that finds its way to this dark side of
crafting, however, and it isn't always the women of the house who
stir up trouble with their powerful domestic tools. What about
those elves who made the shoes for that guy? Or the sorcerer's
apprentice who enchanted/enslaved a broom? Hephaestus wove
magic itself into the glittering thread of a girdle for his wife
Aphrodite, making her irresistible to all who saw her. (Okay, I am
down with handmade lingerie for your life partner, but this was
not the smartest move by a jealous husband.) With the exception of those
little elves, things don't turn out so well for crafty heroes who attempt to
acquire power through domestic skills.

I think the coolest example of a boy doing an evil version of a girl craft and
thereby ending up in hell is Rumplestiltskin. His is the story of a Miller, a Girl, a
King, and a Troll. Of sex, greed, betrayal, dark secrets . . . and crafts! Yes, the tale
of Rumplestiltskin is one of deals gone sour and promises unkept. However, it
isn't the villain who engages in the deceit.

The miller, on a visit to the king, boasts that his daughter can spin straw into gold (which, duh, she can't). Naturally, the king is intrigued and is eager to meet the girl. A couple of questions surface at this point. In what kingdom can a miller just call on the king unannounced? And why does the miller make such an outlandish claim? Does he think that he won't be found out? It seems kind of like fake boobs or stuffing your crotch—as soon as the ruse works, the jig is up. In some versions of the tale, it is the miller's plan that the king, upon meeting the girl, will be so taken with her beauty that he will forget about the miller's promise of gold. Needless to say, the girl is pretty pissed at the miller for telling such a lie and is reluctant to meet the king. In a less than shocking turn of events, the king is not enchanted and still wants the girl to work her magic on the spinning wheel, locking her in a tower until she can finish the task.

So locked in a tower with a huge pile of straw and a spinning wheel, the girl is terrified because the king has declared that, oh, by the way, she must die should she fail in her task. Enter Rumplestiltskin. The little man materializes from the shadows and tells the girl that for a price he can, in fact, spin the straw into gold for her, saving her from death and endearing her to the greedy king. This goes on for two nights, and indeed the king does fall deeper in love each morning as he is greeted by large sums of gold. On the third and final night of the test, the girl has no ruby ring or necklace left to offer Rumplestiltskin in exchange for his magic. Rumplestiltskin offers his crafty skills once more, asking that the girl hand over her first-born son in exchange. The whole marriage/baby thing seems so far down the road that the girl agrees to the trade, never really considering its consequences. That's the generous reading. I think she just flat out lied and never intended to give up her fruit of the womb.

Some years go by, the king married the girl, and they have a baby boy. Sure enough, Rumplestiltskin returns to the girl to claim the child, but when he arrives, the girl (now the queen) has no intention of handing over the royal goods. She offers the riches of the kingdom, but Rumplestiltskin holds her to the promise she'd made. Now aside from Rumplestiltskin, all of the characters are pretty much lying, greedy, morally bankrupt individuals. Only our title character is a straight shooter when it comes to his intentions.

Worn down by the queen's pleas, he agrees to back out of the deal *if* she can guess his name. So she guesses and guesses unsuccessfully. Melchior, Balthazar, Caspar, Sheepshanks, Laceleg, and Shortribs. To the queen's chagrin, none of these classic names was the imp's (I, however, have been inspired to name my first child Shortribs). Tipped off by one of her servants patrolling the woods of the kingdom, she learns secondhand the gnome's moniker. She confronts Rumplestiltskin and he becomes irate, claiming that the devil told her. In a fit of rage, he stomps his right foot with such magical troll strength that his leg plunges deep into the earth. Trying to extract himself, he is actually torn in two and descends into hell.

When domestic and thereby feminine skills are imbued with power (like magic), they threaten to unbalance gendered cultural hierarchies. Of course, then it's necessary to demonize power that springs from a feminine source. It's this logic that allows the one honest person in a story to be seen as the villain. Of course, it probably doesn't help that Rumplestiltskin is a whimsically dressed single man who seeks to gain custody of a young boy.

KNITTING

CRAFT

PROJECT: CAP

ARTIST: *Simone Alpen*

Simone, believe it or not, has only been knitting for about four years, and she's already designing her own garments. But then that's the kind of person she is: When available packaged offerings fail to satisfy, a BazBiz gal's gotta take patterns into her own hands. A common complaint among knitters, according to Simone, is that there are tons of patterns with all kinds of "bells and whistles," and yet a paucity of unfussy fundamentals that one would actually wear. Not to say that bells and whistles aren't a great way to learn and try new techniques, but I think we all know what road that takes us down: Think shoulder-padded, bedazzled, metallic patchwork, faux-angora casino-wear and a home-shopping-hostess French manicure. Or worse yet: *The Cosby Show.*

So we're left wanting some basics. Now here I'd be tempted to quote Coco Chanel and say something about dressing shabbily and people noticing the dress, dressing well and they notice the woman, and so forth; but in all honesty, I'd just be paraphrasing Sigourney Weaver in *Working Girl* (NOTE TO SELF: Do not go through Tess). My point, and I think here Coco would agree with me, is that style is how you put it together, not how flashy any one piece might be. Enter Simone's simple unisex winter hat. Here's a basic knit cap that you can embellish any way you want, and according to Simone, it's worth the hat hair.

BAZAAR BIZARRE
ALPEN, $IMONE
19730714
KNIT HAT

I met Simone in 2000 when I moved back to Massachusetts from Bloomington, Indiana, and we quickly hit it off. Over the few years that I have known her, we've come to discover that we seem to have almost exactly the same taste in everything—music, art, food, fashion, and all the finer things. Everything that is, *except* boys! Could there be a more perfect galpal?

Simone's involvement in Bazaar Bizarre is more than that of your basic participant. She was one of the crafters from my gang of Somerville friends that really made the first Bazaar Bizarre a reality. Now she's headcheese—wait, yuck—rather she's head honcho when it comes to the Boston BazBiz since I live in Los Angeles. I really consider Simone a partner. We're working together (along with fellow BazBiz cast members Mary Jo Kaczka and Leah Kramer) to get our nonprofit Craftopolis off the ground. As if that weren't enough, she co-owns Magpie on Huron, a Cambridge boutique specializing in antiques and handmade goods. And she even has a job!

What is the difference between an "art" and a "craft"?
Art hangs in museums? Crafts may or may not be displayed in museums. This is a tough question because I'm not sure I know the difference. More significantly—I'm not sure I care all that much as

it relates to my own crafting. I would say that I live for crafting because I love having beauty in my life. I certainly don't think that a knitted scarf is art, but it does bring kindness into the world. And not to get too gloppy about it, but giving a friend something you've made with your own little mitts says more about how you feel than any Old Navy garment ever could.

What is your earliest crafting memory?

Sadly, I have few early memories of actually crafting myself. But my German grandmother (my oma) was a crafting genius. She knitted, crocheted, sewed, and made gorgeous tapestries and rugs. While looking at childhood photo albums, I inquired of my mom about each outfit. "Where, at age three, did I get this fabulous matching jade-green crocheted dress and hat?" Every time, the response was Oma.

What is your best crafting moment (idea, inspiration, etc.)?

I'm hoping I haven't hit that moment just yet!

What was your worst crafting moment (a huge mess, project gone horribly wrong, etc.)?

My worst crafting horror story was from last winter. Being ever so fashion forward, I decided I really wanted to make a poncho. This was slightly before the present poncho trend; so knitting patterns were hard to come by. At long last I found one in some "hip" knitting book—basically, it was two large seed stitch rectangles sewn together. Easy, right? So off I went, with the correct gauge, nice yarn, and my little pattern. I finished the project quickly and completed it during my bitch and stitch session. Silence. My friends were like, "Um . . . it's interesting, I guess" and "You kinda look like a superhero!" The poncho looked more like a tiny capelet, like a gray minicape! It's currently buried at the bottom of one of my yarn baskets.

What is your favorite craft you've ever seen?

At the American Craft Museum a couple of years ago I saw a few pieces by Ray Materson (http://www.americancraftmuseum.org/). While in prison he taught himself to embroider. Using threads from socks, shirts, and whatever else he could find, he started creating these totally beautiful, moving scenes. Prison scenes rendered in tiniest detail. Now he's out of prison and continues to embroider.

His pieces are showcases in many museums and are worth thousands.
http://www.npr.org/programs/watc/features/2001/010128.materson.html
Sins and Needles: A Story of Spiritual Mending by Ray Materson and Melanie
Materson

Who made you the crafter you are (who introduced you to crafts, taught you crafts—whether or not it is the one you do now)?

My crafting guru is most certainly Stacie Dolin. She's a pro knitter, bookbinder, and
overall craft rock star. That girl can seriously do anything she tries—and swimmingly
well! She jumps right into projects without fear of failing, which is the most
important thing in crafting.

What are your crafting goals?

I read somewhere that you should create something every day. That's definitely a
good place to start.

Kraft or Kraftwerk?

Kraftwerk.

Who is your fave crafty celeb?

Martha Stewart.

What is your fave craft resource (Web site, store, dumpster, etc.)?

www.craftster.org

www.craftivism.com

www.knitty.com

www.sublimestitching.com

www.ashidome.com/blogger/craftybitch.asp - Crafty Bitch blog

www.bitter-girl.com/knitblog/knitting.html - Bitter Girl blog

www.theredsweater.com/cms/index.html - The Red Sweater blog

www.plainmabel.com

Global Techniques

Excluding any potential eye-gouging-with-knitting-needle scenarios, I doubt many people would consider knitting fraught with peril. I, however, find knitting to be dangerous. For me there is a delicious precariousness to the whole shebang. Allow me to explain:

I'm an intelligent person—hell, I'm a Mensa member—but there are certain intellectual concepts I still can't get my head around. Take algebra, for example. I failed algebra *twice* in high school. I finally had to face my math demon in the form of a zero-credit remedial algebra prep course during summer session of my senior year at Indiana University. I earned an A, but it required as much labor as a full-time job. Point being, I just don't get algebra. The harder I try to figure out why it works, the more my head hurts. The *truth* of algebra is just something I have to accept on faith; like sea monkeys.

Knitting's mystique is remarkably similar—I don't know why it works, but it just *does*. First, there is the magic of using needles to basically tie knot after knot until one strand of yarn becomes an entire piece of cloth. Second, you have two (at least) slippery needles manipulating your yarn. I always feel as if my project is about to break free and fly off into space. Finally is the unravel factor—it seems as if there's never a point at which your project isn't frighteningly close to complete collapse, but still we knit and we succeed. One basic note of caution: Do not let your fears shine through by knitting too tightly. Casting on, the first real stitches of your project will be tight and difficult enough without your added tension. Plus, you can tell a lot about a crafter from her crafts. If you're uptight, it's gonna show.

This pattern assumes a medium knitting level; meaning, basically, that you can knit and purl. Anytime the pattern calls for circular needles, you can always substitute double pointed needles of the same size. And if you've never used double-pointed needles before—don't be scared! Here are some helpful diagrams:

DOUBLE CAST ON

- Take some yarn off the ball. You will need three times the length of one row of finished project.
- Tie a slip knot around needle and hold in your right hand.
- With tail in front and the ball end in back, grab both strands with your left ring and pinky fingers.
- Place your left thumb and index finger together and through the two strands.
- Open thumb and forefinger so that your hand is making a pretend gun. The ball end will cascade down behind left index finger and the tail end will come down in front over left thumb.
- Gather and hold snug both strands with your left middle finger. Keep both strands from the right needle to your left hand snug and do not let the right-hand needle stray too far from your left hand. By now your hands, the yarn, and needle should all look something like a drawn crossbow.
- Pass your needle under the strand of yarn in front of your left thumb from the bottom of your thumb to the top.
- Draw the yarn across your left hand and use the needle to grab the strand that's in front of your index finger by passing your needle under the strand from the bottom to the top.
- If done correctly, you will now see a strand coming off the needle and around your thumb back to the needle.
- Draw the needle tip through the thumb loop.
- Release the loop from your thumb and pull the tail end with your left thumb to tighten and secure the yarn (and your first stitch) onto the right needle.
- Congratulations! You have just cast on your first stitch. Now just repeat this process as many times as there are stitches required by your pattern (for Simone's hat it'll be 88).

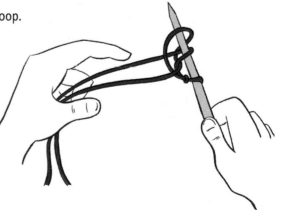

KNiT STiTCH

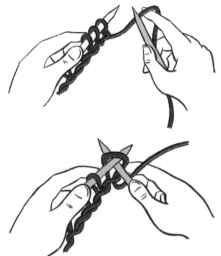

- We'll start with an empty right-hand needle and a piece in progress on the left. Grip the free strand of yarn between your bottom three fingers, then around the outside of your pointer finger. Hold the needle in your right hand so that it points over the top of the yarn.
- Insert your right needle left to right (or "up" due to the angle) through the end stitch on your left needle, behind the left needle, so that they are pointing the same way (despite their being crossed).
- Using your right index finger, wrap the ball yarn counterclockwise around the right needle tip.
- Pull your right needle carefully from the back to the front until you are able to slide its tip in front of the left needle.

- Use your right needle to lift the new stitch up off the tip of the left needle and onto the right needle. You have just knit one stitch!

PURL STITCH

- Doing the same way as you would for a knit stitch, except that the ball yarn should go over the right needle, not under. Purling always begins with the yarn in front.
- Insert your right needle right to left (or "down") through the end stitch on your left needle, keeping the right needle in front of the left.
- Using your right index finger, wrap the ball yarn counterclockwise around the right needle tip.
- Pull your right needle carefully until you are able to slide its tip behind the left needle.
- Use your right needle to lift the new stitch up off the tip of the left needle and onto the right needle.
- If you are going to resume *knitting*, remember to move the ball yarn between the needles to the back of the project.

DECREASE

- Decreasing is super easy in this project. When it is time to decrease, make a regular knit stitch, but be sure to grab 2 stitches at once from the left needle.
- You are effectively knitting 2 into 1, thereby decreasing your stitch count by 1.

KNITTING RESOURCES

- **http://knitting.about.com**

Good basic instructions for knitting.

- **http://www.interweave.com**

This is one of the best knitting magazines, according to Simone. There are only a few free patterns, but plenty of pix to drool over!

- **http://www.knitty.com**

Knitty provides a bevy of free patterns of all skill levels.

- **Rebecca Magazine (http://www.rebecca-online.com)**

A German knitting magazine that's surprisingly hip!

- **Craftster (http://www.craftster.org)**

Craftster is a crafting geek's heaven, and the brainchild of BazBiz crafter Leah Kramer. The knitting forum is particularly active and will provide lots of fun, free patterns along with loads of pix of people's projects—disasters and all!

KNITTING MATERIALS (IN SIMONE'S OWN WORDS)

- **Yarn** How can I sing the praises of Cascade 220? It's a great wool yarn that comes in billions of colors. It wears extremely well.
- **Needles** Addi Turbo is a brand of metal circular needles that are so glorious. Most knitters have strong preferences about whether they use bamboo or metal needles. I'm not normally in favor of metal needles (the yarn slides around so darn much!), but Addi's are the best. For some reason the Turbo part of the name seems particularly true. I can whip out this hat in no time flat!

KNiT CAP DIFFICULTY ☆☆☆☆☆

TiME LiNE For a beginner knitter, this project could take quite a bit of time. The casting on to the circular needles is definitely tricky the first go-round, and the switch to double-pointed needles is challenging until you do it for the first time and realize that it's not impossible by any means. According to Simone, a beginner could complete this project in a few 2-hour sessions. It really all depends on how quickly you knit. It takes some people a long time to ramp up to a quick speed. This project assumes at least a beginner level of skill. It takes an intermediate knitter like Simone about 2 to 3 hours total. Once you get into the groove, all the knitting, knitting, knitting is really passive and can be completed during a lengthy TV watching/movie watching session.

 The Smiths: *The Smiths;* Buzzcocks: *Singles Going Steady;* The Pixies: *Surfer Rosa*

The Women (Rosalind Russell knits throughout the movie!); *Waiting for Guffman; Umbrellas of Cherbourg*

SHOPPiNG LiST

CRAFT/YARN STORE

- 125 yards of worsted weight yarn (recommended yarns: Cascade 220 or Brown Sheep)
- Size 6 U.S. 16-inch circular needles
- Size 8 U.S. 16-inch circular needles
- Size 8 U.S. double-pointed needles
- Stitch markers
- Tapestry needle (large plastic needle for yarn)

Step by Step

Simone tells me that any veteran knitter would be really irritated by the fluffy, yet charming, step-by-step format I have been using for the other chapters of this book. So for you more knowledgeable knitters, I present here the unfettered pattern in its purest form:

Cast on 88 stitches on #6 circular needles, being careful not to twist the stitches. Place marker and join.

BEGIN RIB PATTERN:

Round 1: *K2, P2; * to end.
Continue in rib pattern for 8 rounds total.
Switch to #8 needles.
Knit all rounds.
Continue for 6 inches.
Set up for decrease rounds by placing a stitch marker after every 11th stitch for one round.

DECREASE ROUNDS:

Round 1: *Knit 2 together (K2tog), knit to marker; *repeat from *
Round 2: Knit all stitches

Continue, repeating rounds 1 and 2 six more times. Switch, as needed, to double-pointed needles when hat has decreased to a size smaller than your circular needles. 11 stitches remaining.

Cut yarn, leaving a long end for sewing in. Pull through stitches remaining on the needles; pull tightly to cinch top and secure inside.
Weave in all your ends.

MY VERSION OF THE INSTRUCTIONS

Okay, so to me that looks a lot like algebra, but I have it on good authority that it's proper knitting pattern protocol. However, for a Mensa member I can be kinda dumb.

You see, I actually did *fail* algebra twice in high school (with the same teacher!), but then, of course, that could've been because my illustrious educator (let's just call him by his student-assigned moniker: Silky) seemed interested in the budding female Fibonaccis of the class more than quadratic formulae or asymptotes (see, I remember a couple things). Regardless of my factorial failings, here is the pattern again, this time numerated and peppered with my witty commentary and helpful advice.

1. Cast on 88 stitches on #6 circular needles, being careful not to twist the stitches.

Place marker and join. Be careful to leave the marker between stitches. Mine tend to get actually stitched into the project, which is not what you want. Begin rib pattern.

2. Round 1: *K2, P2; * to end.

This means knit 2, then purl 2. * is a shorthand symbol. It stands for whatever instructions immediately follow the * in the directions. In this case it means to repeat the knit 2, purl 2 pattern.

3. Continue in rib pattern for 8 rounds total.

A round is the same as a row, except here we are knitting on circular needles, so you know you've completed one round when your stitch marker comes up on your left needle again.

4. Switch to #8 needles.

This seems a bit intimidating, but you just drop your right hand and start with an empty #8 circular needle and keep going. You are just transferring from one set of needles to another in this step.

5. Knit all rounds.

So once the ribbing is done, you're gonna proceed knitting all the way for each round instead of K2, P2.

6. Continue for 6 inches.

Keep knitting and knitting until you've knit 6 inches worth of hat *after* the ribbing. Remember to finish off a round by reaching the stitch marker. Don't stop in the middle of a round just because you've reached 6 inches.

7. Set up for decrease rounds by placing a stitch marker after every 11th stitch for one round.

Now you will decrease the rounds.

8. Round 1: *Knit 2 together (K2tog), knit to marker; *repeat from *.

Every 1st of 11 stitches, you're going to pick up 2 stitches (decreasing) instead of just one (normal knitting).

9. Round 2: Knit all stitches.

After knitting one round of decreasing every 11 stitches, knit one round of straight knitting.

10. Continue, repeating rounds 1 and 2 six more times.

Each time you'll be decreasing and ending up with smaller and smaller rounds.

11. Switch, as needed, to double-pointed needles when hat has decreased to a size smaller than your circular needles (you will use 4 double-pointed needles).

Here again this switch seems intimidating. You won't realize how doable it is until you try it. When you get to a point that is too small for the circular needles and is divisible by 3, transfer one-third of the stitches to one needle. Drop it and transfer the next third to the second needle. Drop that and transfer the last third to the third needle. Now you just continue this process, using your fourth empty needle as your first needle, allowing your project's diameter to get smaller and smaller, yet still be comfortably knittable.

12. Keep going until you have only 11 stitches remaining.

13. Cut yarn, leaving a long end for sewing in.

Using a yarn needle or crochet hook, pull the long end or "tail" through stitches remaining on the needles; pull tightly to cinch top and secure inside.

14. Weave in all your ends.

Again, using your yarn needle, weave or sew your tail through the inside stitches of the hat to secure it.

15. Ta da! You are now the proud owner of a fab new winter hat!

SERVING SUGGESTIONS

Make beautiful felt flowers for your hat. First, cut out 5 identical petal shapes out of whatever felt you like. Baste the bottom of each petal so that you have a chain secured at one end with a knot. Pull the thread tightly through the beginning anchor knot, gathering the petals together in the center to form a flower. Don't cut the thread at this point. Use a button to create the flower's center. Just sew through the button's holes and knot on the back once it's secure. Now you can snip. To attach the flower to the hat, you can just whipstitch around the edges of the petals or pick a few places to anchor. You can achieve a variety of looks, from a blossom firmly attached all the way around or one with freer floating petals.

Contact Info

Simone is very accessible—and in a number of ways. You can reach her via e-mail at simonealpen@yahoo.com. Check out Magpie (her store) at 368 Huron Avenue, Cambridge, MA 02138. Their site is http://www.magpie-store.com/. Visit http://www.chicka-dee.com/, her own personal site, where she'll be chronicling her crafting adventures and selling a few items. And of course there's always http://www.bazaarbizarre.org.

Crafty Snacks

Wednesday evening has arrived and it's your first time hosting the gang for craft night. Do you really think you'll be able to satisfy your fellow Bazaar Bizarros with a mundane snack like chips? Something right outta the bag simply won't cut it if you want your reputation to be truly crafty. Why not take some of the wisdom and daring creativity you've acquired in these pages and pair 'em up with some pantry staples for a treat that'll wow your guests?

CRAFTOID

EGG & OLIVE PENGUINS

Our very own illustrator, Craig Bostick, shared with me this gem sure to fill your guests' tummies and warm their hearts.

12 baby carrots
12 black olives
6 peeled hard-boiled eggs

Start by using a veggie peeler to sharpen the end of one of your carrots. Insert your sharpened carrot into one of the black olives so that the pointy end is sticking out. Voilà! A penguin head. Use a toothpick or toothpick segment to fasten this to the top of an egg. Cut your remaining olive in half lengthwise and attach each half to either side of the egg for wings. Finally, cut your remaining baby carrot in half lengthwise to create feet with a flat side so you can stand your penguin up. Again, use toothpicks to attach. What a cute and delicious friend! So much more impressive than a plain old cracker or crisp.

Makes 6 whimsical penguin eggs

LUCILLE BALL DEVILED EGGS

Okay, one more: I love Fran Drescher, and in her movie *The Beautician and the Beast* she makes Lucille Ball deviled eggs.

6 peeled hard-boiled eggs
3 tablespoons mayonnaise
1 teaspoon mustard
salt and pepper to taste
12 pimentos
2 black olives
1 carrot

Cut hard-boiled eggs in half lengthwise and remove the yolks. Mash yolks in a bowl with a fork and then add mayonnaise, mustard, salt, and pepper. Scoop yolk mixture back into each half of the egg whites. Create a mouth by adding a pimento as the lips. Slice the olives into rings, then halve them. Use each half as an eye. With your vegetable peeler, make curly carrot slices to give each egg that signature coif. Now if only I could come up with an Ethel-based appetizer we'd be set.

Makes 12 deviled eggs

PEAR MOUSE

I remember another visually stunning taste sensation from a cookbook of my youth.

1 canned pear
2 leaves lettuce
2 marshmallows
6 cloves

Take the pear half and lay it flat side down on a leaf of lettuce. Slice a marshmallow to create two round mallow discs. Affix these pieces about 1 inch from the pointy end of your pear. You may need to use a toothpick if the moisture from the pear is not enough to adhere the marshmallow ears. Use whole cloves to make eyes and a nose and you have a tasty mouse. Can you think of something to use for whiskers?

Makes 2 mousy treats

SiLK PAiNTiNG

PROJECT: SiLK-PAiNTED PATCH

ARTIST: *Karen Carnegie*

When Karen Carnegie's 2003 Bazaar Bizarre vendor application originally floated across my computer screen, I was hesitant, to say the least. No offense, Karen, but "silk painting" sounds like some serious hippie and/or new age hoo-ha. I began to envision menopausal midwestern moms batiking Kokopelli onto poofy blouses. There was no way I was going to support this. Fortunately, I know myself well enough not to put too much stock in my reactionary snap judgments. I did a little poking around Karen's Web site and was relieved and excited to see what she was doing with silk and paint. I didn't see any blurry washed-out ravens, horses, coyotes, or cacti. On the contrary, I saw bold saturated pop-art colors, crisp clean lines, and cute cartoon kitties. Have a great time making this project, but if it comes out looking like something you'd buy at a Phish concert or head shop, I'll swear I don't know you.

CRAFTER BIO

Montville, New Jersey, Party girl Karen "KC" Carnegie describes one of her favorite activities as "rolling down hills with eight-year-olds." During her college summers, she worked as a YMCA camp counselor in the Catskills in New York where she picked up this sordid addiction. KC went to college at the University of Delaware and graduated with a degree in business (risky business, perhaps?). During her tenure at the U of D she "studied" abroad in Hawaii for a semester. A radical change of gears then found her at the Rhode Island School of Design (RISD), where she graduated with a BFA in illustration.

Since her departure from Providence, she's worked in animation, as a storyboard or character layout artist, including a stint doing time in graphic design and communication for a nonprofit organization (HOBY). Animation credits include: MTV's *Daria*, *The Oblongs* (premiered on the WB, then aired on Cartoon Network's Adult Swim), and Disney's *way* cute *Teacher's Pet*. Her season won an Emmy for best daytime animated program. Currently, she spends her nine-to-fives working on *The Simpsons* (along with a few other BazBiz vendors). She's always doodled and drawn, and started only recently selling her own designs online.

My favorite thing about Karen—aside from her talent—is that she *seems* to love kitties as much as I do (although no one but my buddy Stephanie Melikian has proven that degree of kitty love thus far). Wait till you see Karen's kitty illustration for this chapter—you'll plotz.

What is the difference between an "art" and a "craft"?
The confidence of the artist in presenting their work. Every craft is an art and every art a craft.

What is your earliest crafting memory?
My parents enrolled me in some sort of exploratory art class when I was six. The one part I remember was when we made some prints from copper plates! We each got two little copper discs (about two inches across) and drew/etched on them. My parents still have the two prints hanging up at home—one's a cat and the other is someone flying through space in a "supershoe."

What was your best crafting moment (idea, inspiration, etc.)?
Any one that works!

What was your worst crafting moment (a huge mess, project gone horribly wrong, etc.)?
Spilling dye on an otherwise almost finished silk piece . . . black dye.

What is your favorite craft you've ever seen?
Oh, that's tough. Every time I go to a craft/art show I'm in awe of the creativity of my peers. Is that too wimpy of a response?

Who made you the crafter you are (who introduced you to crafts, taught you crafts—whether or not it is the one you do now)?
My good friend Nicole introduced me to the silk painting process. She's amazingly talented and is always an inspiration. I suppose my mom, though, introduced me to crafts. When my brother and I were *really* little, she took various crafting courses to keep herself sane. They included such trendy classes as macramé and painting ceramics. (It was the 70s after all!)

What are your crafting goals?
Have fun, express creativity, and grow the opportunity to share my artwork to bring others joy.

Kraft or Kraftwerk?

Kraft individually sliced singles. No wait—cannolis. It's tough to find a good cannoli over here. Ask me again tomorrow.

Who is your fave crafty celeb?

I don't know if he'd be considered "crafty," but the person who keeps coming to my mind as I ponder this question is Gary Baseman, creator of the *Teacher's Pet* cartoon and Cranium board game artwork. He makes a living pushing the boundaries of his creativity, paints for fulfillment as well as for paycheck, and is a prolific keeper of a sketchbook, which I have a lot of respect for.

What is your fave craft resource (Web site, store, dumpster, etc)?

Art stores, fabric stores, bead stores, etc.—anyplace I can touch everything. I'm a very tactile person. Once I know what I want I'll look online or get a catalog to see if I can get a better price. Here are some specific places I like:

- www.dharmatrading.com for silk supplies
- Surma Store in NYC for my electric wax pen
  http://www.surmastore.com/order.html (I prefer item #14—the medium point)
- Pearl Paint stores for general poking about in

Global Techniques

When looking for source material for almost any project, I usually suggest that one's own imagination is the best resource. You can't draw? Perfect—it'll look like outsider art. However, I realize that this can be a real obstacle for some. If you can't seem to get past the idea of making an image from nothing, well, there are tons of sources like clip art, comics, tracing—you name it. For silk painting (and many other projects), you want to start with very clear black and white line art. This could mean that you have to re-create an image, removing color and shading and adding distinct lines.

After selecting your line art, you need to transfer the design in wax onto the silk. I don't know that there's a proper technical term for this process, but I use the words "tracing" and "edging." Tracing is just what you would expect after years of being a crafty individual: You make a line of wax on the silk directly on top of the line of the pattern, replicating it exactly. When you apply the dye to the surrounding fabric, the line you traced with wax will remain undyed.

Edging is somewhat trickier. You use this technique when you want to create a line of color. You can't paint fine lines of dye directly onto silk because of the bleeding factor. To edge a line of the pattern, you encircle the line with wax, ensuring that there are no gaps in your enclosure. Then when you apply dye to the fabric inside the enclosure, it won't bleed past the wax border. This takes patience and steadiness. You will also use this technique when you want to color a shape or design. In this case, you simply edge the outline of the shape you want to fill in.

In silk painting, wax performs the function of a "resist." Generically, a resist is used to control the flow of pigment on any porous material like paper or fabric. When you apply dye to the silk, it will just keep bleeding outward on all sides until it reaches some kinda moisture equilibrium with the receiving silk (dries out) or until it bumps up against a resist. A resist will basically "clog up" your material so that nothing can be absorbed where it has been applied. However, if there is enough dye, the bleeding will simply continue *around* the wall you've penned. That's why complete, connected outlines and shapes are very important when designing. Many times you'll be working in very small areas, and if there's an unintended gap in the wax, dye is gonna bleed out where you don't want it. The upshot of this is that there is no need to fill in large white areas with wax as long as your outlines connect end to end.

Gutta is another type of resist that comes in a little fine-tipped squeeze bottle. Wherever your draw with the Gutta, dye will not absorb. It has some interesting applications since it comes in colors like gold, but I'd stick with good old beeswax for the bulk of your project, if for no other reason than price. Additionally, the backside of your project will come out differently than the front when you use Gutta. With wax, the two sides will be identical. Something to consider when making, say, a scarf as opposed to a patch or wall hanging.

SiLK-PAiNTED PATCH   DiFFiCULTY ✡ ✡ ✡ ✡ ✡

TiME LiNE Silk painting is a pretty involved technique, but a project this size should only take about 2 hours of active time. As far as passive time, you're gonna want to let the dyes dry overnight before steaming and heat setting the finished piece (which takes about an hour). And of course there's the whole dry-cleaning thing, so plenty of time to check out the following:

Indigo Girls: *Rites Of Passage;* The Beatles: *Anthology;* Stray Cats: *Greatest Hits*

High Fidelity; Say Anything . . . ; Bring It On

Shopping List

When Karen first started to paint on silk, she spent a lot of time tracking down her supplies and eventually moved to catalogue shopping when she became familiar enough with what she was using to order items unseen. I want you to go out and try to find the stuff before you follow suit. It'll build character, and I bet in the process you'll find other cool materials and places you didn't even know you needed or existed. When you do find yourself up against a wall without an attractive playmate behind you, and you have to use a catalogue, Karen recommends the Dharma Trading Company catalogue. Art and craft supply stores do not always stock such specific items. Worse yet, they will sell you the one tiny thing you need *only* as part of some freaking kit. They end up making twenty-five bucks off you for an item that would cost just a buck or two on its own. However, you need to really know exactly what you're looking for. Here's the breakdown:

ARTS AND CRAFTS SUPPLY STORE

- **Silk dye** For this project, Karen uses royal blue, sapphire blue, apricot, magenta, and chocolate brown. The brand that Karen uses is called Jacquard. There are different types of dyes, so ask for help with "silk dye" at the store unless you are very certain you have what you need. Again, the specificity of the product *may* send you packing to the Web or a catalogue.
- **High-quality nylon fabric brush** If you lay out the bucks ahead of time, you will need only one of these. You could buy a broader brush for filling in larger areas with pigment and a very fine pointed brush for detail, but you can easily get by with only one brush if you invest in a nice one. A mark of quality is that a larger brush's bristles will come to a nice point by themselves when you get them wet.
- **Plastic watercolor palette** The brand Karen mentioned by name is Daisy. This is one of those cheap round plastic palettes that remind me of some kind of deviled egg plate. They're very useful, so stock up even if you need only one for this project.
- **Silk tacks** They're used to tack silk. I think you can get these at a fabric place like Jo-Ann's.
- **Silk** You can buy this off the bolt, or sometimes you can find it in premeasured panels. "Crepe de chine" 12 mm is the classification that Karen prefers for its texture and its translucency (so you can see your trace lines are visible from the pattern). I would stick with white. The dye will not be opaque, so the darker the color silk, the less you will see what you're painting. Prewashing optional but not required.
- **Wax pen (electric kistka)** Okay, I did a little research and the authentic name for this device is a "kistka." It is what is used to make the intricate designs on Ukrainian Easter eggs (aka *psyanky*). Sometimes crudely referred to (by me) as an "applicator" or "wax pen," the plug-in self-heating version Karen uses would be called an "electric kistka" and you can find 'em on the Web, no sweat. Karen happened to find hers at a Ukrainian gift shop, so you may have luck in your town. Originally, she'd used a *tjant* (the wax-dispensing tool used in batik), but it was not precise enough. Beware when choosing a kistka of the one with the

larger reservoir that uses a mechanism to release the wax. You have to apply pressure to the tip, and this can easily snag on your silk. Stick with the small one—it'll work fine.

- **Beeswax** Beeswax is nicer than your old candle scraps because it's very easy to cut into extremely small pieces with an X-acto knife.
- **Canvas stretcher bars** These come in pairs of varying lengths. You shouldn't need anything larger than a 12- x 12-inch bar for this project, but you might wanna go larger since they are useful for a lot of things—including bigger versions of this project.
- **Mini squeeze bottles (optional)** These are ideal for conserving new colors you have mixed from preexisting dyes.

JUST LYIN' AROUND

- **Medicine dropper** I bet you have one in the bathroom somewhere—just don't grab the one with the dinosaur DNA in it. The medicine dropper is an essential tool for getting dye in and out of the bottles very neatly. Especially important is its conservation factor. Sometimes you literally need just a drop of dye. Try *pouring* one drop from a brand-new, full bottle of dye and lemme know how that turns out. If you don't happen to see a medicine dropper in your travels, you can swing by the drugstore and pick one up on your way home.
- **Plastic cups** You know the cup you got to hold all those beads when you were flashing your business down in New Orleans? Or how about the one you stumbled outta Circus Circus with? You'll need something on that order to fill with water; one for clean water, one for cleaning your brush.
- **Chopsticks** These will be used for heat setting your project. I am gonna smack the face of anyone I catch actually *buying* chopsticks. I shouldn't have to tell you where to find them either unless you are a weirdo who doesn't love Chinese food.
- **Paper towels** I love to take an old Brawny and make him make out with a new Brawny. They are such a cute couple, and so domestic!
- **Pot** The boiling water kind (do I *look* like a hippie?)

Step by Step

1. Tack your silk to the stretcher bars.

Begin at the center of each edge. Try to keep the warp and weft square. Stretch so that it is taut, but has a little bit of give. It works best if you start with the top, then bottom, and then try to do the left and right sides simultaneously. This will keep distortion to a minimum. Add tacks in between, about 1½ inches apart all the way around, working with the silk to keep the weave straight.

2. Prepare your design.

Of course, you can use your own drawing, but these steps will assume you've xeroxed the cute cat illustration that Karen drew for this project. Laminate your design with contact paper if you plan to reuse it so that the paper won't absorb the water and distort the image.

3. Tape your design to a book and place on your work surface. Place your silk on top of the design.

The book should be slightly thicker than the wooden stretcher bars so that the silk maintains consistent and constant contact with the book.

4. Use wax to draw the border of your patch.

This is important because you want the dye to remain within the bounds of your design. Make sure to leave a seam allowance that will let you sew the patch to something else. I'd say allow for a ¼-inch to ½-inch seam.

5. Begin by outlining the cat with wax.

Remember that lines made in wax will remain white (or the color of the silk). Trace the whiskers, too. Remember to connect your outlines because the wax acts as a physical boundary through which the dye cannot pass. Gaps could lead to seepage.

6. Edge ears, eyes, nose, and mouth with wax.
Take your time with this. Outline the pattern line or shapes for each of the facial features with wax so that you can fill in each line with color. It's a subtle but important difference between tracing and edging. If you trace where you should be edging, your kitty will look anemic.

7. Trace the cat outline #1 from the pattern.
This will create a canal for the orange dye border.

8. Lift silk and frame off the design to check.
Hold your silk up to the light to double-check wax coverage. The wax lines on the silk will be clearly visible and should appear lighter and more transparent than the fabric itself.

9. Use black dye to color the eyes and mouth.
Touch your brush gently to the silk rather than "brushing" per se. The silk will suck up the dye more than you might expect. The black dye may require 2 to 3 coats before it reaches full saturation. Let the dye dry in between each coat.

10. Use magenta dye to color the cat's nose.

11. Use the orange dye to color the border closest to the cat.
Remember to keep working while it's wet to avoid an unwanted hard edge between strokes.

12. Use your sapphire-blue dye to color the background of your patch.
This may take more than 1 coat to achieve the saturation you want, depending on the exact shade of blue you choose. You can use a larger brush to fill in this big area. Make sure to keep your strokes wet so you don't get any unwanted edges (wet strokes? I'm dying here—I'm also actually dyeing). Once it's dry you can place a piece of white paper underneath the silk to gauge the color more effectively.

13. Color the ears, legs, and tail with the chocolate-brown dye.

You can achieve a faded/gradient look on the ears, legs, and tail by wetting the silk with a brush before applying the dye. Wet the specific area in the *opposite* direction of your desired fade. Wherever you apply water, the dye will be faded. So to fade the tail, the tip should be completely dry, and then become increasingly wet as you move to the right toward the cat's body. When you are finished coloring, wet the rest of the remaining white areas of the cat's body with water to ensure even coloration of the undyed silk (otherwise there will be a hard edge from where you stopped fading and the rest of the cat's body).

14. Let your piece dry.

15. Trace cat outline #2 from the pattern onto the silk with wax.
This will "lock in" the blue color that is already on the silk. This process is *slightly* similar to batik (but much cooler) in that you can lock in a color and then add another layer of color over it without affecting the original hue.

16. Use the brown dye to color in the space between cat outline #1 and cat outline #2.

17. Use royal blue to darken the background.
Apply royal blue to the area of silk on the outside of cat outline #2. The outermost outline of the cat will remain the lighter sapphire blue with which you began while the background will be slightly darker.

HEAT SETTING YOUR PROJECT

18. Set out a length of paper towel.
You can use newsprint or actual steamer paper. Whatever it is must be semiabsorbent.

19. Lay your silk on top of the paper towel and lay 2 more layers of paper towel atop the silk.

20. Roll the layers together like a jellyroll, making sure the silk does not come into contact with itself.
The heat will temporarily disrupt the dye, so if 2 dyed areas are in contact, the colors will bleed and make a big mess.

21. Fold the towel/silk roll into a small, neat bundle.

Clear packing tape works best to wrap and seal this bundle of joy. Be sure not to tape up the entire bundle so that there is room to push the chopsticks through the folds in the roll.

22. Skewer the bundle onto chopsticks.

Wiggle and force two chopsticks through folds in the bundle in an *x*. If you can't make a perfect *x* or fit the chopsticks through the folds, you could attach them in any number of ways. You can tape the chopsticks to the outside of the bundle in an *x*-shape or along the sides like a stretcher. The goal is to create a means by which to suspend the bundle above the boiling water. The bundle should rest in the middle of the length of chopstick when the chopsticks are laid across the top of the pot. The *x*-configuration just happens to work really well.

23. Balance atop a pot of boiling water.

Set the chopsticks flat across the pot so that the bundle hangs in the middle without touching the water. The heat from the boiling water is what will set your design. Cover the whole shebang loosely with more paper towel. Let it set for an hour, flipping your bundle every 15 minutes or so.

24. Dry clean your finished piece.

This will remove any remaining wax, finalize the setting process, and remove any steamed-in crinkling from the texture of the paper towel.

SERVING SUGGESTIONS

In this chapter we're making a patch to be sewn to a T-shirt or handbag. In the color photo (see insert) you can see that the patch is sewn onto a black T-shirt. If you're going to present your piece on top of a nonwhite surface (like a black T-shirt), always lay an opaque white piece of fabric or interfacing between the surface and the patch. This will ensure that the colors will be true and "pop," as they say. Had we sewn the patch directly onto the shirt without any opaque white material in between, the colors of the patch would be far less vibrant.

Contact Info

I have to say that Karen isn't the easiest person to get hold of, but your best bet is checking out her Web site at http://www.takkat.com, where you can find out more about her and her business. You can also drop her an e-mail at karen@takkat.com.

Word Search

```
C L C H I L D L E S S M E T D T
G O A F R Y I N G P A N G G N O
N S M I R E T S I G E R G O R R
O H E M R C I T E H T S O R P R
I O P G O T D T K E N H C A R A
T R U C R D S N S N E K C I D C
U T P O M A I U S P I N D L E D
L R P R I S F F D D G T L N I L
O I E P L U Y E I N I L T M N O
V B T S L L I S D C I E M I T O
E S M E E L T S N B A E N T N M
R C A F R A N K E N S T E I N G
K R S T F H N N Y D R P I P T T
I O T F C P O M A M E S U O M N
N N E T T H P L I G I E R S N V
G E R L P H E Y R T S E P A T F
```

ARACHNE
CARROT
CHILDLESS
COMMODIFICATION
CORPSE
CRONE
DEFARGE
DICKENS
DIMMESDALE
DISTAFF

EGG
FRANKENSTEIN
FRYINGPAN
GEPETTO
INDUSTRIAL
KING
KNITTING
LOOM
MILLER
MOUSE

NYMPH
PHALLUS
PHONEBILL
PROSTHETIC
PUPPETMASTER
REGISTER
REVOLUTION
SHORTRIBS
SPINDLE
TAPESTRY

CRAFT

ViNYL ACCESORiES
PROJECT: ViNYL CUFFS
ARTIST: Una Mano Lava La Otra, Lo Olivera, and Ben Harris

My love affair with records began as a kid. It's difficult to fathom the number of hours I spent sitting on the orange shag carpet of my bedroom with my beige Fisher-Price record player and *Thriller* picture disc. *Disco Duck, Strawberry Shortcake's Tea Party Sing-Along,* and *Pac-Man Fever* gave the king of pop a run for his money in the rotation. What was so neat, I think, was that there was this self-contained form of entertainment technology released into my complete grade school control. The records were mine to care for, scratch up, or even break by throwing them against the wall when playing *Krull* and *Tron,* and I didn't have to ask Mom or Dad before playing with them. They weren't so lax about their first CD player. I couldn't be trusted not to drop Lego men in the vaporizer motor or melt Smurfs on my desk lamp, so it seemed like a big honor to have my own record player.

Aside from the occasional picture disc, it wasn't until college that I became acquainted with colored vinyl. The thrill then was to find the import edition of such-and-such on the orange vinyl, for instance. It seemed, however, that a lot of singles and LPs were put out on colored vinyl to spark interest and raise collectibility because the music simply wasn't that hot. My solution was to steal a lot of colored vinyl records from the Indiana State University radio station where I had a show with my best friend, Shannon. I never got busted for poaching platters, but I was frequently yelled at in regards to my Mixmaster scratch efforts. Some people are so uncultured.

Ben and Io's vinyl record jewelry and accessories are a perfect project because you get all the tactile and visual pleasure of the candy-colored records without having to listen to them. And trust me when I say that there is plenty of colored vinyl out there that will have a much more fulfilling life *post-op* as a bowl, pair of earrings, or in this case a sexy and futuristic wrist cuff.

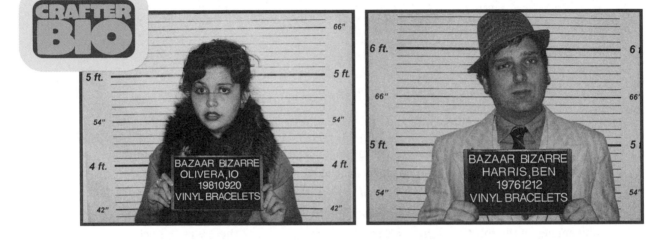

CRAFTER BIO

The crafting super team known as Una Mano Lava Otra is the love child of Ben Harris and Io Olivera. Both attended Otis College of Art and Design but did not know each other until after graduation, when they became roommates. Ben studied fashion and Io studied sculpture. After various evenings of talking about how much they liked making things, it was inevitable that they started dating. Ben and Io have miscellaneous and complementary skills, so they decided to join forces.

According to this dynamic duo, Los Angeles is their main inspiration. What started Una Mano Lava La Otra was a desire to make beautiful and functional things without a huge investment. The phrase "Una mano lava la otra" is Spanish, which literally translated means "One hand washes the other." It was Ben's idea for the project's name since Io's and his crafting is such a communal activity. In fashion and in fine art it seems that only one person gets the credit, though many work on its execution. Ben and Io want people to know that most great endeavors are rarely the work of just one person. Believe me, their endeavors *are* great. Their work with vinyl records is intricate, beautiful, and exceedingly relevant to any potential concept of a punk-rock crafting scene.

What is the difference between an "art" and a "craft"?

The difference between art and craft lies in intent. Crafts are closer to hobbies for us. That is, you do them for no other reward than that of making something that rocks your world. We're really into making accessories and working with fabrics. The difference between making fine art and crafting really lies in intent. When you are making something as craft, you can get away with taking less responsibility for the symbolic meaning of what you're making. When you are making something as fine art, you are totally liable for the content of your work; it's like the difference between writng paper that is going to be published and writing an entry in a journal.

Io: When I was kid growing up in Mexico there was a lot of crafting going on around me. In Mexico crafts are seen as a national treasure. Every region has a particular style and the objects are always a reflection of the resources that are naturally available in the area. As a kid I remember collecting small toys and trinkets during outings to rural towns. Someone had spent time creating an object that was one of a kind and for that reason they were truly valuable to me.

But crafting is more than a hobby for the artisans, and a lot of crafts have derived from technologies of yesteryear. So in essence, function is a big part of crafting whether that function is practical or purely decorative. In my family, all my relatives have developed some sort of craft either out of boredom or necessity, so crafting is very much a family activity.

What is your earliest crafting memory?

Io: My earliest crafting memory involves a Barbie and some toilet paper. I think I was probably about four years old. My mother had just bought me a knock-off Barbie doll and it was my first doll with little plastic breasts. So I soon decided that she needed a hipper outfit than that stupid little dress that cheap knock-off Barbies always come with. So I took my new doll to the bathroom and with the help of my favorite friend, masking tape, I went to work with the scissors and the toilet paper.

I created a devastating ensemble complete with custom-made high heels of tape, marker, and matchstick pieces. I was thrilled at the sight of the gorgeous little white dress I had just made. So I ran out of the bathroom and went to show my dad the fabulous outfit. He was really impressed and then he told me that only "exotic" women wore outfits like the one I had just made. I was totally heartbroken.

What is your best crafting moment (idea, inspiration, etc.)?

Ben: I learned how to sew while helping my mom on a community service project. We were making sheet and blanket sets for people from the shelter that had just received housing and little else. I didn't pick up the necessary skills that quickly, but after a couple of Saturdays, the work seemed effortless. I don't think anyone's life was that much better after receiving a homemade sleeping bag, or some sheets made out of kid's pajama fabrics, but I definitely got something out of it. My clothes became covered with rock patches, even polo shirts (style took a little longer than sewing I guess), and I continued sewing.

What was your worst crafting moment (a huge mess, project gone horribly wrong, etc.)?

Io: It is the consensus between Ben and me that learning how to knit is the biggest craft disaster. Picking up the stitches is easy but when that perfect little rectangle you were knitting turns out to be some sort of trapezoid there is nothing left to do but start over. This is the worst feeling in the world. You have not just made a simple mistake; you spent a great deal of time making that mistake.

What is your favorite craft you've ever seen?

Ben: At the Cultural Center in Chicago there's a cigarette-style vending machine full of artifacts and other handmade trinkets. You buy a five-dollar token in the gift shop, pull the lever, and then . . . It's almost like buying the mystery pleasure packet from the condom machine in seedy bathrooms—you can never really tell what you're getting until you unwrap the package. We got some really cool presents—quality trinkets, hand-painted cocktail pins made out of bottle caps, miniature drinking cups waiting for assembly. I guess it's not really the product that grabbed me the most. Buying crafts from a machine catches me as so ironic; I had to give my approval as a consumer, and buy.

Who made you the crafter you are (who introduced you to crafts, taught you crafts—whether or not it is the one you do now)?
Ben: Mom, definitely for the both of us. My mom and my grandmother were both quilters, so I grew up around constant piles of colored and patterned fabric. I eventually learned to sew; I've always been caught by how fabrics can complement each other. I work as a designer now, and I often feel like they helped me practice putting things together visually.

What are your crafting goals?
Io: We're into the joy of making things. Ben is sick; he wants to own goats, and move back to the land. Mostly though, just learning how.

Kraft or Kraftwerk?
Io: Kraftwerk of course, because it's all about "fun fun fun on the autobahn," though I do have a fixation with a tuna-size can of Kraft processed cheese with all the printing in Arabic—a real find. I sometimes buy cans just because I like the way they'll look in the cabinet, though I rarely think of eating any of the contents.

Who is your fave crafty celeb?
Io: MacGyver is our fave . . . I mean come on, the guy gets by on an army knife and duct tape. Who can deny the awesome craft potential of duct tape? This was a really hard question to answer because celebrity tends to be anticraft. Our other favorites, at the risk of sounding like total nerds, include Brini Maxwell because crafts should be charming and Soleil Moon Frye as Punky Brewster.

What is your fave craft resource (Web site, store, dumpster, etc.)?
Ben: Going home to the Midwest and visiting the thrift stores to liberate handmade country artifacts from the bric-a-brac is a favorite craft resource. But downtown L.A. is our real favorite. Michael Levine is nice for fabric, and Michaels-Moskatels Wholesale (usually referred to plainly as Moskatel's) is wonderful for useless holiday junk. Maple is great if you like to haggle. There are tons of junk wholesalers of all varieties, so just checking it out is enough to get motivated to make some stuff. If you want to learn how to do anything, the craft how-to books at the thrift store are an awesome resource. Since a lot of the craft books at the thrift store are from the hippie days, the projects are really easy to pick up and affordable.

Global Techniques (My Little Squib About Vinyl)

I think the number-one most interesting aspect of audio recordings on vinyl has to be the lingo. Neither CDs, cassettes, nor MP3s even come close to vinyl in terms of nomenclature. Record, platter, LP, EP, single, 45, 78, 33, 12-inch, 10-inch, 7-inch: Each title contains some information about the origins of its namesake. Punk rockers and size queens, for example, usually refer to records by diameter in inches while connoisseurs of orchestral or classical music reference RPMs. I never even knew that my "record player" was a "turntable" until college.

The icy academic in me wants to eschew sentiment, but I can't help but feel pity for kids who don't even know what a record is. Usually I am wary of nostalgia, and I avoid reminiscing about the good old days, but as codependent as I am with my iPod and its six-thousand-song capacity, it pains me that you never got to *touch* the songs. Where in the life of an MP3 do you come into contact with anything besides your computer keyboard? The few CDs and tapes that try to include any kind of design element are immediately hidden inside their players once you start listening. On the other hand, I probably could have spearheaded a bipartisan national health-care initiative or discovered a viable alternative to fossil fuel with the hours I spent getting lost in the spinning eyes of Nick Rhodes, John Taylor, and Simon LeBon. But hey, what's a punk rocker without misspent youth? The point is that there is an exposed visual and tactile interactivity with vinyl that you don't get with most audio document formats.

Here are some tips for working with vinyl:

- Vinyl has an extremely low melting temperature. Keep your physical interactions with the vinyl brief. Make your cuts and holes quickly, so as not to overhead the record and cause it to melt. Conversely, when you're bending the vinyl, keep in mind that it will cool just as quickly as it heats up, so you'll want to stop bending it after a few seconds to avoid snapping.
- There are varying thicknesses of vinyl records. Thicker allows for deeper grooves and thereby higher fidelity. That's why you're going to see thicker vinyl on an LP than of an EP or single. Classical recordings will often be much thicker than popular music to achieve an "audiophile" sound quality, but unfortunately I have never seen a classical

recording on colored vinyl (and yes, I own a large number of classical recordings).

- When making vinyl cuffs or accessories of any kind, try to incorporate the existing edges of the record into your design. It's more organic and lets you make one less cut.
- When installing a coping or jeweler's saw blade into the handle, make sure that the saw teeth are pointing "down" toward the handle and that the blade is taut.
- A Dremel is much faster and much more suitable for vinyl than a power drill. A power drill must be very fast and have very sharp bits to be usable on vinyl records. Either should be used atop a wood block or other surface in which you don't mind having holes.
- If you make a mistake when shaping heated vinyl, all you have to do is drop your piece into the simmering water and it will flatten completely, allowing you to begin again.

ViNYL CUFFS DiFFiCULTY ✪✪✪✪✪

TiME LiNE Io and Ben can make a bracelet pretty quickly—in about an hour, but it might take you longer, since there are two of them, and you might need time to get used to working with the vinyl. Passive time is divided up into small chunks, mostly waiting for water to boil. And since a watched pot never boils, watch something else.

Roxy Music: *Avalon;* Elton John: *Don't Shoot Me I'm Only the Piano Player;* Thelonious Monk: *Criss-Cross*

Pretty in Pink; Return of the Jedi; The Warriors [AUTHOR'S NOTE: *The Warriors* absolutely rocks]

SHOPPiNG LiST

I'M ON THE HUNT, I'M AFTER YOU . . .

- **12-inch colored vinyl records** Who's to say where you're gonna find these? Aside from DJs and punk rockers, not that many people buy vinyl records anymore. Chances are you're not gonna have much luck at the mall or a department store.

If you can't find any at yard sales, thrift stores, or your closet, you'll have to seek out a bona fide record store. It's yet another opportunity for a BazBiz adventure. The colored/clear vinyl is definitely more expensive to produce. The coolest colored vinyl is either superrare import stuff from Japan and Europe *or* the lamest of the lame corporate singles that just never hit it big. The people with the most money tend to make the crappiest music, and the megalabels often spend a lotta dough for colored vinyl to distract you from how bad the music actually is. Make sure to stick to the bargain bins when trolling for colored vinyl.

HARDWARE STORE

I would normally direct you to an art supply store for at least part of your project, but I'd be shocked if you couldn't find every single one of these items at the hardware store—especially a big Home Depot-type place.

- **Coping saw** A coping saw is a small handheld saw with a removable blade. You'll be using it to do the bulky, nondetailed cutting in this project. Just ask at the hardware store for a little lesson if you haven't used one before. Make sure to get extra blades!
- **Jeweler's saw** This looks just like a smaller version of a coping saw. The blades, however, are much more fragile. Using a jewel's saw takes more skill and practice, but allows for more intricate cuts. Extra blades are even more important for this saw.
- **Assorted files** Of course you can pick up a set of files at the hardware store, but I'd look around the house, a junkyard, or a thrift store first. This project does not require the high level of precision you get from buying brand-new tools, so why shell out the bucks? In general you'll want a big, flat file and a few little ones to finish detailed edges. You can also substitute assorted grit emery boards for the smaller detail files.
- **X-acto knife** Our trusty friend is back to help us remove burrs and stray pieces of vinyl. You could also use a utility knife for some of the heavier duty tasks like scraping.
- **White colored pencil** These work great for marking your records because you can wipe off any excess pigment once your pieces are cut (not so with a

Magic Marker). You could also use a grease pencil or Chinese marker.

- **Masonite board (about 24 x 36 inches)** This is a great, cheap, portable work surface if you don't have a dedicated cutting area.
- **Oaktag or poster board (optional)** Paper templates make fitting your designs a lot easier. Go ahead and try out your designs with oaktag first before investing all that time only to come out with a cuff that would only fit your neighborhood stick person.
- **Dremel high-speed rotary tool (optional)** You could conceivably use a power drill here, but it would need to be very fast and have extremely sharp bits. I can't think of a low-cost, punk rock substitute for a Dremel, but its application here is purely decorative, so if you can't get your hands on one it's not gonna stop you from doing this project.

RIGHT AT HOME

- **Old T-shirt** Not everyone has a dedicated workbench. If you're like me you're working at a table you use for a million things. So to avoid scratching it up, lay down a T-shirt to work on. This will also protect your record from unintended scratches.
- **Pot of hot water** To soften things up. I guess I'm assuming you already have a stove or at least a primitive form of fire à la Cro-Magnon man.
- **Ruler**
- **Tape measure**

Step by Step

1. Lay your T-shirt out on your work surface.
This will protect your surface if it's not a proper bang-em-up workbench and it will prevent unintended scratches on the underside of your vinyl.

2. Determine the length for your cuff.
Measure your wrist snugly, but comfortably, with a tape measure. Add 1½ inches to this measurement to allow for the opening and the filing down of the edges.

3. Make a template for your cuff.

The template you are making is going to end up looking like an elongated football. Using a record edge as a guide, trace a semicircle onto a piece of oaktag. Find the area of the record where the distance between the edges is the same as the desired length for your cuff. Make hash marks on the oaktag along the curved line at each end of this length.

Now you are going to draw a curve that bulges in the opposite direction. Place the record on the oaktag so that the edges intersect the hash marks you just made. When you trace the curve, it will make a line that joins the hash marks to complete the football shape. Cut out your cuff template.

4. Using a colored pencil, draw your cuff on the record.

Lay either side of the template flush with the record's edge and trace it with the colored pencil.

5. Keep half of your record on the table with your nonsawing forearm and use a coping saw to cut halfway inward from each cuff endpoint on the record's edge.

You must keep the blade exactly perpendicular to the surface/plane of the record to avoid catching the vinyl. This is very difficult at first as the blade will most likely seize up on you, but you can work into a rhythm. Do not rush things—practice makes perfect.

6. Remove your cuff from the record.

When you get good and fast at sawing, the vinyl will actually melt as you cut, making it difficult for you to get your blade out from between your vinyl pieces. But if you gently wiggle as you remove the blade, it should release without breaking. Then you can snap off your cuff from the rest of the record.

7. Remove any burrs from the edge of the bracelet.

Use your X-acto or utility knife to shave/scrape along the cut edge of your cuff. Be careful and try to work moving the blade away from you rather than toward you.

8. Use your large file to smooth the cut edge.

The best approach here is to lay the large file flat on the table and then drag the cuff across it. This will give you more control, and the T-shirt will grip/stabilize the file on the table.

9. Give extra attention to rounding off the ends of your cuff.

The corners of your cuff are going to be sharp. You can use a jeweler's saw to round off the corners before you file them down. You don't want them to dig into your skin.

10. Do a second round of filing with a smaller, finer grit file or emery board to make things extra smooth.

You'll find you'll have a lot more control over the file and the bracelet once you switch to the smaller file, but don't skip filing with the large file.

11. Rescrape your cuff edge.

You may have caused some extra tiny burrs or rough spots when filing, so give it another go with your blade.

CUTTING OUT SHAPES WITH A DREMEL (OPTIONAL)

12. Use your pencil to draw the shapes for any cutouts.

Keep in mind that you're going to need a Dremel to complete these. Simple geometric shapes like hearts and stars are a good place to begin, but you can really do anything once you feel comfortable enough. Don't be surprised, though, if your attempts to cut out the words "foxy lady" don't turn out right away.

13. Use your Dremel to make holes in your cuff.

Hold your cuff down and use a quick stamping motion to make your hole. Remember to keep the Dremel running as you remove it from the record (this makes it release easily). For nondrillable (nonround) cutout designs, drill a starting hole, and then use a jeweler's saw to cut the shape. To do this, you have to remove the blade from the saw handle, thread it through your drilled starting hole, reset it into the handle, and start sawing. This is definitely a more advanced technique than just drilling.

14: Keep your bits clean as you work.

Keep your eyes peeled for stray burrs stuck on the drill bit each time you pull your Dremel from the vinyl. Remove them

15. Make sure to finish off all of your cutouts with a small detail file.

Small files come in a number of shapes like round, square, and triangle. Use the shape of file that's going to fit closest with the cutout you're working with. For instance, if your shape is an angular cutout like the bottom point of a heart, you're going to have a much easier go of it using the triangle file.

SHAPING THE VINYL PIECES INTO CUFFS

16. Heat water to a simmer and then reduce heat slightly.

Keep your water just shy of bubbling. A pot with a larger diameter will give you more space in which to work and help you avoid burning your wrists on the pot rim.

17. Dip each end of the cuff in the hot water to soften it for shaping.

Holding one end of your cuff above the water between your thumb and index finger, dip the cuff in the water, applying slight pressure to the end against the bottom of the pot until you can sense it beginning to bend.

18. Alternately curl each end of the cuff.

Repeat the dipping and bending process alternating ends of the cuff. You will only have a few seconds to shape the heated vinyl until it starts to stiffen. You should soon end up with a canoe shape when looking at the bracelet edge on.

19. Hold the ends and dip the middle of the cuff.
Begin to shape an arch in the center of the cuff.
Keep dipping and shaping until the bracelet profile
looks like a bowl rather than a canoe with a flat
section in the middle.

20. Curl the cuff ends inward to finish your bracelet.
Once you have a smooth round shape, begin to bring the cuff ends
toward the center to achieve a closed loop. This will actually keep the
bracelet on. Make sure to leave enough space to fit your wrist
between the cuff ends. The vinyl will bend very slightly, even when
completely cool, so don't be afraid to make the cuff closure a little
snug. Now you're styling. Go ahead and make another so you can be
like Wonder Woman!

Contact Info

E-mail Io and Ben at unamanolavalaotra@yahoo.com or visit their Web site
www.unamanolavalaotra.com for lots of more cool ideas of treasures to make out of
old vinyl records (do you have to actually say that a record is made from vinyl these
days? Seems like a lot of kids aren't sure what "records" are).

CONCLUSION

A lot of this book—most, in fact—has been about the *how* of crafting. I can't in good conscience leave you without taking a few paragraphs to detail some of the *why*. In a way, crafting is about exercising self-expression not through what you buy, but what you create. But I wouldn't be telling you anything new if I said that "opting out" or simply removing yourself from the traffic of American commodity culture is an impossibility. Further, who would want to? I don't really think a reactionary withdrawal on that order would be much fun—it's called being a hippie. Looking back through this book, I don't see even one crafter who regrets being molded at least in part by pop culture. Theorist Fredric Jameson wrote about living in the "belly of the beast," his term for employing strategies that allow us to participate more critically in the exchange between individualism and mass culture instead of simply trying to hide from it.

In the most vulgar and capitalist sense of the word, everyone is a consumer (including you, dear reader, sorry). That is to say, we are all pleasure-seeking consumers who buy beyond our requisite needs such as food and shelter. Some of us avoid the label of "consumer" because we listen to the Clash and tune in to the notion that the left is no place for traditional, rampant materialism. Consumption, however, is scarcely restricted to the tangible. While not as obviously concrete as a Benz or a set of Vuitton luggage, a specific combination of aesthetics and credibility exists that we counterculturalists strive for—an underground, secret, punk lifestyle whose trappings we are aching to possess.

Unfortunately, the relationship of counterculture signifiers (ironically frumpy, nerd chic, tattoos, piercings, what have you) to an implicit value system has dissolved completely. Any "underground" or "alternative" cultural production begins by running parallel to—and is often driven by—an anxiety about commodification and misappropriation. But capitalism pursues an ever-growing search for new markets and consumers, and in this process packages, advertises, sells, and mainstreams cultural production that was once specifically *counter*cultural. Not too long ago I saw a TV ad for Kraft (appropriately enough) mac and cheese that featured the T-Rex classic "Bang a Gong." I am not sure I can think of something as inappropriate—or as funny—as using a drug-and-sex-themed glam-rock song to sell easy-to-prepare mac and cheese to rosy-cheeked latchkey kids, none of whom are older than twelve.

As technology extends the reach and immediacy of capitalist interests, there is an ever-waning lag time between a practice's status as alternative or underground and its commodification as mainstream. In simpler terms: The time it takes for one of your own countercultural craft ideas to appear on a department store shelf is getting shorter and shorter. All, however, is not lost. The hypersaturation of the mainstream marketplace by misplaced kitsch and a zillion other crappy products that miss their mark reminds me of why I came back to my crafty roots.

It is only a matter of time before you find yourself putting a colorful and glittery bric-a-brac emblazoned with faux sass ("princess," "angel," "bad girl," and so forth) into your basket and remembering that you used to *make* cool stuff as opposed to shop for it. When you bottom out like this, just take your shopping spree down to the craft supply store and go nuts.

I am the first to admit that I love to buy things. Spending some dough is a great way to brighten up a rainy day, and you can still have that therapeutic retail experience. Hell, I *live* for it. Think about the all-important ritual of consumption as identity: gift giving. Despite our obsession with buying certain objects of status or beauty, there are remnants of a premium placed on handmade gifts. The golden rule of gift giving is that "it's the thought that counts." Handmade gifts, no matter how simple, rustic, cheap, or janky, still retain major credibility as being the most thoughtful. It's almost chic to showcase some ugly thing someone *made* for you.

Take, for instance, a recent television commercial where a man shops for a refrigerator, and he has but one requirement for purchasing the big ticket appliance: The in-door ice dispenser must accommodate the ugly monstrosity of a coffee mug his kid made for him. Take sixty seconds and I bet you can come up with a dozen similarly motivated scenarios from television, film, and your own life.

So who could really fault you for buying supplies in an effort to at least partially unplug yourself from the routine of consumption as expression? You can still have a blast fondling the pretty fabrics and tubes of glitter because you are reclaiming the tools that corporations have stolen to forge a testament to lameness.

I guess my big point here is that the BazBiz way of life isn't about the denial of guilty pleasures, nor is it about the condemnation of American consumerism with which you were raised. You don't have to boycott your favorite store, beat yourself up for liking television, or stick a really stupid KILL YOUR TV sticker on your bumper. You no longer have to pretend that you'd rather curl up with Jane Austen than with *America's Next Top Model.* Critical consumption—and production—is the cornerstone of *Bazaar Bizarre.* Turn on your brain, fire up that sense of rabble-rousing, and always realize that you can do better than what's on the shelf.

INDEX

Page numbers in *italics* refer to illustrations.

ABOUT THE AUTHOR

He's come a long way, baby. Picture it: Tabriz, 1975. An adorable olive-skinned baby is adopted by an Armenian-American couple and brought to the New World (Acton, Massachusetts) to enjoy an idyllic suburban upbringing replete with soccer practice, scout meetings, viola lessons, and lots of therapy. Gregory Nazareth Der Ananian stumbled his way through the Acton public school system, pursuing a career as class clown and getting into plenty of trouble along the way. He attended Indiana University originally as a viola performance major, but ended up with a triple major in English, Gender Studies, and "Electronic Culture and the Politics of Representation." He was recognized for his limit-testing video installation "Gaze (W)rites: Making the Visible Pornographic." Recognition included the Individualized Major Program's Outstanding Project Award, as well as a lot of lecturing about using so much hard-core gay porn in a public setting. During his tenure in Bloomington, Indiana, Der Ananian worked with adults living with severe mental illness and was in a band called Prettypony. Mind you, these were not always separate endeavors.

After moving back to Massachusetts in 2000, Der Ananian founded the punk-rock crafts fair called Bazaar Bizarre with the help of crafty cronies he'd originally met while touring with his band. A surprising success, it went on to become an eagerly anticipated annual event. Der Ananian moved to L.A. in 2002, starting a left-coast edition of his brainchild in 2003. Cleveland joined the ranks in 2004, and Bazaar Bizarre continues to grow. Der Ananian, a proud mouth breather since birth out to dismantle cruel stereotypes, is a card-carrying member of both Mensa *and* the Subway Sub Club. Greg lives in Silverlake: the trucker hat of Los Angeles neighborhoods.